Pelican Books

Helping Troubled Children

Professor Michael Rutter completed his basic medical education at the University of Birmingham, qualifying in 1955. After taking residencies in internal medicine, neurology and paediatrics, he proceeded to the Maudsley Hospital, London, for training in general psychiatry and then child psychiatry. He spent the 1961–2 year on a research Fellowship studying child development at the Department of Pediatrics, Albert Einstein College of Medicine, New York, returning then to work in the Medical Research Council Social Psychiatry Research Unit. In 1965 he took an academic position at the University of London's Institute of Psychiatry, where he became Professor and Head of the Department of Child and Adolescent Psychiatry in 1973, a post he still holds. During the academic year 1979–80 he was a Fellow at the Center for Advanced Study in the Behavioral Sciences, Stanford, California. His research interests include stress resistance in children, psychosocial development in an ecological context, schools as social institutions, reading difficulties, interviewing skills, neuro-psychiatry, infantile autism and psychiatric epidemiology. His published work includes some fifteen books and scores of scientific papers. *Maternal Deprivation Reassessed* and *Juvenile Delinquency* (written with Henri Giller) have also been published in Penguin.

Michael Rutter

HelpingTroubled
Children

Penguin Books

Penguin Books Ltd, Harmondsworth, Middlesex, England
Viking Penguin Inc., 40 West 23rd Street, New York, New York 10010, U.S.A.
Penguin Books Australia Ltd, Ringwood, Victoria, Australia
Penguin Books Canada Limited, 2801 John Street, Markham, Ontario, Canada L3R 1B4
Penguin Books (N.Z.) Ltd, 182–190 Wairau Road, Auckland 10, New Zealand

First published 1975
Reprinted 1976, 1977, 1979, 1980, 1982, 1984, 1987

Set, printed and bound in Great Britain by
Cox & Wyman Ltd, Reading
Set in Intertype Times

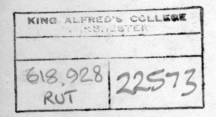

Contents

Preface

Emotional and behavioural problems in childhood are very common, and anyone dealing with children is likely to encounter many with psychiatric difficulties. For the most part these difficulties constitute exaggerations of or deviations from the normal rather than mental illnesses or diseases. This book aims to provide an account of the thinking and principles underlying the understanding and treatment of these common problems. Because it is primarily intended for the general reader and for non-psychiatric professionals who care for children, the focus is on the psychiatric difficulties of the everyday child rather than on psychoses or the more severe and rare conditions met with in hospital in-patient practice. Nevertheless, it is hoped that the book may be of interest to students (medical and non-medical) who want an introduction to child psychiatry.

In order to keep the main emphasis on ways of thinking about emotional and behavioural problems and on ways of helping troubled children, discussion has largely been restricted to the difficulties presented by youngsters in the middle years of childhood from ordinary schools attending out-patient clinics. As a result the important problems of preschool children, of older adolescents, of mentally retarded or physically handicapped children at special schools and of residential care are not specifically discussed. Nevertheless the principles and manner of working described here will have relevance to all these other groups.

The roots of child psychiatric disorder lie not only in the child himself but in his family, his schooling and his social environment. Because of this, the assessment and treatment of child psychiatric disorders involve a multidisciplinary approach.

Much of the treatment described in the book was devised and carried out by psychologists and psychiatric social workers rather than psychiatrists, and a collaboration between equals is an essential part of the professional approach. As a result, except where I have wanted to indicate the special contribution of one discipline, the clinic team members are usually referred to by the general terms of 'clinician' and 'therapist'.

The fact that a child is referred to a psychiatric clinic does not necessarily mean that there is any problem in the child himself. The first chapter describes how the clinic team set about assessing whether the child has a disorder and, if he has, what its nature is. The next four chapters provide more detail on some of the elements which are essential to that assessment, namely the course of the child's development, his individual characteristics, the family setting and the broader socio-economic context including his school and group of friends. The next three chapters give an account of some of the commoner psychiatric disorders occurring in childhood, and the last chapter brings together some of the main issues involved in planning treatment. Complaints are sometimes made that psychiatry is befogged by jargon, speculation and vague generalities. I have attempted to avoid these faults by using ordinary language, by referring to the available evidence and its limitations and by using specific clinical examples. The case-histories are taken from both general population studies and from clinical notes. All names are fictitious and family circumstances have been disguised, while still retaining the psychological reality of the child's situation. In order to avoid the tedium of 'he/she' the word 'he' has been used throughout the text to refer to both boys and girls and to both male and female therapists. The true sex has been retained only when referring to a specific child and when particular emphasis is being given to differences between the sexes.

As a guide to further reading, a short list of other relevant books is provided. More numerous references are given to substantiate points made in the text, as it is considered essential that clinical practice should be firmly based on knowledge rather than on opinion and supposition. Nevertheless, in order to avoid burdening the book with too extensive a bibliography, wherever possible preference has been given to readily available review articles or books.

April 1974

Acknowledgements

For many years I have worked as a member of an inter-disciplinary team in a child psychiatry department. This book owes much to what I have learned over the years from working with members of other disciplines and I am deeply indebted to many colleagues who have done much to increase my understanding of children and of their problems. Special thanks are due to the psychiatric social workers, Fraida Sussenwein and Daphne Holbrook, and to the clinical psychologists, Michael Berger, William Yule and Evril Silver, with whom I have worked most closely. They have all done much to develop better ways of helping children and their families and they were responsible for planning and undertaking many of the treatments described in these pages.

Each of them provided constructive advice and critical comments on an earlier draft of the manuscript. Helpful suggestions were also made by Antony Cox, Lionel Hersov, David Quinton, David Shaffer and Celia Tupling. My wife, Marjorie, was invaluable in helping me to clarify both my thoughts and their expression in print.

I am most grateful to Joy Maxwell, Danuta Votolato and Khim Brown for skilled secretarial work, and especially to Joy Maxwell for checking references and helping with indexing.

Figure 3, 'Growth Curves for Different Parts of the Body', is reprinted with permission from J. M. Tanner's *Growth at Adolescence* (second edition, Oxford: Blackwell Scientific Publications, 1962).

1 Understanding Children's Problems

Numerous studies have attested to the fact that most children show isolated psychological problems at one time or another and that many have transient periods of emotional disturbance or behavioural difficulties. [166], [177] To a considerable extent these are part and parcel of growing up and are not in themselves a cause for concern. On the other hand, some children have psychiatric disorders which interfere with normal development and which require treatment, although not necessarily from a psychiatrist. So, one of the first tasks when a child is referred to a clinic is an assessment of whether or not he has some kind of disorder which warrants treatment. The very fact that the child has been referred means that someone is concerned and proper attention needs to be paid to that concern. But it should not necessarily be assumed that concern equals psychiatric disorder, for it does not. It may be that the parent has become worried about something which is a perfectly normal stage in development, or it may be that quite minor problems in the child are being used as a reason for seeking help with serious family difficulties.

Kanner[90] has described how symptoms – that is, people's complaints to a doctor – serve several different functions. First, they are an 'admission ticket' indicating that there is a problem to be studied. Second, they may be a signal that something is wrong within the child. Third, they may act as a safety valve, as when rebellion and defiance are used as a response to an intolerable situation. Fourth, they may be a means of solving problems as when a child copes with his anxiety about school by complaining of a belly ache and going to bed. This is not a very adaptive or useful solution but its importance lies in the need to understand what the problem is which gives rise to the symptom. Fifth, the symptom is a nuisance, as when fighting and aggressive behaviour at school cause annoyance to teachers. It should be appreciated that with children the initial complaints or symptoms do not usually come from the child himself — instead they come from a parent, or teacher, or someone else who is worried about the child's behaviour. This means that it is also necessary to understand the dynamics of the referral itself. Who was concerned about the child? Why was he concerned? Why was he concerned *now*, rather than at some other time?

Although most children referred to clinics have a psychiatric problem, it has been found that the reasons for referral often lie in the parents or in the family as well as in the child. This has been demonstrated by a study which compared children attending clinics and those not attending clinics, the children in both cases having roughly comparable disorders. This showed that clinic mothers were more likely to have suffered nervous complaints themselves and to be worried about their children, and more of the clinic children came from 'broken homes'.[177]

Accordingly, diagnosis must focus as much on the social context and manner of referral as on the child himself. The need to understand referral may be illustrated by two brief examples. Mrs Smith asked us to see her four-year-old daughter, Rachel. Mother had many complaints about the child's behaviour but none seemed to amount to very much. Rachel's supposed 'over-activity' was no more than normal exuberance, her 'sleep difficulties' simply arose as a result of being put to bed far too early and her 'tantrums' were merely the normal childish assertions of individuality. Discussion with Mrs Smith soon made clear that she was seriously depressed and drinking heavily. She had become aware of her rising irritation and intolerance of Rachel and was concerned that her own problems were making it difficult for her to be a good mother. Rachel's referral reflected this concern.

The second example involves not one referral but several. Over the course of a couple of months there was a steady stream of requests by the headmaster of a special school for us to see various pupils of his. Although all the referred boys had definite enough psychiatric problems, it was unclear why so many were being referred all at once, until it emerged that there were serious staff conflicts at the school. Each boy needed help in his own right but the school were also implicitly appealing for assistance in resolving their own difficulties.

This illustrates the point that the issue is not 'who is ill?' or 'who is to blame?' but rather 'what is the problem?' and 'how did it arise?' However, because referral almost always involves complaints or worries about a particular child's behaviour it is convenient to begin by discussing the principles underlying the assessment of this behaviour. The diagnostic issues with respect to the child may be illustrated by considering two ten-year-old children who were both seen as part of a general population survey. Neither was attending a psychiatric clinic but both presented problems. Nevertheless it was thought that only one had a disorder which warranted treatment.

Over the last year Gordon had developed a habit of shrugging his shoulders and clicking his teeth. This began after he started at a new school and it only happened during term time. It was more marked if he was worried about something, it did not occur at all when he was playing and it had gradually lessened in recent months. Shortly after he started at the new school he developed a 'nervous cough' which, like the tics, was most marked when he was anxious. This habit lasted a few months and then disappeared. Also, after changing schools, he began to bite his nails. He was a generally happy boy with no particular worries or fears, his relationships at home were good and he had a lot of friends. He played football after school every day and children were often calling for him to go out to play. There was some irritability and scrapping with his brothers but generally they got on well. Gordon was friendly and affectionate but self-sufficient and not physically demonstrative. His concentration was good and he was making good progress at school. Father was a cheerful, level-headed chap but rather a worrier, especially over his work which he took very seriously. This made him irritable sometimes. Mother was a more easy-going person and family relationships were generally good.

Gordon was basically a normal, well-adjusted boy who experienced some anxiety and tension with respect to changing schools. He followed after his father in taking work seriously and his concerns about school showed themselves in the tics, as he had learned to keep his anxiety under control. These anxieties were diminishing and the tics were becoming less marked as he gradually adapted to the new situation. His psychological and social development continued to proceed normally throughout this phase of mild emotional difficulties and at no stage was he handicapped or impaired in any way. For this reason he was thought not to have a psychiatric disorder, although he was experiencing some difficulties in adaptation.

Toby, in contrast, had always been a difficult child to bring up. From early childhood he had been a nervous, irritable, sensitive, worrying boy. He slept poorly, irritated his parents through his constant anxious questioning and he was not very affectionate or responsive. This made it much harder for his parents to deal with him and they both got angry with him more often than with their other children. When he was nearly three years old they saw a paediatrician because he would not sleep, seemed withdrawn and was generally difficult to handle. Recently the family doctor had suggested psychiatric referral, but the parents had not acted on this suggestion. The parents were most concerned over Toby's worrying. He worried about school, about mother leaving him and about meeting people. When worried, he tended to ask endless questions, seeking reassurance but usually eliciting irritation. When he got in a panic with fear, as he did frequently, he tended to lash out in all directions, becoming uncontrollably aggressive. He was terrified of the dark and had to have the light on at night. Often at night he would keep calling down to his mother. When meeting new people, but not otherwise, he stuttered and could not get the words out properly. There were numerous food fads and he would try to transfer the food he did not like to his father's plate. Toby was a restless, fidgety boy who could not settle to anything and was always wandering around. He had some friends, but he was always falling out with them, was jealous of others, got into daily fights and frequently complained of loneliness. He rarely smiled, he seemed miserable and he moped about. There was a serious obsession with germs, such that for the last two years he had washed his hands at least thirty times a day. He washed his hands before he put the kettle on, before touching a plate and before shaking hands. He avoided parties or other social gatherings. If it seemed that there might be pressure on him to go, he screamed, shouted and protested. There were frequent clashes with his father, especially over the last five years since father developed a serious neurological disorder which caused episodes of dizziness. Father was a lonely person who often sat looking into space but also had severe tantrums. He had numerous fears and recently had suffered from quite serious depression with sleeplessness and unreasonable feelings of jealousy. The marital relationship had progressively deteriorated and there were frequent rows. Two years ago mother had seen a psychiatrist because of depression and worries about a lump in her throat. She was very scared of the dark and of spiders.

There was no doubt that Toby had quite a serious psychiatric disorder. His problems differed from those of Gordon in that the symptoms were more varied, more severe and more persistent. In addition his overall psychological development was not progressing normally and his symptoms caused social impairment in that they interfered with his everyday life in numerous ways. Temperamentally Toby had been unusual right from infancy and his difficult temperament meant that his parents found it much harder to love him than their other children. When they were irritable it was Toby they took it out on. Both parents had had psychiatric problems and it may be that Toby had inherited an increased psychological vulnerability, but also it was striking that the development of his obsessional symptoms closely followed the onset of his mother's neurotic disorder and coincided with the deterioration in the marriage and in father's bad temper. Whatever the genetic factors, the disturbed family interaction was also playing an important part in the genesis of the problems. If this child had been attending a clinic, one of the tasks would have been to work out just how this might be happening.

Although Toby was not attending a psychiatric clinic, few people would have any doubt that some form of treatment was needed. However, other cases are less obvious and it is necessary to consider what are the various factors which need to be taken into account in making a psychiatric assessment.

Children are developing organisms

The first point is that children are developing organisms so that assessment needs to be made in the context of a developmental framework. This means that clinicians must have a good knowledge and understanding of child development, both normal and abnormal. Children behave differently at different ages and it is necessary to know what behaviour should be expected at each age. Of course all children are not alike, so that some knowledge of the range of variability is also required. Different stages of development are associated with different stresses and different susceptibilities. These too must be understood. It is not only a question of when things happen during development, but it is also a matter of how they happen and what processes are involved. Last, any psychiatric assessment must consider the extent to which the child's symptoms are or are not associated with any interference with the course of psychological development. That presupposes a knowledge of what that source is. An outline of some of the findings and issues concerning child development is given in chapter 2.

Particularly because children are developing and changing all the time, children's disorders need to be thought of in terms of the whole of their course. It is not enough to know what the child is like at the time he comes to the clinic. The psychiatrist has also to find out what he was like when he was younger, when the difficulties began and how they got better or worse.

In looking at the course of child psychiatric disorders, one must make a distinction between the factors that engendered the disorder in the first instance and the factors which are currently causing the disorder to persist. These may be quite different and, regardless of the origin of the child's problem, careful attention always needs to be paid to current influences.

Epidemiological considerations

Before turning to the question of the guidelines which might be employed in assessing whether or not a child suffered from some form of psychiatric disorder, it is necessary to have some idea of the dimensions and nature of the problem. For this, we need to turn to epidemiological studies looking at the distribution of disorders in the general population. They show that over the course of one year, somewhere in the region of five to fifteen per cent of children suffer from disorders of sufficient severity to handicap them in their everyday life.[158, 162, 166] We need not concern ourselves too much with the exact figure, but we can conclude that child psychiatric disorders are very common. Only a minority of children with these conditions get to see a psychiatrist, and it is evident from the prevalence figures that it would not be realistic (even if it were desirable, which it probably is not) to expect psychiatrists to deal with all psychiatric conditions in childhood. The very size of the problem means that family doctors, paediatricians and non-medical professionals, such as teachers, social workers and psychologists, working outside clinics must also be expected to deal with some kinds of psychiatric disorders.

The next point that arises from epidemiological research is that, for the most part, the disorders do *not* constitute diseases or illnesses which are *qualitatively* different from normality. There are a few conditions, such as infantile autism, which might be termed diseases in this sense, but this is not true of the great majority of disorders. Most conditions differ *quantitatively* from the normal in terms both of severity and of associated impairment, but minor variations of the same thing can be found in many essentially normal children.

A corollary of this is that isolated 'symptoms' are extremely common and usually of little clinical significance. Disorders are diagnosed not on the presence of single items of behaviour which are diagnostically specific, for these are rare indeed, but on the basis of patterns of multiple symptomatology which are persistent and socially handicapping.

Another important finding is that it is quite common for disorders to be partially, or even entirely, specific to certain situations.[114, 166] Children may wet their beds at home but never when away from their parents, or they may be aggressive and disruptive at school but not at all with their family. This has practical implications in terms of the need to obtain reports of the child's behaviour in both settings, but it also has implications concerning the nature of child psychiatric conditions. This situation-specificity implies that disorders must be regarded in *interactional* terms. That is to say the problem lies in the *interaction* between a child and his environment, and not just within the child himself. This is an important conclusion which influences both diagnostic formulations and treatment plans, but it should not be taken to mean that factors within the child are irrelevant. That is far from the case, as will be discussed in chapter 3.

Assessment of the presence of psychiatric disorder

These considerations mean that the severity of a disorder is a crucial part of the psychiatric assessment. In this connection severity involves two different elements: abnormality and handicap. The first issue is whether, in terms of its frequency or pattern, the child's behaviour is abnormal in statistical terms. The second issue is, given that there is some abnormality, is it associated with any handicap or impairment in the child's social functions. Let us consider these in turn.

Is the child's behaviour abnormal?

In assessing the possible abnormality of any behaviour, several different criteria have to be employed. These include:

(a) Age and sex appropriateness.

Many behaviours are normal at one age but not at another. Thus all babies wet themselves, and many children do not stop wetting the bed until they are four or five years of age. On the other hand bed-wetting is distinctly uncommon at age ten years, and therefore would be regarded as abnormal then. Similarly separation anxiety is a normal phenomenon in toddlers (indeed a total lack of anxiety at leaving his parents would be a cause of some concern in a child at that age). But separation anxiety in an adolescent would be quite unusual and therefore abnormal.

There is a very substantial overlap in the behaviours shown by boys and by girls, even in later childhood. Most boys show some supposedly 'feminine' traits and most girls have some 'masculine' ones. That is quite normal. However, it is distinctly rare for a boy to show *all* feminine traits and therefore this would be statistically abnormal. Whether it should also be a cause for concern is a matter to be decided on the basis of the other criteria of abnormality and on the presence of social impairment.

(b) Persistence.

As already noted, if a survey is taken at any one point in time many children will be reported as having fears, tantrums or other kinds of troublesome behaviour. However, it is much less common for these behaviours to persist over a long time. Thus almost every child goes through a phase of being reluctant to go to school. This may be just the odd day or it may be something that lasts for a week or so. On the other hand a reluctance to go to school which persists for many months or even years is much rarer and thereby more of a cause for concern.

(c) Life circumstances.

Transient fluctuations in children's behaviour and emotional state are quite common and normal. Psychological 'efficiency' has its peaks and troughs so that at some times the child may be quite vulnerable and yet at others resilient and adaptable. Development does not proceed entirely smoothly and plateaux and transient regressions are part of normal development. However, these fluctuations are more likely to occur at some times than at others, so that attention to the child's life circumstances is important. Many children revert to more immature patterns of behaviour when a new baby brother or sister arrives. They may return to sucking their thumb or wanting the bottle and they may become more demanding and attention-seeking at this time. Starting a new school or joining a new class is another common stress which may be associated with increased anxiety and dependency. Some increase in emotional and behavioural difficulties is to be expected in many children at times of stress.

(d) Socio-cultural setting.

Behaviour can not be judged normal or abnormal in an absolute sense. Rather the way the child behaves must be assessed in terms of the norms for his immediate socio-cultural milieu. An understanding of the many cultural variations in our society is important, but assessment is always more difficult in a child from a very different cultural background.

(e) Extent of disturbance.

Isolated symptoms are very much commoner than the simultaneous presence of many symptoms. Indeed this is so much the case that only occasionally will symptoms occurring on their own be of any psychiatric significance. More attention always needs to be paid to the child with many items of emotional or behavioural disturbance, especially if these extend over several different areas of psychological functioning.

(f) Type of symptom.

However, the nature of the symptom will also, to some extent, determine its likely significance. Surveys have shown that some symptoms are very much more likely to be associated with generalized psychological malfunction than are others.[166] Thus nail-biting is *not* indicative of psychiatric disorder; it is a behaviour which is just as common in normal children as in those with psychiatric disorder. That is not to say that it has no meaning. On the contrary those who bite their nails tend to do so particularly when they are tense. However, everyone is tense sometimes and tension is not synonymous with psychiatric disorder. In contrast disturbed peer relationships are more commonly associated with psychiatric disorder and, as such, warrant more serious attention.

(g) Severity and frequency of symptoms.

Mild, infrequent difficulties are much commoner than severe, frequent ones. Accordingly, when a child is said to have nightmares, temper tantrums, tics or some other symptoms, it is crucial to determine how often these occur and to obtain a clear description of what actually happens. Does the tantrum consist of shouting for two minutes or does it involve lying on the floor screaming for half an hour? By 'nightmare' does the parent mean that the child reports in the morning that he has had a bad dream or did he awake in the night screaming and covered in sweat? Do these occur nightly or only once a month?

(h) Change in behaviour.

A somewhat different consideration is whether there has been a *change* in behaviour. In other words is the current behaviour normal for that child (rather than for children in general)? Of course lifelong behaviours can be serious in their implications, but attention should always be paid to an alteration in a child's behaviour which is not of a kind expected in terms of ordinary maturation and development.

(i) Situation-specificity.

In general a problem which is manifest in all settings probably reflects a more fundamental disorder than one evident in only one situation. However, the degree of situation-specificity is not a good guide to the abnormality of a behaviour. Nevertheless the presence of situation-specificity is important in terms of the light it throws on the dynamics of the child's problems in interacting with other people.

It will be appreciated that, in deciding on the abnormality of a behaviour, judgement should be made on a combination of all these criteria and not just on one. Even so, it is not enough to consider abnormality in purely statistical terms – in terms of its frequency. It is also necessary to consider how far the abnormality is associated with impairment.

Impairment

Judging behaviour in terms of its abnormality simply means assessment on the criterion of rarity. This gives some measure of its significance but it is also necessary to ask whether the behaviour is doing any harm, whether it matters to the child. This is a quite separate type of criterion and in the ultimate analysis more fundamental and more important. Whereas, in general, a behaviour which is rare is more likely to indicate psychiatric disorder than one which is common, it is immediately obvious that this does not necessarily follow. To turn to a medical example, dental decay is so common as to be almost universal but nevertheless it is a disorder leading to destruction and eventually loss of teeth, and it is quite properly regarded as a disease. Statistical considerations, actually, do help to indicate this in that there are populations (such as the islanders of Tristan da Cunha before they were drawn into western civilization) where dental decay is very rare. Conversely there are rare phenomena which cause no impairment and are not disorders in any sense of the word. Thus very high intelligence is rare but not a disorder, whereas very low intelligence is equally rare (actually slightly less rare) but is a disorder because it is associated with malfunctioning and social impairment.

It should be said that social impairment is necessarily a relative judgement and it has no meaning in absolute terms. This is because it can only be judged in relation to a person's social environment, and if that changes, so will the level of impairment. In our society an inability to read is a serious cause of impairment, but in a non-literate society there would be no impairment. It is essential to bear in mind the limitations imposed by this relativity of judgement but the assessment of impairment is, nevertheless, of considerable utility. Four main criteria of impairment may be employed: suffering, social restriction, interference with development and effect on others. Let us take three common symptoms (a dog phobia, aggressive behaviour and social withdrawal) and see how these criteria may be applied.

(a) Suffering.

There is a wide range of normal temperamental variation. Some children are cautious and restrained, others are adventuresome and exuberant. Both patterns are acceptable and normal and it is important not to try to impose on children any stereotypes we may have of 'the healthy personality'. There are many healthy personalities. Accordingly, with a child who is said not to join in with other children and to be socially withdrawn, one of the first questions is whether this is associated with any suffering. Is the child self-sufficient and perfectly content or is he anxious and miserable because he cannot join in? Is he a child who is by temperament rather introverted or is he suffering because he wants to participate but does not know how to or is too frightened to make the initial overtures? In the case of the child said to have a dog phobia, the distinction might be between someone who just does not like dogs but who is not afraid of them (and is therefore not really phobic) and someone who is petrified with anxiety when a dog approaches. In the case of aggression, the psychiatrist would need to ask himself whether this is a child whose aggression stems from unhappiness and discontent or whether the aggression is rather the result of overexuberant assertiveness.

(b) Social restriction.

With any of these three symptoms the question is whether it prevents the child from doing things that he wants to. There is a world of difference between the child who is anxious in the presence of dogs, but who still manages to go out and play when dogs are about, and the youngster who is house-bound in case he might meet a dog when he leaves the house. Similarly it is important to determine whether lack of social involvement or aggression is preventing the child from engaging in activities which are important to him.

(c) Interference with development.

As children grow older they need to progress in their psychological development, to cope with various life crises, to pass through certain phases and to advance in their mastery of the environment. It is not a rigid or fixed sequence but it is to a considerable extent predictable. For example, a child learns first to play on his own, then alongside others and finally with other children. Friendships in early childhood are transient and of little depth, but as he matures the child's friendships become more stable and long-lasting, and more of himself is invested in them. He learns to give and to receive confidences, to become empathic with other people's feelings and to quickly appreciate non-verbal signals and signs of social communication. Parallel with these changes, as an infant he first becomes attached to other people and is anxious if they depart. Gradually the attachment becomes firmer and the child is able to maintain bonds even while the other person is away. His dependency on his parents becomes less exclusive so that relationships with his peers and with other adults grow in importance and there is an increase in the child's autonomy and independence. In the same way the process of emotional or cognitive or linguistic development may be seen to move forward in a systematic fashion. Symptoms must be viewed in terms of the extent to which they are associated with interference with these developmental processes either in terms of a slowing down of progress or in terms of abnormal or deviant developments. The psychiatrist will want to determine whether the child's social withdrawal or aggressiveness have interfered with the process of social development. What has happened to the development of friendships and where is the child in terms of dependence and independence?

(d) Effects on others.

Finally, all of us live in a social environment in which our interaction and relationships with others are of vital importance to us. The essence of humanity lies in communication with other people, and in common with other social animals the development of personal ties and group relationships is fundamental. Accordingly symptoms must also be considered in an interpersonal context. What is the child's behaviour doing to those about him? Is his aggression souring his relationships or is it causing psychological damage to others? It is not at all infrequent to find that a child's main problem lies not in his personal behaviours as such, but rather in the manner of his deviant and maladaptive interaction with other people.

Diagnosis
Conceptual framework

Having decided, on the basis of the criteria we have discussed, that a child has some kind of psychiatric disorder, the next step is to make a diagnosis, to determine the nature of the disorder. Traditionally, in medicine, the model is of one diagnostic term to cover everything. Doctors talk about a patient having mitral stenosis (a type of valvular disease of the heart) or tuberculosis of the lung. The term refers to a disease or illness and there is an implication of one main cause and a fairly unitary approach to

prognosis and to treatment. Thus tuberculos
bercle bacillus and treatment consists in the adm
one of the drugs which is active against the bacillus. The
disease term conveys a lot of information, and a straigh
forward diagnosis using a single term works reasonably well in
practice. However, as doctors are well aware, the true situation
is more complex than that and there are many elements which
are not taken into account by a diagnosis of that type. For
example, although TB is due to the tubercle bacillus, susceptibility to the disease has an important hereditary component, diet and physical surroundings play some part in the
course of the disease, and psychosocial factors may also modify
the prognosis.

In general psychiatry, at least in the past, there has been a
tendency to use the same model. Diagnoses such as schizophrenia or manic-depressive psychoses also imply a disease or
illness and researchers are carrying out investigations to determine *the* cause of these diseases. To some degree this framework is applicable to a few of the rare psychiatric disorders in
childhood, but it is not appropriate for the majority of commoner disorders. The disorders are not diseases – psychiatric
problems have many facets not easily encompassed in a single
term, and typically the disorders are multifactorily determined.
It does not make sense to search for *the* cause for there are
usually several.

This will become more apparent later in the book as further
case examples are discussed, but let us take two examples to
illustrate the point. At times psychiatrists have talked about 'the
brain damage syndrome' or 'the brain-damaged child' or the
syndrome of 'minimal brain damage'. These sound like medical
diagnoses but they are seriously misleading in their implications. There is not one brain damage syndrome but many,
and the form of these disorders is usually indistinguishable
from that seen in children without brain damage. Furthermore
brain damage does not usually lead *directly* to psychiatric disorder.[161] The presence of damage greatly increases the child's
susceptibility to psychiatric disorder, but it does so through
interaction with a variety of psychosocial influences, as we will

...past have argued over whether a
...y retarded, in the same way that
...differential diagnosis between rheu-
...congenital valvular defect. But the
...different. Psychosis refers to the child's
...ioural state whereas mental retardation
...ctual level. Both are essential elements in
... ...y are *different* elements. A child may be
psych... ...t retarded, retarded and not psychotic, psychotic and re... ...d or he may have neither problem. The two terms
refer to quite different aspects of the child's disorder and are
properly thought of in terms of different *axes* or dimensions.

Considerations of this kind, together with the finding that
a single medical type diagnosis did not work in practice, led a
World Health Organization group a few years ago to suggest a
multi-axial approach to classification in child psychiatry.[163, 187]
This has been widely taken up by child psychiatrists, as it so
closely follows the style of thinking used in clinical practice,
and preliminary studies of this approach suggest that this is a
workable and useful scheme.[165] The system described here is
modelled on that suggested by the WHO, although it differs
from it in a number of respects.

The axes which may be employed are five: (1) clinical psychiatric syndrome, (2) intellectual level, (3) associated or aetiological biological factors, (4) associated or aetiological
psychosocial factors, and (5) developmental disorders. A diagnosis on this scheme would say something about the child's
problems on all five axes, even though the information might be
negative. For example, the diagnosis might be of (1) conduct
disorder in (2) a child of normal intelligence, who suffers from
(3) epilepsy and comes from (4) a family characterized by discord, quarrelling and disruptions. There is the associated problem of (5) specific reading retardation.

In this book we will not be concerned with the details of how
to classify biological conditions or how to classify psychosocial
factors. However, their important influence with respect to the

development of child psychiatric disorders is discussed in some detail in chapters 3, 4 and 5.

Intellectual level

Neither will we be concerned to any extent with the problems associated with mental retardation. These are certainly important and very much the province of the child psychiatrist (as also of the paediatrician and other specialists), but they mainly involve children attending special schools, whereas this book focuses primarily on the problems of youngsters going to ordinary schools.

Nevertheless it is important to know something about the meaning of variations in intellectual level.[153, 187] For most practical purposes four levels may be defined: (a) normal, (b) mildly retarded, (c) moderately retarded, (d) severely retarded. First, there is intelligence within the normal range, that is above the IQ of 70 or thereabouts. That includes about ninety-seven per cent of the population and variations within the normal range are undoubtedly important. In general the lower the intellectual level the higher the risk of psychiatric disorder. Also, an IQ above about 110 or 115 is required for most types of academic education. However, there are no clear demarcations within the normal range and the average child goes up or down by some 15 points during the 10 or so years of his schooling. Therefore a particular figure for IQ should not be taken too seriously in spite of its importance as a predictor of later scholastic success.

The next level is of mild intellectual retardation in which the IQ is within the range of roughly 50 to 70. Children with mild retardation should be able to acquire the basic skills of the 'three Rs', but many will need special schooling in order to do so. The great majority will go on to obtain and hold a job of some kind (albeit at a low level) after leaving school, and many will subsequently marry and have children. In this group the low IQ will have been determined in part by genetic factors, in part by social factors (most of the children come from poor homes lacking in intellectual stimulus and interests) and a few of the children will be of low intelligence because of overt brain disease or damage.

The situation is quite different with respect to moderate intellectual retardation, roughly a range of IQ 35 to 49. These children too will need special schooling, but it is unlikely that more than a few of them will learn to read and write at a useful level. After leaving school, many will be capable of a very simple job in a sheltered work setting but only a tiny minority will be able to hold a regular job on the open market. Very few will marry and many will be infertile (i.e. incapable of having children). In the vast majority of cases the low IQ will be attributable to some form of disease or damage to the brain.

The position with regard to the severely retarded (an IQ below about 35) is similar to that of the moderately retarded except that the prognosis is worse and most will not be employable even in a sheltered work setting.

It should not be thought that there are qualitative distinctions between these levels, or that there is anything magical about the boundary figures of IQs 70, 50 and 35. As with IQs at any other level, the actual test scores will fluctuate up or down to an appreciable extent as the children develop. On the other hand, if the groups at each level are compared, there are major differences between them with respect to aetiology, educational prognosis, employability and fertility, so that it is evident that the distinctions have meaning and are of considerable practical utility both medically and educationally.

Clinical psychiatric syndromes

Clinical psychiatric syndromes will be considered in more detail in chapters 6, 7 and 8, but an outline is given here in order to show why the disorders are subdivided in the way they are.

(a) Emotional disorders.

The two largest groups of common conditions consist of emotional disorders and conduct disorders.[166] Emotional disorders, as the name suggests, are those in which the main problem involves an abnormality of the emotions such as anxiety, fear, depression, obsessions, hypochondriasis and the like. In practice a psychiatrist will usually refer to the condition according to the particular form that the emotional disorder takes, so that he will speak of a phobic state or a depressive disorder. These are often termed 'neuroses' but that term is probably best avoided in view of the limited continuity with adult neuroses (see chapter 6).

Toby, who was mentioned on page 14, had an emotional disorder, as had Jane, who was seen during a general population survey. At about the age of nine years she became increasingly worried and unhappy, felt very miserable, went quiet and withdrawn, thought she was shunned by the other children and came home from school almost every day in tears. She was tense and frustrated and temper tantrums occurred three times a week. Her teacher described her as the unhappiest girl she had ever seen and the child begged her mother to take her away from school. At interview she was tearful, appeared markedly depressed and talked of her worries over her relationships with others, saying that sometimes she didn't care if she was dead or alive.

(b) Conduct disorders.

Conduct disorders are those in which the chief characteristic is abnormal behaviour which gives rise to social disapproval. The category includes some types of legally defined delinquency, but it also includes non-delinquent disorders of conduct as shown by lying, fighting, bullying and destructive behaviour. The mere fact that a child has transgressed the law does not, of course, mean that he has a conduct disorder. It is also necessary for the behaviour to be abnormal in its sociocultural context and for there to be social impairment. Surveys of the general population show that nearly all boys have at some time done something which is technically against the law. Most of these are perfectly normal youngsters who do not have any kind of disorder. Also, as already noted, the designation of conduct disorder does not necessarily involve a delinquent act at all. Many children with conduct disorders have not appeared in Court and some of the disorders are restricted to the home. Children with conduct disorders often have some emotional difficulties (particularly depression), but it is the socially disapproved conduct which predominates.

For example, George was a ten-year-old boy, also seen as part of a general population survey. He had pilfered small sums of money from his parents in the last year and had stolen a larger sum of money which his parents had put aside to pay the gas bill. On several occasions he had stolen from a near-by shop, from which he was now barred by the shopkeeper. He squabbled with his brothers and frequently got into fights on his way home from school. He wet his bed occasionally, also tended to soil himself and regularly wet his pants. There were daily temper tantrums, he was easily upset and cried when reprimanded. At interview he was fidgety and miserable, lacked emotional response and showed many facial mannerisms.

Logically the category of conduct disorder is unsatisfactory in that the diagnosis depends on social norms. It also includes a quite heterogeneous mixture of disorders. Nevertheless, in spite of that, it has been shown to be a meaningful and useful designation, and children included in this group have been found to have a lot in common. Conduct disorders are very much more frequent in boys than in girls and they are often associated with specific reading difficulties. The prognosis is much worse than that for emotional disorders, and there is a fairly strong link with the development of adult personality disorders.

In practice a sizeable proportion of children have disorders which share to a great degree the characteristics of both emotional and conduct disorders. For this reason there has also to be a category of 'mixed disorders'. In many respects these mixed conditions have most in common with the conduct disorders, but in other respects they occupy an intermediate position.

(c) Hyperkinetic syndrome.

There is a much less common disorder known as the 'hyperkinetic syndrome', which is chiefly characterized by very poor concentration, as shown both by short attention-span and distractibility, and abnormalities of motor function.[31] When younger, the children are characteristically very overactive in an uninhibited, disorganized and poorly regulated way so that they tend to be 'on the go' all the time. In adolescence this overactivity often fades away and is replaced by an inert under-activity. Impulsiveness, marked mood-swings and aggression are also common and disturbed relationships with other children are usual. In many cases the children have had delays in the development of speech or of other functions, reading difficulties are usual and often intelligence is somewhat below average. This disorder is very much commoner in boys than in girls in a ratio of four or five to one. The prognosis is poor and, although the overactivity lessens, the great majority of the children still show severe social handicaps in adolescence.

Robert showed the hyperkinetic syndrome. From infancy he was very accident-prone, the accidents mostly involving impulsive actions leading to disaster, such as when he fell out of an upper-storey window and when he ran out into the road in front of a motorcycle. In addition he was generally clumsy and was always bumping into things and breaking things. Since early childhood he had been very active. He rushed about like a whirlwind, was never still for more than a few minutes and was constantly fidgeting. His concentration was very poor. Robert wanted to do things with other children but he was always squabbling and fighting and no one wanted to play with him. At his last birthday party, when he was ten years, not a single child turned up. Tantrums were frequent and he often broke things in temper. He had various fears and, when he was younger, there was a phase of playing truant.

(d) Infantile autism.

Even rarer is a condition known as infantile autism. It is a severe disorder, present from the infancy period, in which there are three main abnormalities.[155] First, there is a failure in the development of social relationships, so that the infant appears unresponsive and fails to become attached to his parents until well after the usual age. Later he totally fails to develop friend-ships and shows an odd stilted way of interacting with people. Second, there is a severe delay both in the understanding of language and in the use of speech. When speech does develop (and in nearly half the children it never does) it tends to be stereotyped and full of echoed phrases and reversal of personal pronouns. Third, there are a variety of compulsive and ritual-istic activities. These may include such things as carrying around odd objects, finger-flapping mannerisms, severe food fads like only eating marmite sandwiches and preoccupations with numbers and timetables.

Like the hyperkinetic syndrome, it is also very much com-moner in boys. In about three-quarters of autistic children there is associated mental retardation and even in those of normal intelligence there is often a problem of understanding. Most of the children need special education but a few of the less handicapped ones can go to ordinary schools. Very few children with this disorder recover but, of those with normal intelli-gence, about half will improve sufficiently to make a reasonable social adjustment and hold a job. Scarcely any marry. The prognosis for those with mental retardation as well as autism is very much poorer and children with an IQ below 50 are likely to need lifelong close supervision and care.

(e) Schizophrenia.

Unlike autism, schizophrenia does not begin until later child-hood or, more usually, adolescence and cases before seven years are very rare.[155] Like the condition in adults, the onset is often insidious. The adolescent becomes perplexed and disturbed in his thinking, his school work falls off, his relationships with other people become more difficult, and he develops halluci-nations (especially of voices talking about him) and delusions. He may feel his thoughts are being controlled by an outside agency. Sometimes the onset is quite acute, often with the sudden development of ideas that he is being persecuted, that ordinary events have a special significance, and with either de-pression or excitement.

In the population as a whole it is not a very uncommon condition. Ultimately almost one person in a hundred will suffer from schizophrenia but the great majority of these disorders begin in late adolescence or early adult life after the person leaves school.

(f) Other disorders.

In addition there are a number of other common conditions

which do not fall into any single well-defined category. For example, bed-wetting (or enuresis) is one of the commonest childhood disorders. It is a troublesome condition which often occurs on its own, but sometimes it forms part of a wide psychiatric problem. Soiling (or encopresis) is less common and is more often associated with severe emotional disturbance. Both enuresis and encopresis are commoner in boys, encopresis very much so. Tics – a disorder in which the main feature consists of quick, involuntary, apparently purposeless and frequently repeated movements which are not due to any neurological condition – are also fairly common, again especially in boys.[40] A rare, and much more serious, condition is anorexia nervosa in which the main features are a persistent active refusal to eat and marked loss of weight, often with a degree of activity and alertness which is surprising in relation to the emaciation. Typically the disorder begins in teenage girls but sometimes it may begin before puberty and, rarely, it occurs in males. A stopping of the menstrual periods is usual. Some of these conditions will be considered in more detail in later chapters.

(g) Adjustment reaction or adaptation reaction.

Sometimes the term adjustment reaction is used for mild transient disorders, which are often relatively circumscribed and situation-specific and which may occur in response to acute stresses. There is no significant distortion of development and the problems are not of sufficient severity to consider them as full psychiatric disorders. Gordon (see page 13) presented problems of this kind.

(h) Developmental disorders.

Finally, there is an important group of problems, usually called developmental disorders. They are rather different in several respects from other psychiatric disorders, but they frequently coexist with them (especially with conduct problems). For this reason I have suggested they most appropriately form a separate fifth axis of classification. However, they are conveniently considered here for the moment. They constitute a group of disorders in which a specific delay in development is the main feature. The aspect of development which is delayed is related to biological maturation, but it is also influenced by non-biological factors. The two commonest varieties are a specific developmental speech disorder (shown by either speech delay or by gross abnormalities in pronunciation) and specific reading retardation (in which reading and spelling skills are seriously impaired in spite of adequate intelligence). All disorders in this group are very much more common in boys (in a ratio of about four to one) and similar problems are often present in other members of the family.

Principles and rationale of classification

It has already been stated that, for the most part, child psychiatric disorders do not constitute diseases or illnesses. In the past all these disorders have often been pooled together under some general term like 'maladjustment' or 'behaviour deviance'. What is the justification for dividing them up in the way they have been? Is it purely arbitrary or does it matter how they are classified? It does matter and it is not arbitrary. However, it does require justification. Classifications have sometimes been based on armchair theories, but that is no longer good enough. For a classification to be of any general use it must be based on facts, not concepts, and it must be defined in operational terms.[149] Second, it must convey information which is relevant to the clinical situation and which has predictive value. Third, it must classify disorders rather than children. Just as children may have measles one year and scarlet fever the next, so children may have one kind of psychiatric disorder at five years and another sort at twelve years. You do not talk about a measly child or a mitral stenotic person, and for the same reason it is better not to talk about a maladjusted child or a neurotic child. In the first place, it sounds rather degrading. The child is a unique individual with his own personality and not just the exhibition of a disorder. But also, and this is more important practically, a label of 'neurotic' on a child, rather than on his problems, suggests that he will always be neurotic. As labels can bring about self-fulfilling predictions, and because most children with psychiatric disorders do recover, this should be avoided.

Bearing these principles in mind, how may we decide whether the form of classification used is valid and useful? Several criteria need to be employed, and the more criteria that are met the more support is provided for the classification.[149, 166] It should be added that different classifications may be needed for different purposes. That which is most useful in planning schooling may not be the same as the one most useful in deciding upon the form of psychiatric treatment.

The first approach might be to examine what symptoms intercorrelate or 'go together'. If you are anxious, do you also tend to be depressed? If you steal, are you also likely to play truant? Several studies of this kind have been carried out.[77,86,198] They show that there is a group of emotional disorders which tend to hang together and which differ from other sorts of problems. Within this group a distinction has sometimes been found between anxious, fearful behaviour and depressed, inhibited behaviour. There are then one or two 'clusters' (i.e. groups of symptoms) concerned with conduct disorders. In some studies there has been no differentiation within that overall group, but in others a distinction has been found between aggressive behaviour and delinquent behaviour and in yet others between 'unsocialized aggressive behaviour' and 'socialized delinquency'. The meanings of these distinctions will be discussed in chapter 7. A further 'hyperkinetic' grouping has also been reported, although its differentiation is less clear-cut than that of the other groups. Finally, a cluster of items representing enuresis and encopresis has been found. In summary, statistical studies of the grouping of symptoms provide some justification for the classification, but they also emphasize the considerable overlap of groups of symptoms.

However, it is not enough to show that symptoms cluster together in diagnostic categories. If the categories are to be at all useful, it is necessary to go on to ask: Do the differentiations between categories have any meaning? Do the categories differ in other respects, such as age of onset, sex distribution, association with scholastic problems, aetiology, response to treatment and outcome? Only if they do, is the classification worthwhile. The results of using this variety of approaches to examine

Table 1 Variables differentiating diagnostic categories

Diagnostic Groups	Age of onset	Sex	Reading difficulties	Organic brain dysfunction	Family discord	Response to treatment	Adult state (if impaired)
				Variables			
EMOTIONAL	any	=	−	±	−	++++	neurosis/depression
CONDUCT	any	male	++	±	++	+	delinquency/personality disorder
HYPERKINETIC	<5 years	male	+++	+	+	+	personality disorder/psychosis
AUTISM	<2½ years	male	+++	++	−	+	language and social impairment
SCHIZOPHRENIA	>7 years	−	+	±	±	+	relapsing or chronic psychosis
DEVELOPMENTAL	infancy	male	+++	+	−	++	educational difficulties

differences between categories is summarized in Table I for a selection of six disorders.

The first distinction concerns the age of onset. The developmental disorders are present from infancy; autism always begins before thirty months of age; the hyperkinetic syndrome has an onset before five years; schizophrenia rarely begins until after age seven years, and both emotional and conduct disorders can begin at any age.

In terms of sex ratio the two disorders which stand out as different because of a roughly equal incidence in boys and girls are schizophrenia (which is slightly commoner in boys) and emotional disorders (which are slightly commoner in girls). All the other conditions are *much* commoner in boys in a ratio of at least three or four to one.

There is a general tendency for psychiatric disorder and educational difficulties to go together. This tendency is especially marked in autism, the hyperkinetic syndrome and the developmental disorders, but it is also marked in the case of disturbances of conduct. Emotional disorders stand out as different in having no particular association with reading difficulties.

The presence of organic brain dysfunction or damage is associated with an increased rate of all psychiatric disorders, but it is found in only a tiny minority of children with emotional disorders, conduct disorders and schizophrenia. In contrast it is much more frequently found in children with autism, the hyperkinetic syndrome or a developmental disorder.

Family variables also differentiate between the disorders. Family discord (quarrelling, marital difficulties, etc.) is fairly strongly associated with conduct disorders and shows a lesser association with the hyperkinetic syndrome. It is not associated with any of the other conditions. A family history of schizophrenia is associated only with schizophrenia and a middle-class background only with infantile autism. Parental constraint and overprotection are probably connected with emotional disorder, and parental neurosis is also.

Not only do the categories differ in causation, but they also differ in response to treatment. The outlook is best for emotional disorders, most of which clear up completely. It is worst for the hyperkinetic syndrome, autism and schizophrenia, in which most individuals are left with some degree of handicap in spite of improvement. To some extent the categories also warrant different forms of treatment, although the distinctions are far from clear-cut. Individual psychotherapy has only been shown to be useful for children with emotional disorders, although it is sometimes also indicated for children with other disorders. Stimulant drugs are probably only of value with the hyperkinetic syndrome and the major tranquillizers are mainly employed for the same condition and for schizophrenia. Among the behaviour-modification treatments (see chapter 9 for a description of these) techniques of desensitization and 'flooding' are useful mainly for emotional disorders, whereas, on the whole, operant approaches apply more to the other conditions. Educational methods of treatment apply especially to children with autism and those with developmental disorders.

The long-term outcome differentiates the disorders in broadly similar fashion to the short-term response to treatment.[141] Most children with emotional disorders recover completely, and about a third to a half of those with conduct disorders do so. Of the youngsters with developmental disorders most are free of psychiatric problems in adulthood, although many are left with educational difficulties (see below). In contrast the majority of children with autism, the hyperkinetic syndrome or schizophrenia remain handicapped to some degree.

Finally, among those who are left with some form of disorder in adult life, the type of disorder indicates important distinctions between the childhood categories. In the minority of children with emotional disorders who have persisting or recurring problems, the adult disorders mostly take the form of neuroses or depression. Among the children with conduct disorders who remain handicapped as adults, the problems mainly concern criminal behaviour or personality disorders. But, also, some involve depression. The outlook for children with hyperkinetic syndrome is worse and to some extent different. A personality disorder is the usual outcome but a few of the children become psychotic in adult life. Children with autism will continue to show severe social impairment and in many cases language difficulties also persist. Some youngsters with schizophrenia recover completely, but often the course is of a relapsing or persisting psychosis. Within the group of children with developmental disorders the main problem tends to proceed from speech difficulties to reading difficulties to spelling difficulties. Those with milder disorders may recover completely, but in the case of severe disorders some difficulty in spelling and reading is likely to remain.

In summary, although many problems remain, the research findings clearly indicate that a rational, and useful classification of child psychiatric disorders is possible and necessary.

Diagnostic formulation

Diagnosis and classification are a means of stating what a child's disorder has *in common* with other disorders. It picks out the certain key features of the disorder which enable a grouping and labelling of the disorder according to the denominators which it has in common with other similar disorders. This is a useful thing to do both because it narrows down the field in terms of causes, treatment and prognosis and because it provides a short-hand language of communication with other professionals. If a psychiatrist says that he has just seen a child with a phobic state this conveys meaning to other psychiatrists. However, because classification is based on the lowest common denominators, it necessarily provides a crude grouping, which disregards all that is unique about the child. Accordingly a further process is required to bring out these qualities. That consists of the diagnostic formulation which, unlike classification, emphasizes what is different and distinctive about this particular child.

The formulation puts forward ideas and suggestions about what psychological or biological mechanisms might be operative, what the underlying causes and the precipitants of the disorder for *this* child are, what the factors leading to a continuation of the disorder are and, on the basis of these considerations, what treatment approaches are likely to be most effective. Essentially it is a process of generating and testing hypotheses, which requires all the creativity and rigours of research. The hypotheses about mechanisms and treatments must, of course, be put to the test so far as possible and this means a careful monitoring and evaluation of the treatment process. It is essential to have some means of determining whether the treatment which is employed is being effective.

The process of coming to a diagnostic formulation may be illustrated by first considering overall syndromes (when the process is still very akin to diagnostic classification) and then individual behaviours (when the approach is more individualistic).

Syndromes

Each diagnostic category includes within it an assortment of syndromes which arise according to different psychological mechanisms and which require different forms of treatment. For each of his patients the clinician has to undertake a detailed analysis of the characteristics of the disorder in order to decide which psychological mechanisms probably apply. This process may be complex and difficult, and often it is not possible to be sure exactly which mechanisms are operative. However, it is essential to proceed as far along this path as possible. The procedure may be illustrated by taking two different presenting symptoms. In each case the diagnostic process will be followed through from the symptom to the overall psychiatric category and on to the particular sub-syndrome. To simplify the procedure, a branching-tree approach will be followed in which a single item decides which branch to follow in each case. It will be appreciated that in practice it may not be quite as straightforward and tidy as this. In particular it is common for there to be several different psychological mechanisms operating simultaneously.

(a) Non-attendance at school.

Non-attendance at school is an important cause of psychiatric referral,[74] which may arise in several quite different ways. The child may be kept at home by his parents to look after a younger brother or sister, he may be playing truant or there may be school refusal as part of an emotional disorder. If it is school refusal, this too may be due to a number of different mechanisms. Let us see how these may be distinguished one from another. The procedure is illustrated in Figure 1.

The first question is whether or not the child is remaining at home when he is not at school. If he is not at home, but at the cinema, playing with his mates or doing something else away from the house, the likelihood is that the problem is one of truancy. If it is, then the parents will probably not be aware

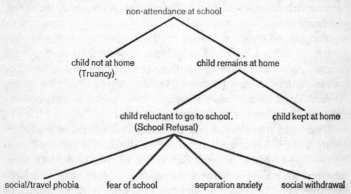

Fig. 1

each time the child plays truant and there may well be other indications of delinquent acts or of socially disapproved conduct. If the child has a psychiatric disorder (and many truants do not), the diagnosis will probably be one of conduct disorder.

If the child remains at home with his parents' knowledge, then the probability is that either he is being kept at home by his parents or he is refusing to go to school. If the latter, there will be indications of *his* reluctance to attend school; if the former, there will be reports of the parent keeping him off school.

If the problem is one of school refusal, it is an emotional disorder. However, it may arise in several different ways. It may happen because the child is afraid of school, because he is anxious about separating from his parents, because of a social or travel phobia or because of general social withdrawal. In each case there are one or two key questions which help decide which mechanism is operative. First, it is helpful to inquire what the child is like when he is *not* at school, that is, how he behaves when at home or with his friends in circumstances where the question of school does not arise. If he is cheerful, lively and in all respects his normal self, that rules out the possibility of general social withdrawal. On the other hand if he is said to be withdrawn, miserable, lacking in interest, not wanting to go out with his pals and concentrating poorly, that immediately suggests that the school refusal is part of a more widespread emotional disorder such as depression (or much more rarely schizophrenia).

The second question would be: Does the school refusal vary with the school curriculum? If the answer is that it always occurs on the day when the child has his French lesson, or PE or when he has to stay to school lunches, this provides a strong indication that the school refusal is connected with anxiety about something that is occurring at school.

The third question would be: Does the school refusal vary with what is happening at home? Is it worse when mother is depressed or when father is ill and off work? Did it start when mother took a job outside the home? If it does vary with happenings at home, this is a pointer to the probable importance of the child's anxieties about something in the home or family. Anxiety about separating from parents is probably the commonest mechanism of that kind and there the key question is: How does the child respond to other separations? Unless there is something very special about separating *vis-à-vis* school, the expectation is that, if there is separation anxiety, it should also show itself in other ways. The child may be anxious when his mother leaves him at home to go out to the shops or to visit friends; the child may be reluctant to go to stay with relatives or to go to play at a friend's house. If there is no anxiety with respect to other forms of separation then this makes it less likely that the school refusal arises on the basis of separation anxiety.

Less commonly, school refusal may arise because of social phobia or travel phobia. In the former instance there is a general fear of social situations and meeting people and in the latter a fear of going on buses, trains and the like. In both cases school refusal arises because it happens to be one instance of a situation involving meeting people or travel. This would rarely occur in the young child, but it is an occasional cause of school refusal in the adolescent. It can be distinguished from separation anxiety by asking whether the child is anxious meeting people or going on buses even when his parents are there (he will not be if it is separation anxiety), and conversely whether he becomes anxious with separations which do not involve either travel or meeting people.

Having made this preliminary sorting out of possible mechanisms the next stage is to ask why? and how? How did separation anxiety arise and why has the school refusal begun now? This means a careful study of factors in the child, in the school and in the home.

With respect to the child, have temperamental attributes helped determine his response to the separation involved in school attendance? Has he always been timid, fearful and dependent? Has he had previous unpleasant or stressful separation experiences? Has his experience of normal, happy separations been unusually restricted? Have difficulties at school arisen because of scholastic problems, because he is poor at sport or because he is lacking in social skills?

Regarding school, has there been a recent alteration, such as a change of teacher or of class? Are there particular difficulties with school meals (because the child is faddy or because of religious dietary restrictions)? Have there been difficulties about being allowed to go to the lavatory? (One child I saw had become preoccupied with anxiety because a medical bowel disorder meant that he had to go to the lavatory frequently. The teacher was unaware of this and had introduced restrictions on the number of times he could go, the child being too timid and self-conscious to explain.) Are there problems with bullying or with an unsympathetic teacher?

As regards the home, how do the parents deal with the child's anxieties about going to school? Do they get very anxious and worried and convey this to the child? Eisenberg,[49] in a study of families in which school refusal occurred because of separation anxiety, gives a vivid description of the many ways in which parents convey to the child *their* anxiety, by fussing, by unnecessary wiping of noses, by excessively repeated, tremulous reassurances that everything will be all right, and in a myriad other ways. Has there been a recent change at home? Is one parent ill or has there been a change in work pattern? Is either parent unduly dependent on the child? Are the parents fussily overprotective and restricting or conversely are they unconcerned and not providing support?

Overlapping with all these areas is the question of possible relevant factors in the way school attendance itself has been handled. Has the child been kept off school for all sorts of minor physical complaints? Has the school been punitive or mocking when the child has returned following a period of absence? Has the child's anxiety been intensified by other people responding with anger or by showing anxiety themselves? Is the situation such that this is the only way the child can gain attention and concern from his family? Some examples of how this procedure may be applied in actual practice are given in chapters 6 and 9.

(b) Faecal soiling.

Another example of the procedure of diagnostic formulation is provided by the problem of the child who soils his pants or passes his motions in inappropriate places. This too is a problem that may arise in several quite different ways, some of which have an origin in medical disorders and some in psychological disturbances. Figure 2 outlines the main steps in differential diagnosis. The first question is whether or not the motions are normal in appearance and consistency. If they are abnormal, we move to the right-hand side of the diagram and there is the further issue of why the motions are loose or slimy or whatever is wrong with them. The next question is whether the child has got masses of constipated motions. If he has, then there is probably the condition known as 'retention with overflow'. Here the basic problem is one of constipation which becomes so severe as to lead to partial blockage of the bowel. As a result of the blockage some of the motions liquefy and seep past to produce faecal soiling, the soiling occurring because the child has lost

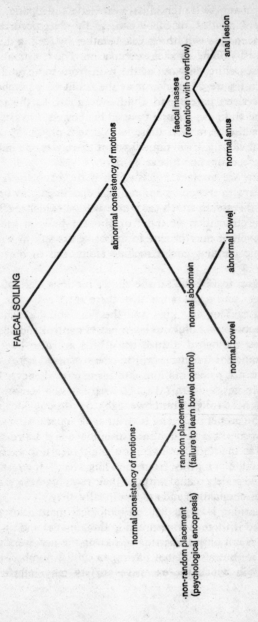

Fig. 2

the normal anal reflex through the excessive constipation and the subsequent dilation of the bowel. If this has occurred, then the faecal masses will be noticeable either by feeling the child's tummy or by doing a rectal examination. The constipation may have arisen either because of the pain from some anal disease such as a fissure or fistula, or as the result of a psychological battle between parent and child over going to the toilet, in which the child has refused to open his bowels. Physical examination will determine if there is a current physical lesion (although obviously it will not tell you if there was one in the past when the constipation first arose).

If there are no faecal masses, then the problem is one of diarrhoea with secondary soiling. The diarrhoea may be due to physical disease, in which case there will be evidence (from the history, examination or tests) of abnormalities in the bowel. Alternatively it may be due to excessive anxiety in which the autonomic nervous effects include alterations in bowel function.

To return to Figure 2, if the child's motions were of normal consistency and appearance, then there is no reason to suspect bowel disease of any kind and the differential diagnosis lies mainly between a failure to learn bowel control and encopresis due to psychological disturbance (there are also one or two rarer conditions but those will not be discussed here). At first the infant just passes motions into his nappy whenever he feels like it. He has to learn (a) to be aware of the sensation indicating his need to open his bowels, (b) to postpone opening until he is in the proper place and (c) what the proper places are. This learning process is not confined to humans and Laird has provided a fascinating account of how piglets learn to excrete in a corner of the pen away from the lying area.[96] Interestingly, it seems that piglets reared without their mothers have a random pattern of elimination and are continually dirty.

The learning is dependent on biological maturation (it may be delayed if there is widespread brain damage) and on experiences. It is not only a question of having the necessary positive experiences but also of not having an undue number of negative ones in which the excessive anxiety may interfere with learning. If the child has failed to learn bowel control adequately, then the soiling will occur randomly – that is, the child will soil whenever the need to defecate arises and the soiling will take place wherever he happens to be at that time. The fact that the soiling is randomly placed does not necessarily mean that it is due to a failure of learning. Instead it may be occurring as a response to psychological stress. In this case the timing may help. If bowel control was well learned and then lost ('discontinuous encopresis'), or if it started following some stress or intrafamilial disturbance, then a psychological explanation is more likely. However, although random placement does not prove a failure of learning, the converse cannot be the correct explanation. When there are disturbed parent–child relationships, the child may react by soiling and by placing his motions in the most unlikely places. In my experience these have included cupboards, under the bed, in mother's chest of drawers and even in the piano! If this occurs, a psychological explanation is certainly required!

As with school refusal, this preliminary diagnostic sorting-out must then lead on to the usual questions of why? and how? There is a fuller discussion of a child with the problem of soiling in chapter 8.

Individual behaviours

Much the same issues arise with respect to individual items of behaviour. The therapist must understand the meaning and function of each behaviour, and this requires an analysis of the various factors in the child and in his environment, which either increase or decrease the likelihood of the behaviour occurring.

Apparently similar behaviours may have quite different meanings and serve different functions, and these must be taken into account when planning treatment.[57] Let us take the common problem of temper tantrums or aggressive outbursts as an example. This may arise in several different ways. On the face of it, it is simply an expression of anger, but that is an inadequate explanation. In the case of Toby which has already been discussed (see page 14), his tantrums nearly always arose as a direct result of panic. He had many serious and handicapping fears, and when fear reached a crescendo in a situation from which he could not escape he gave way to an ill-coordinated outburst of shouting and hitting out in all directions at whatever or whoever was in his vicinity. In his case the treatment of the tantrum would mean finding a treatment for his fear. Once his fear was reduced or eliminated, the tantrums would stop without anything further being required.

Henry was a severely autistic adolescent, of normal non-verbal intelligence but entirely without speech and with very little understanding of spoken language. Following the onset of epileptic fits he was admitted to hospital. These were brought under control and his behaviour posed no severe problems except that at meal-times there would sometimes be severe tantrums resulting in broken dishes and blows directed at staff and patients alike. This seemed inexplicable until one of the nurses observed that it only occurred when certain foods were being served. It then became obvious that Henry did not want to eat particular foods which he disliked but, having no means of letting staff know that, he responded in a more primitive way by means of tantrums. As soon as observation established Henry's likes and dislikes in foods so that he was not presented with the latter, the tantrums rapidly grew less frequent.

This was a different sort of phenomenon from that shown by Toby. Although in a sense it would be true to say that both were responses to frustration, the mechanisms were different and different solutions were required. If it had been possible to teach Henry some simple gestures to indicate his wants and needs this might have helped even more with his communicative problem which had resulted in tantrums.

With John the tantrums served still another purpose. He was a ten-year-old boy who had frequent outbursts of temper at home, when he would cry and shout and generally create a hullabaloo. His mother would immediately go to comfort him and talk to him until he calmed down, when she would leave and return to her own work and interests. However the tantrums began in the first place, it was clear that they now served the main purpose of gaining his mother's attention. Whenever he had a tantrum she would immediately go to him, whereas when he was behaving himself he was left to his own devices. In his case it was not so much prior events bringing on the tantrum, it was what happened after which provided a reward and an encouragement for having the outburst.

The answer to John's tantrums was to get the parents to pay *more* attention to him when he was *not* having a tantrum, and to ignore him completely during the tantrum. Then, as soon as the tantrum stopped, they should go to him. The net effect was to increase the attention given to him so that there was less need for attention-seeking behaviour, and also to alter the timing of when attention was given so that there was maximum encouragement for his good behaviour and discouragement by lack of attention for his tantrums.

Mark's problem was different. He was a twelve-year-old boy who was referred because of severe temper outbursts in which he smashed furniture and threw things around the room creating havoc. These outbursts occurred only at home and his behaviour at school was perfectly normal. Although somewhat reserved, he had friends and got on all right with other children. In contrast, at home, relationships with his parents were severely strained. In addition to the tempers there were several episodes of destructive acts, carried out deliberately many hours after a family quarrel. On one occasion he made deep gouges in his mother's favourite coffee table and on another he spread glue all over the living-room carpet. He had always been a clinging child who was very close to his mother and dependent on her. When younger he used to cry for hours at night, calling out for her. He was still very close to his mother and was sometimes jealous when his parents kissed or were affectionate with one another. His relationships now with both parents, but especially with his mother, were a mixture of love and overwhelming hate.

Mark's temper consisted of hostility directed against his parents and it was all too obvious that this stemmed from deeply disturbed parent–child relationships. There had always been an ambivalence in these relationships, with a mixture of dependence and resentment, love and hate, and, with the additional stresses of adolescence, an upsurge of sexual feelings and jealousy and increased strivings for autonomy, the negative aspects came more to the fore. Treatment consisted of psychotherapy which aimed to resolve the conflicts and tensions between parents and child.

Finally, Theresa was a five-year-old girl already attending the clinic with a speech problem. In the course of treatment, mother brought up with the social worker the problem of a recent change in Theresa's behaviour. Having previously been well behaved, she was now difficult and demanding and there were frequent minor tantrums at home. It emerged that this behaviour began shortly after mother discovered she was pregnant. This was an unplanned and unwanted conception and gave rise to a good deal of tension, anxiety and indecisive heart-searching. Mother was irritable and low-spirited and this was reflected in her interactions with Theresa. After some weeks mother decided on a therapeutic abortion. This was undertaken, mother soon recovered her spirits and Theresa returned to the usual easy, cheerful state.

In this case the timing of the change in Theresa and the nature of her behaviour, which was like the normal response of a young child to a stressful situation, indicated that the explanation probably lay in mother's depression following on her unwanted pregnancy. The correctness of this explanation was confirmed by Theresa's improvement as soon as mother was better.

In each of these cases the clinician needed to use a combination of knowledge, experience and imagination in working out what the underlying mechanisms might be. The possible factors which may play a part in determining particular behaviours or disorders are infinite and often personal. With each child the clinician must seek to gain an understanding of his particular situation and of 'what makes him tick' in order to have a better idea of where to look for possible causation factors. However, there are certain general areas which always require study: prior circumstances, precipitants and contingencies.

By prior circumstances is meant the more long-lasting conditions which play a part in determining behaviours. For example, with Henry his serious lack of communication skills made him more vulnerable to frustration, and with Theresa it was the mother's depression which increased the likelihood of problem behaviour. With John it was the lack of attention from his parents which led to his using tantrums as a means of gaining attention.

By precipitants is meant the happenings which immediately precede the problem behaviours and seem to trigger them off. Thus with Toby the lights going out or his unexpectedly meeting someone he did not know were enough to send him into a panic. With Henry, being given food he did not want in circumstances where he could not explain that he didn't like the food regularly and predictably served to trigger off a tantrum.

By contingencies is meant what immediately *follows* the behaviour in question, in circumstances where the behaviour seems to bring usually about a certain result. This was apparent in John's case where maternal attention every time a tantrum started acted as a means of encouraging tantrums. The effect was just the same as if John got a prize or reward every time he had a tantrum, and we know that people will work hard to get rewards. John had tantrums in order to do so.

All the examples given refer to negative effects, but positive effects are equally important. Dominic was very afraid of dogs and would cringe if one appeared, but he was very much better if he was with his elder brother. Dominic was very fond of his brother and looked up to him. The brother was not in the least afraid of dogs and his good example served to protect Dominic against his fear. This suggested the use of modelling in treatment (see Chapter 6). Penelope was very difficult, demanding and disruptive at school except in the class with the art teacher. She was good at art, the teacher liked her and gave her a lot of praise and responsibility. These qualities were rather lacking in the other classes where Penelope was a poor scholar and regarded by the other teachers as untrustworthy. When given encouragement and when entrusted with responsibility, Penelope blossomed, as was shown when the other teachers were encouraged to alter their approach to her. Her scholastic failure made for difficulties, but her behaviour was much improved.

Psychoanalysts have sometimes argued against a psychiatric approach based on observations and descriptions of overt behaviour. They have maintained that this results in a disastrous misinterpretation of what is going on and that instead a 'meta-psychological assessment' is required. I hope that the examples given indicate that such a view is mistaken. In each case hypotheses about psychological processes have been derived on the basis of a functional analysis of observable behaviour. Of course it goes without saying that in making observations the clinician needs to use all his powers of empathy, intuition and understanding. He needs to know *what* to look for and this requires experience and art, as well as science. Then, having made hypotheses on the basis of these insights, he must proceed to test them in a logical systematic manner. This process is closely similar to that of scientific inquiry and research. The eminent biologist, Peter Medawar, has shown that there are two stages in science, first, the intuitive and imaginative creation of hypotheses and, second, the systematic testing of these hypotheses.[112] Writers have tended to focus on the second of these and to ignore the first when describing the scientific method, but both are essential. Medawar draws the parallel with clinical medicine and I cannot do better than quote him:

'The ... clinician always observes his patient with a purpose, with an idea in mind. From the moment the patient enters he sets himself questions, prompted by foreknowledge or by a sensory clue; and these questions direct his thought, guiding him towards new observations which will tell him whether the provisional views he is constantly forming are acceptable or unsound. Is he ill at all? Was it indeed something he ate? An upper respiratory virus is going around; perhaps this is relevant to the case? Has he at last done his liver an irreparable disservice? Here there is a rapid reciprocation between an imaginative and a critical process, between imaginative conjecture and critical evaluation. As it proceeds, a hypothesis will take shape which affords a reasonable basis for treatment or for further examination, although the clinician will not often take it to be conclusive.'

There could be no clearer description of the diagnostic process, and this applies just as much to child psychiatry as it does to general medicine. The whole burden of this chapter has been to give some 'feel' of what the process is like. The branching-tree outline of the diagnostic process with respect to syndromes was misleadingly mechanical because it assumed that there was a finite set of categories or baskets and it was only a question of obtaining predetermined pieces of information in a logical order and, click, into the basket the syndrome would go. The logic behind the branching-tree outline was real enough and it gave a fair representation of the business of testing hypotheses. That is exactly how it is done, searching for situations which can provide a test to determine whether explanation *a* or *b* is more likely to be correct. What was misleading was the implication that you could predetermine the set of baskets. In practice, of course, you cannot. Human beings are infinitely varied and the problems of each child are a bit different from those of every other. The purpose of the examples of separate symptoms was to illustrate how essentially the same diagnostic process may be applied to unique terms of individual behaviour.

On the other hand, as Medawar himself points out, the quotation above is also misleading because it implies that the imagination works *in vacuo*. It does not. As he argues, there must be something to be imaginative about, a background of observations and experimentation, before the exploratory dialogue can begin. That presupposes a knowledge of likely factors and mechanisms which have been examined and tested through research. The next four chapters aim to provide an outline of some of the knowledge which all the members of the clinic team need to have in making a diagnostic formulation. Only by appreciating the influences which impinge on a child and the factors which the child himself brings to any particular situation can the therapist hope to understand the unique problems of each individual.

2 Child Development

The biological basis of development

This chapter will be concerned largely with describing the changing pattern of children's behaviour as they grow older, together with some of the main psychological processes involved. However, to a considerable extent psychological development is dependent on physical growth and maturation, so that it is appropriate to begin by making a few comments on the biological basis of development. At birth the baby does not yet have the equipment needed for speech, for coordinating hand and eye, for walking or for understanding mathematical concepts. The development of these skills will depend both on physical maturation (especially brain growth) and on life experiences.

Growth spurts

In order to understand the psychological implications of physical development it is important to have some understanding of the timing of development. This varies according to the different body organs, as shown in Figure 3.[109, 186] The body does not grow at the same rate in all its parts, but for most body tissues there are two spurts of growth. The first occurs in the early years of life as a continuation of the very rapid development which takes place in the womb before birth. There is then a period of relative quiescence during the middle years of childhood followed by the well-known growth spurt of puberty. Obviously this second spurt is most marked in the reproductive organs concerned with sexual functions, but the increased output of sex hormones is also associated with a major acceleration in bone growth and general body development, as shown by the familiar shooting up in height during the years sur-

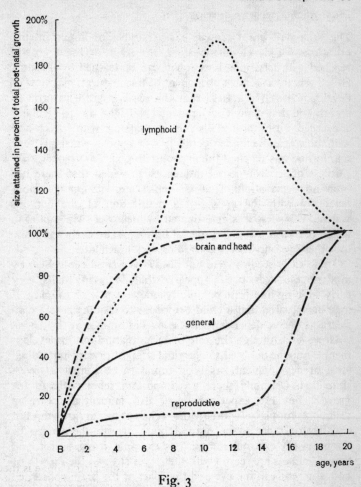

Fig. 3

rounding puberty. The first growth spurt is greatest in the case of the brain which differs from other organs in having its major development during the infancy and toddler age-period. Even by six months the brain has reached half its final mature weight whereas the body as a whole does not do so until about ten years. Indeed by five years the brain has already reached ninety per cent of its adult weight.

Maturational view of development

The timing of brain growth has a number of important implications for development. First, the stage of brain growth reached will determine how much can be learned by training. Gesell was the foremost proponent of this maturational view of development.[64] He argued that the basic impulse to grow is inborn and that many developmental skills (he was particularly concerned with motor skills such as walking, with speech and with bowel and bladder control) will appear when physical maturation has reached the appropriate point, more or less regardless of environmental influences, provided that there has been no deprivation. That is, behaviour will emerge spontaneously with the appropriate maturation of the nervous system. This view was investigated by means of twin studies in which one twin was given special training at an early age while the other one only received training very much later.

These early studies were not always very well controlled, by modern standards, but it appeared that, for many skills, very early training had little or no advantage over later training. It may be accepted that a child's response to training is to a considerable degree dependent on the level of brain growth.

However, although the role of brain maturation in development cannot be doubted, the original straightforward 'unfolding' view of development has been found to be somewhat oversimplified. Certainly there are important inborn stimuli for growth, but life experiences are also influential. Learning cannot take place without the relevant brain growth, but equally for there to be normal brain growth there must be the necessary external stimuli. For example, it has been found that if animals are reared with their eyes covered the growth of both the retina in the eye and that part of the brain concerned with vision is impaired.[137] Recent studies with rats have even suggested that the chemistry of brain development may be affected by stimulation or deprivation.[145] More familiar examples are afforded by the withering of an arm or leg which is not used or by the greater bone development in a limb subject to much strenuous exercise. Undoubtedly *lack* of normal stimulation can actually hold back physical growth. Whether *supra-normal* stimulation can accelerate growth is much less certain.

Quite apart from physical effects on maturation, stimulation or privation may influence the development of particular behaviours. Thus how much babies babble and how quickly they learn to talk is normally influenced by the extent to which adults talk to them and show interest in their vocalizations. For instance, Irwin found that infants who were read to for fifteen to twenty minutes each day produced more spontaneous babble than a control group who did not receive this experience.[84] Cazden showed that two- to three-year-old children given daily language training at a day centre made more progress in language than a similar group who received an equal amount of playtime at the centre but who did not get the language stimulation.[24]

Given apparently normal brain growth, stressful experiences may interfere with the emergence of behaviour which would otherwise have followed maturation. For example, this seems to be the case with enuresis. It has been found that many children who experience 'stresses', such as severe burns or surgical operations during the first five years of life when bladder control is usually established, continue to wet the bed for much longer than is normal.[96]

Variations in growth rates

Just as some body organs mature early and some mature late, so some parts of the brain mature in advance of other parts.[109] The lower (and more primitive) parts of the brain tend to develop earlier than the higher and more complex parts. The brain fibres for hearing develop early, but the parts of the brain concerned with the use and understanding of what is heard develop later. The brain pathways for vision also tend to develop a little before those concerned with hearing. This could mean that a child will usually understand what he sees rather before he understands what he hears, although this has not been shown directly. In short, it is normal for one aspect of brain development to be somewhat out of step with other aspects. This may be relevant to cases of children who are seriously behind in just one developmental function but who seem otherwise normal (see chapter 8). For example, there are children of normal intelligence who do not learn to speak until age three or four years – much later than usual.[164] It has been suggested (although direct evidence is lacking) that this may be due to a specific delay in the maturation of one part of the brain – an exaggeration as it were of what is in any case a normal tendency. This would be the equivalent in brain development of the otherwise normal child who is very late in getting his teeth. This appears to be an extreme example of the general trend for children's rates of development to vary considerably. However, these extreme degrees of a specific delay in development seem to be rather more than just exaggerations of normal, in that severe specific delays, unlike mild delays, are very much commoner in boys than in girls. The view that these specific delays in development are due to delays in the maturation of specific parts of the brain is a plausible hypothesis for which there is a certain amount of circumstantial evidence. Nevertheless it is just a hypothesis, in that for obvious reasons no one has actually examined the brains of the children during this stage of development. Much has still to be learned about the associations between brain structure and brain function during development:

It is appropriate at this point to emphasize the very marked individual differences in the rate of development, in both brain maturation as such and the various milestones of development such as sitting, walking, talking and so forth. Often people talk about the 'average' age or the 'usual' age for achieving these milestones. While such statements may well be accurate, they sometimes give rise to unnecessary anxiety because of a failure to appreciate the extent of the normal range. For example, the normal age for walking extends from about ten months to eighteen or nineteen months and there is a similar range for other functions.

Vulnerability to damage

Other implications also follow from what is known about the

timing of brain growth. In general, tissues or organs which are still developing, and therefore immature, tend to be more susceptible to damage. This is one of the reasons why infections of the brain and its surrounding tissues (encephalitis and meningitis) are usually more serious in the infant than they are in the older child. There are other reasons as well, such as the greater difficulties in diagnosis in the very young, but the vulnerability to damage of immature tissues is one of the most important. Dobbing has suggested that susceptibility is generally greatest at the point of most rapid growth.[46] This would make brain damage most likely in the first two years of life. One of the circumstances where this may be relevant is when there is severe malnutrition (either not enough food or the wrong kinds of food). In Britain this is quite uncommon in children but in many parts of the world it is distressingly frequent. If the malnutrition lasts only for a short period and there is an adequate food intake afterwards, the child will usually catch up by an increased rate of growth when he again gets enough to eat. However, the process of catching up may not be complete and studies suggest that malnutrition early in life may lead to permanent impairment not only of brain growth but also of mental development.[14, 15] In impoverished areas this is one of the causes of a lower level of intelligence or even of mental retardation.

Recovery of brain function after damage

While the immature brain is more susceptible to damage, it is also more capable of adapting to damage so that the practical consequences of brain injury in the young child may be less severe. In the adult each part and each side of the brain has rather specialized functions. Thus the left side is particularly concerned with speech and language, whereas the right side tends to be more involved with visuo-spatial functions. Within each side there is further specialization, so that the rearmost portion of the cortex (the occipital lobe) deals with the organization and understanding of things which are seen, and the temporal lobe is particularly concerned with memory and with emotions. But these specializations are not absolute. At one time it was thought possible to make detailed maps of the brain, allocating individual functions to each small area. It is now realized that this is an oversimplification. The brain consists of a complex set of connections, so that even quite simple functions involve circuits extending across several parts of the brain. For this reason it is misleading to localize speech or vision or any other function to just one limited portion of the brain. Nevertheless it is true that these circuits include key areas with specialized characteristics. If one of these areas is damaged or destroyed in the adult, it has a particularly serious effect on those specialized functions. Other parts of the brain cannot readily take over. If an adult receives a severe injury to the part of the brain specializing in speech, there may well be improvement later, but it is very unlikely that he will ever get back to his previous level of fluency and mastery of language.

The situation is quite different in the child.[161] With lesions confined to one side of the brain there is usually extensive recovery due to the ability of the immature brain to transfer functions from one side to the other. If the left side is damaged, the right side will take over speech function to an extent that is not possible once brain growth is complete. Transfer does not take place with equal ease for all functions, so that damage to one side of the brain in infancy may lead to partial paralysis of one side of the body whereas it will not lead to an inability to speak. So far, knowledge is lacking on how readily transfer takes place in the case of functions concerned with emotions and behaviour.

This period of recovery is a long one and children may continue to improve for a couple of years or more after a severe head injury or an attack of encephalitis. For example, Peter, the boy described in chapter 3, was unconscious for a long time after a severe head injury. When he recovered consciousness, he could not speak, he could not feed himself and in all respects seemed as helpless as a baby. However, ultimately he made a good recovery, returned to an ordinary school and proved to have normal intelligence. People commonly underestimate the degree of recovery which is possible in young children and so give an unduly gloomy prognosis.

Infancy and the first year

Capacities

It was once thought that babies were passive creatures of little individuality, at the mercy of their environment and with little or no ability to understand their experiences. This is now known to be a mistaken view. Babies have been shown to be active, capable and individual. They are active in the sense that their characteristics help shape what happens to them. Mothers respond to their children according to what their children are like. For example, it has been shown that mothers' nursing behaviour differs according to whether the child is awake or asleep, content or crying, when brought for feeding.[104] Babies who, for biological reasons, are more active or cry more will elicit different maternal behaviour from that elicited by the passive, quiet, contented infant. This effect on the mother is most striking in the case of the infant who has some congenital defect or handicap.[44] Mothers also respond differently to the premature infant, who is both more fragile and less responsive than the normal mature baby born at term. Of course maternal behaviour is also strongly influenced by the mother's personality, social background and past experience. But it has to develop and the development is part of a reciprocal interaction with the child, in which the child's characteristics and the child's experiences play a part in shaping the mother's behaviour. It is well known that in some animals a short separation of mother and infant may seriously impair or even abolish maternal caretaking. More recently it has become apparent that something of the same kind (although to a lesser degree) occurs in humans.[94, 100, 101] Mothers unable to handle their premature babies may show less attachment to their infants and express less confidence in dealing with them. The issue of mother–child interaction is considered further in the next chapter.

Babies are capable in the sense that they have considerable powers of visual and auditory discrimination; they are also able to learn and are generally much more in control of their environment than was once thought. Some of the studies showing these skills are both fascinating and ingenious. Most of them rely on apparatus which allows a very simple action well within the baby's powers to produce quite complex changes in the environment. In this way it is possible to show the types of sensory discriminations of which babies are capable. For example, in one investigation babies were placed in a special chair in front of a television screen and given a teat to suck. The teat was wired up to the screen in such a way that the baby had to suck at a certain rate to bring the picture into focus. If he could learn to do that consistently, then he must be able to see when the picture is sharp. Another study did much the same thing with auditory discrimination.[59] Toddlers could work a specially modified tape recorder to choose different tapes. The tapes were made to differ widely (such as speech versus gibberish) and quite subtly (such as tone of voice or stories with and without a lot of repetition). By means such as these it has been found that babies are much more capable than was thought a few years ago.

Of course babies' capacity is still decidedly limited compared with the adult and there are many things they cannot do. Many of these involve the *linking* of two different skills. Thus the baby can see objects and he can move his arm, but not until about five months is he able to combine these two skills to reach for an object and touch it accurately. In the same way, although he can see, hear and touch, the ability to link these different sensory impressions develops only gradually over the course of several years. He can distinguish sounds, but it takes several months for him to be able to understand much of what he hears. While he is responsive to people's interest and attention, at first he is not able to discriminate between different people or between people and objects. When smiling first appears at about two months of age, it does not have any social quality. It may be elicited by two dots on a card. Gradually the smile comes to be elicited only by a human face and by five or six months the infant will usually only smile in response to familiar faces. The young baby does not differentiate between the various people who look after him and it is only about half-way through the first year that he develops specific attachments to particular individuals.

Individual differences

Infants also have highly individual personal attributes.[12] It is quite appropriate for mothers to talk, as many do, of their baby's 'personality'. Obviously it is still a personality very much in the making and it may be very different from that shown when he is older. Nevertheless the beginnings of personality development are very decidedly present and it is a common observation that some babies are naturally more lovable than others. The differences between babies have been shown with respect to a wide range of characteristics including autonomic functioning (heart rate, blood pressure, sweating, etc., as shown in response to various stimuli), amount and type of muscle movement, responses to stimulation, regularity of wake/sleep cycle, type and intensity of emotional responses and sensory threshold, to mention but a few.

There are several different sources for this individual variation. There are vital genetic influences (as shown by twin studies), sex differences are already present (as discussed in chapter 3) and the degree of physical maturity will also have an effect. Physical *sequelae* of the birth process are especially important at this time. It is usual to talk about birth damage or injury as if this occurred during the period of birth itself. Of course such injuries can and do occur, but many of the problems stem from circumstances before and after birth. The baby is more likely to suffer from inadequate nutrition during his period in the womb than he is from injuries received during labour. Research over the last few years has also made clear that one of the particular hazards with very underweight (small for the date) babies in the first few weeks is damage from low blood sugar. Better understanding of the metabolic needs of these very fragile tiny babies has led to such improvement in paediatric care that not only are more surviving but probably there are also fewer damaged survivors. Finally, it is essential to recognize that life experiences are already helping to shape development in infancy. The influence of experience becomes increasingly important as the child grows older, but even young infants can and do respond to what happens to them in a way that in small measure helps shape their future life course.

The importance of these very early individual differences is considered in more detail in the next chapter. At this point it may be sufficient to note that not only may they reflect differences in capacities, propensities and relatively persistent behavioural attributes, but they will also influence how other people respond to the child, will determine what stimuli impinge on the child and will help shape his life experiences.

Oral phase

Many developments take place during the child's first year. In the past, psychoanalysts have usually termed this period the *oral* phase because mouthing and sucking is such a prominent part of a baby's behaviour and because they considered that in infancy the mouth is the main source of sensual satisfaction.[102] In recent years the concept has been much criticized by psychoanalysts as well as by other writers and it is evident that the term is so misleading as not to be helpful.[154] Certainly the oral area is a particularly sensitive one in infants, and undoubtedly infants not only get pleasure from sucking but also tend to suck objects as a form of exploration and satisfaction. However, young infants spend much time in exploratory play activities of a non-oral kind and even at this tender age infants are already getting obvious pleasure from genital stimulation. The timing and method of feeding (breast versus bottle, time and weaning, schedule or demand feeding) seems of very little importance for later development and sucking does not seem to be due to an innate desire. Finally, the development of social attachments which seems the most important characteristic of the first year of life does not primarily depend on sucking and feeding.

Attachment

Development is such a complex and multifaceted matter that to label any period by just one activity is a misleading oversimplification. However, if the first year or eighteen months must be labelled, it is probably best considered as the phase of *attachment*.[18] Erikson describes the same phenomenon in different terms by talking about this as the stage of development of trust.[52] The development of bonds or attachments to particular persons in the first instance requires certain cognitive skills.[170] At one month the baby mainly pays attention to the eyes in faces which he sees. By six months he is able to respond to the face as a whole. Parallel with this he moves from treating all people as alike to an increasing differentiation between people. At first this is chiefly a question of distinguishing the familiar from the strange, but during the second half of the first year he makes increasing distinctions between adults who are equally familiar, sorting out those who mean most to him. At the same time a fear of strangers commonly develops.

Sometime about the age of seven months the infant usually first develops an attachment to a specific person. This age is very approximate and the studies which have systematically examined the matter have found a range as wide as three and a half to fifteen months. Much has still to be learned about the factors which influence this development of attachments, but it is clear that neither feeding nor care-taking are essential features. It also appears that attachments do not necessarily develop to the person who spends most time with the child. The *intensity* of interaction probably has more effect than the duration. Attachment tends to be strongest when someone plays with the child and gives him a lot of attention, particularly if this is associated with responsiveness and sensitivity to the baby's signals. A baby's tendency to seek attachments is increased by anxiety and fear as well as by illness and fatigue, and attachments are particularly likely to develop to the person who brings comfort at such times. The development of attachments also tends to be inhibited by a generally unstimulating environment. Of course the degree of attachment is influenced by characteristics of the child as well as of his environment. Children differ in this respect as in many others.

Because in most families mothers have most to do with young children, the main attachment is usually to the mother. However, one study found that in nearly a third of cases the main attachment was to the father and it may be to a brother or sister or even to someone not in the family at all.[170] Bowlby has suggested that there is a bias for a child to attach himself especially to *one* figure and that this main attachment differs in kind from attachments to other subsidiary figures.[18] However, others have doubted this claim and the necessary evidence is so far lacking.[156] What is undoubted is that most children have *multiple* attachments of varying intensity and that there tends to be a persisting hierarchy among these with some continuing to be stronger than others. Even in institutions children tend to have their 'favourite' adults, but whether the bond that happens to be at the top of the list is different in kind from the others seems very doubtful.[183] So far as can be judged many children have several bonds which seem similar in type and serve much the same purpose. Indeed, it is probably very much to a child's advantage to have several bonds. It means that he will have several people to turn to during times of stress or difficulty and he is also likely to be less upset if the person to whom he is most attached has to go away because of illness, accident or other circumstances (this prediction has yet to be adequately tested).

Children's later relationships with people (friendships, love relationships and family ties) have to build on what has happened earlier in life and, although their exact function remains uncertain, most experts think that these early attachments are particularly important in this connection. There is no sharply limited critical period for the development of the child's first bonds, but the evidence suggests that, if the child has failed to develop attachments by two or three years of age, it will be increasingly difficult later. The situation most likely to cause the child problems in this respect is the old-style institution, where the child is cared for by a large number of adults who come and go without anyone having special responsibility for individual children. Since the dangers of this form of upbringing were pointed out some twenty years ago, conditions in Children's Homes have much improved, but there are still institutions which leave a lot to be desired. Understandably we know more about the circumstances when things go badly wrong than we do when they are just not quite right. However, it is important to recognize that it is not enough for a child to develop any old kind of attachment. The quality of the bond is also important. We know very little about what makes for 'good' bonds, but the security of the attachment and the child's capacity to maintain bonds even during a separation are probably two important factors. Some of the circumstances which may help foster these characteristics will be considered when discussing the two- to five-year age-period (see below).

Other changes

Although the development of bonds is probably the most important feature of the first year in personality development, many other changes are taking place.[19] Motor skills are increasing so that the child has learned to reach for things, to sit without support, to crawl (usually, although some quite normal children omit the crawling stage or instead shuffle on their haunches) and to stand. By twelve months the child may be just beginning to walk, although this usually develops at a later stage, as there is generally a gap of about three months between his being able to stand and walking without support. Perceptual development is characterized not only by the child's increasing ability to deal with complex sensations and to link different sensory modalities but also during the second half of the first year by a gradual progression from mouthing and a general emphasis on the proximal senses to an increasing reliance on the distal senses of vision and hearing. Language development is chiefly notable for the great increase in the child's ability to understand what is said to him and by the increasing range and complexity of the sounds the baby makes. Babble is well established and perhaps the child has spoken his first meaningful word, although often this is not until a little later. Fears are beginning to be present. At first they occur largely in relation to unexpected sights or sounds, such as sudden noises or sharp movements. At about seven or eight months he begins to show some apprehension of strangers and may even panic if one approaches him too quickly before he has the opportunity to size up this new person. At this stage imagination plays little or no part in children's fears.

The second year

During the second year the child's attachments to people become stronger and reach a peak. This is a period when toddlers tend to follow their mothers about the house and sometimes are rather clinging, hiding behind mother's skirt when a stranger appears. Gradually, however, the infant learns to use his mother's presence as a secure base from which to explore the world. When visiting strangers, at first he will stay very close to her. But then he will leave her side for longer and longer periods, only returning from time to time as if for reassurance. However, it is not just the mother's presence which serves as a base. The same phenomenon may be seen with fathers, older brothers or sisters or indeed anyone to whom the child is attached.

This is an age when children are often most upset in a new situation (such as in hospital or at residential nursery) or when away from their parents (see chapter 4). This distress may be considerably ameliorated by someone spending time doing things with them and being generally available for the child to come to for comfort. New attachments quickly develop in such circumstances. However, the greatest relief is provided by the presence of a familiar person, particularly one to whom the child is attached. Parents obviously fulfil this role, but it is of interest and importance that even very young brothers and sisters may also do so. It seems therefore that what is important is not the parental care provided by someone but rather the *presence* of someone familiar.

Over the year most infants are becoming increasingly confident. This shows itself in a variety of ways. Motor development is advancing so that the child is able to walk and move about with increasing speed and agility. Altogether his coordination of large muscles is becoming much improved. Emotionally too there are important changes. The child's fear of sudden noises and movements is diminishing and by the end of the second year he will probably show much less fear of strangers (or may not be afraid of them at all). On the other hand fears of dogs or other animals or objects associated with pain are quite common.[87]

As well as the increasing capacity to do things on his own the child also shows increasing independence of action. About age two years the 'me do it' phenomenon is quite characteristic. The child has discovered that he can do things for himself and insists on exercising that ability. Understandably his wish to do things on his own often outstrips his ability to do so safely and adequately and Erikson has rightly described this period as one in which the development of autonomy and self-reliance is most prominent.[52] The parents have a difficult task in encouraging the child to develop this autonomy and so improve his social competence and aid the growth of confidence while at the same time ensuring that his explorations remain within the bounds of safety and do not too frequently meet with failure. The child's learning to say no is an assertion of his own individuality. It is a necessary step in personality development, but obviously it creates an area of possible conflict between parent and child. He needs to be helped to help himself in such a way that he can learn how to do things without feeling that they are being done for him. Learning needs to be carefully graded so that new efforts usually meet with success instead of over-ambitious at- tempts ending in failure. Parental guidance has to be both skill- ed and unobtrusive for this to work really well, with safety uppermost in mind because of the child's inclination to rush into the road when he sees something interesting and his lack of appreciation of the dangers of stoves and of fires. Burns and scalds are particularly common (and serious) in the pre-school period.

Anal phase

Traditionally in psychoanalytic theory, toilet training is the most crucial feature of this stage of development, which for this reason, and because it was thought that sexual feelings centred around defecation at that age, has been called the *anal* phase.[102] Certainly, in previous generations, this was the issue which most commonly gave rise to a clash of wills between the parent and child, but toilet training probably now involves less parental investment of energies than was once the case. The child's attempts to gain control of his bowels and bladder are important sources of interest and exploration for him but there are no good reasons for regarding the anus as the main focus for sexual interest. Moreover there is no reason to suppose that the timing or methods of toilet training have any marked effect on adult personality.[27] Parent–child conflicts on potty training are probably best seen as merely one example of a wider source of clashes involving autonomy rather than something which is uniquely important.

Emotions

Anger is a common emotion in the second (and third) years, and tantrums involving screaming, kicking or holding the breath are the commonest forms of expression. At this age tantrums are most frequently associated with either parental restrictions or with frustration at failure to accomplish something. Being put to bed, made to sit on the pot, dressed in restrictive or bulky clothing or being forbidden to do something are the usual precipitants of anger. Changes of routine (often associated with visitors to the home) are also liable to lead to tantrums.

In people of all ages mood is much influenced by physical state, but this is particularly marked in the toddler.[87] Temper outbursts are especially frequent just before mealtimes when the child is hungry, when he is tired, when he is cold or when he is unwell. Many a parent has discovered the curative value of something to eat or a period of rest. Parents also learn that a change of mood may be the first indication that a child is sickening for something. Increasing irritability and temper outbursts are often the first signs of an ear infection or one of the childhood fevers.

Increasingly too learning influences the expression of anger and the use of tantrums. In dealing with temper outbursts, it is important not to encourage the child to think that this is the best way of getting what he wants. If parents only pay attention to the child or give what he wants when he has tantrums the child will quickly learn what to do to achieve this desired end. This possibility is greatly reduced if parents are sensitive and alert to the child's needs when he is *not* having a tantrum and if avoidance of known precipitants of anger, diverting the child's attention and providing an alternative activity are used as ways of coping with tantrums. Once an outburst is established (particularly in older children) it may sometimes be best to ignore it until the child settles down and only then provide solace, comfort and attention. However, whether this is the right course will depend on the reason for the tantrum (see chapter 1).

During early childhood there is a shift in the types of emotional problems which are common. In the first year or so eating and sleeping difficulties predominate but during the second year anxieties over separation become more common and also many difficulties centre around clashes of dominance between parent and child. The latter persist throughout the pre-school years, but increasingly in the years leading up to school entry concern begins to focus on the child's difficulty in relationships with other children. Parents may become worried about aggression in this context. Also there is an increase in parental anxieties about delays in the development of bowel and bladder control, and of speech, if the child is falling behind in these.

Language

At the beginning of the second year, after a gap of a month or so following the first meaningful word, there is a gradual increase in vocabulary which markedly accelerates from about eighteen months, so that by two years of age the average child will understand several hundred words and regularly use perhaps two hundred.[59] However, as with other aspects of development, there is wide variation and a few normal children may use only a dozen or so words by their second birthday. A child's first words are little more than reflex responses to an object, but particularly during the latter half of the second year, he develops a flexibility in the use of words that indicates the beginnings of true language. Distinctive intonation patterns may be evident even with single words so that 'Daddy' may be said one way to mean 'Daddy, I want this' and another way to indicate 'Look, there's Daddy'. In a sense this is the beginning of early sentence formation.

During the second year children's understanding of language noticeably increases, so that they are able to follow simple instructions as well as to respond to single words. All the time the child is listening to the speech around him, learning from adult conversation. His enjoyment of the rhythm of nursery rhymes and his pleasure in oft-repeated stories add to the building of language skills. Those aspects of play which reflect language similarly develop. Early in the second year infants begin to use common objects (such as a hair brush or a cup and saucer) in a way that indicates an understanding of their use and function. Some months later the child will extend functional play to involve dolls and large toys and by his second birthday he may be expected to use miniature toys in a similar fashion. The second year is also a time when imitative gestural games such as 'peek-a-boo', 'bye-bye' and 'pat-a-cake' are prominent among the child's activities. The child is probably showing some interest in other children and may play alongside them. But he will not yet play with them and interactions with other children are not yet an important feature of his life.

More than any other individual, Piaget has opened up new ways of looking at children's mental development in terms of its course and various stages.[201] The first major stage, that of sensori-motor intelligence, occupies roughly the first eighteen months and precedes the period when concepts, symbols and language dominate thinking. In the first year there is a progression from simple repetitive movements to deliberate actions for a predetermined purpose, such as when the child knocks down a tower for the pleasure of watching it fall. Just before his first birthday this develops into active trial-and-error experimentation as the first phase in problem solving. He becomes able to group and classify objects and he learns to look for objects that are hidden, following an appreciation that they do not cease to exist when they disappear from view. By eighteen months imagery and symbolization are beginning to have a place in problem solving, in parallel with the child's increasing growth of language.

The two- to five-year age-period

Much happens during the next three or four years leading up to school entry. With almost equal force this could be regarded as the phase of language development, of the growth of play, of identification and the emergence of guilt, of gender identity and of locomotion.

By three years motor development has come a long way. The child is probably running smoothly and is able to jump (although even by five years he still cannot hop or throw properly). Climbing, balancing, running, pushing and pulling are easily accomplished and the child is using these new-found skills to test his abilities in innumerable ways which extend the horizons of his experience. Fine motor coordination is improving but remains more limited. Circular scribbling is followed by an ability to draw straight lines, and drawings begin to have more form, so that by age five years the child can create a recognizable picture of a person or of a house. Detail is still meagre and the child's sense of relative proportions is poor.

Perceptual development is proceeding and the child is becoming able to make quite fine discriminations. Gibson has shown that four year olds can differentiate according to closure (for example the difference between O and C), but still have problems with line-to-curve transformations (for example U to V) or rotational transformations (such as M to W or b to d).[65] Obviously this is very relevant to learning to read and it is fortunate that slope transformations (for instance $|$ to $\setminus$), which are not mastered until after eight years, play little part in the English alphabet. The precise skills which underlie these perceptual discriminations remain uncertain[26] and it is noteworthy that some of the discriminations involve *un*learning as well as new learning. Thus one of the first things a child learns is that a chair is still a chair whichever way it faces. In other words ⊢ is the same as ⊣. In that the retinal image will change markedly according to the distance and angle from which an object is viewed, this is an essential piece of learning if the world is not to be total visual confusion. But, for reading, this has to be unlearned. A letter is *not* the same if written the other way around: *b* is not the same as *d* or even *p*, nor are *u* and *n* interchangeable. Learning to read is the more difficult because it involves unlearning something already well learned.

Language

The growth of language is more impressive during the pre-school period than at any other time.[164] Vocabulary increases from some two hundred words to several thousand, the child learns to talk in sentences and he masters the basis of most of the complexities of grammar. Exactly how this learning takes place is ill understood, although it is clear that the process involves meaning and understanding rather than mere reflex associative learning. Also children learn rules, not just specific grammatical constructions. This is the period of constant questioning, 'what' questions predominating at first, then 'where' and 'who' and then by age four years it is 'why' which holds the stage. While questions are frequently used to seek information, parents are often irritated by the frequency with which children ask questions to which they obviously know the answer. Children seem to be concerned with how the adult phrases his reply – perhaps to learn about language rather than about the thing mentioned in the question. In the same way children spend a lot of time talking to themselves, trying out different word combinations and different ways of saying things.

At the same time as children are learning new words their pronunciation of these words is steadily improving. Some two thirds of children are easily intelligible from the beginnings of speech, but one third go through a phase when they cannot be understood, and one child in twenty-five is still unintelligible on entry to school at five years.

Play

During the third and fourth years the child shows a rapidly increasing use of imaginative or pretend play, in which he practises his skills or acts out his fantasies in games of school, of doctors, of babies, of cowboys and Indians, of cops and robbers and the like.[113] Make-believe play is at its height between about eighteen months and seven years. Imaginary objects are not merely absent real objects, they may also be 'inventions' and many children at this age have imaginary playmates. At first make-believe play is a medley of events – both actual and imaginary – but without much of a coherent story. Gradually the child becomes progressively more capable of orderly sequences and his play comes to represent a meaningful story.

Pretend play has an important role in development and serves many functions. It may be a form of exploring emotions as when the child rushes into the home with a pretended terror of tigers chasing him. Alternatively it may serve as a means of lessening fears as in the case of a child who repeatedly re-enacts some frightening event such as the house being set on fire or a car accident. By repeating the event in safety it may help him come to terms with the experience and so lessen its impact. In other cases children clearly re-enact events, not in the way they actually happened, but as they would have liked them to happen. Play may be compensatory or act as a kind of wishful thinking. Yet again, the play activity may help the child understand some happening. He may pretend to go to hospital or to go to work, over and over, asking his parents to confirm the details or the sequence as if to help him appreciate what really happened. At other times make-believe play may be a way of overcoming boredom in an unstimulating environment or of arousing a crescendo of excitement (which often ends in tears or in a fight). Susanna Millar summarized it by saying that the child may be exploring his feelings, lessening his fears, increasing his excitement, trying to understand a puzzling event by graphic representations, seeking confirmation of a hazy memory or altering an event to make it pleasant to himself in fantasy![113]

Play with other children goes through several stages in early childhood. In the first year most play is solitary and other children are largely ignored, but from about a year onwards children pay increasing attention to others and by age two years they will play alongside other children. During the third year this gradually progresses to associative play in which the children engage in the same game but with each child intent only on his bit of it. By three years cooperative play, in which the children really join together in the same activity, is beginning and this increases over the next few years. At first cooperative play rarely involves more than two children and the pair often do not stay together long. But by age five years a play group may consist of four or five children and the group generally stays together much longer. During this preschool age-period the presence of other children becomes increasingly important both as a source of pleasure and as a cause of dispute. After two years, clashes with others become more important as a precipitant of temper outbursts, and rivalry and competition increase. Learning to share is something that is only slowly gained with experience. Equally, however, children get increasing pleasure playing with their brothers and sisters or with other children. Rough-and-tumble play is greatly enjoyed, but truly cooperative working together also becomes more frequent. Both the child's opportunity to play with other children and the way his parents deal with the interaction will greatly influence social responses and the amount of cooperation.

At this age many children have some object which they like to hold or carry about with them. This may be a cuddly toy, a teddy, a blanket or even just a rag, but usually it is something soft with a pleasant feel to it. The object is usually used as a source of comfort when the child is worried or tired and is most used at bed-time. Frequently, it is rubbed against the face or the threads are used to tickle the nose or the lips. The smell is often important also, and many children either suck the object or hold it in their hand while sucking their thumb. Winnicott[197] described them as 'transitional objects' and it has been thought that in some way they serve as a link with mother, being used as a source of comfort when she is not there and as a stage in the progression from an exclusive relationship with her to a wider range of social relationships. However, this explanation is put in doubt by the observation that the use of such objects is not influenced by the presence or absence of the mother. Nevertheless there is evidence that the object may have some symbolic function and, if the object is removed or destroyed, the child frequently finds another one to take its place.[106] The nature of the child's attachment to this object remains ill understood, but it is an important feature of many (though not all) children's life in the preschool period. During the school years the attachment usually diminishes in importance gradually, but most often it is still used at bed-time for several years after it has been dropped in other situations. The age when objects cease to be used in this way is extremely variable. Generally children stop using the object as a source of comfort in the daytime during the first few years of schooling, but it may be used at night-time (especially by girls) right through adolescence.

Another sort of play consists in the exploration and investigation of objects, and this too grows and develops during the preschool years. Most children like to find out 'how things work' and will spend a long time with a new toy or novel object finding out what it will do. Wheels will be removed, switches pulled, doors opened, knobs turned and moving parts moved. Of course this can be inadvertently destructive, but it is the child's way of learning about the environment and he will be just as interested (although not as competent) in putting things together as in taking them apart. Play with bricks and constructional toys is popular at this age, but just as popular (with the child if not with the parent!) is exploration of dad's tools, mum's household equipment, light-switches, taps and other 'adult' objects. Children vary in how much they explore and boys tend to be somewhat more exploratory than girls. Obviously parents differ too in their response to this sort of play, and children's continued exploration may well be shaped by the family reactions they encounter. This is important, as exploration is one of the main ways in which children learn about 'things', and the extent to which parents aid and foster the child's interest in investigation is likely to influence his intellectual development.

Exploration is different in many ways from other sorts of play: in its characteristics, in when it occurs and in what it leads to. Children explore when they are at ease, whereas they may engage in other sorts of play in order to obtain comfort. On the whole, exploration increases when the object is new and complicated (provided it is not so different as to be frightening, or so complicated as to be outside the child's capacity). But many sorts of play revolve around frequent repetition of the familiar. Young children love to hear the same story over and over again and often will insist that a particular game is repeated exactly in the way that it first gave pleasure. This is an age when children get great comfort and pleasure from anything familiar. Bedtime rituals become very important and have to be gone through in exactly the same way, the child becoming upset if the parents try to cut short the process because they are in a hurry to go out. Many children are also very conservative in their eating habits at this age. One of the stresses in going to hospital or being admitted to a residential nursery is the lack of these familiar routines, and much comfort can be provided by ensuring that they are preserved as well as by having familiar adults present at key times such as meal-times and bed-time.

Use of play in clinical assessment

Clinically a great deal can be learned about a child's development by asking about and observing his play. Many errors in the diagnosis of mental retardation, for example, could be avoided by proper attention to the child's play.[164] Parents and doctors often place most emphasis on speech and motor milestones (age of sitting, walking, etc.) in judging a child's intelligence, but both of these have serious limitations. Specific delays in speech in children of normal intelligence are far too common for speech delay to be a reliable guide to intelligence and motor milestones are far too variable for them to be of much value in this connection. Many retarded children have normal motor milestones and, conversely, motor development may be affected by neurological disorders which do not affect mental function. Of course a child's play is inevitably influenced by the toys and opportunities available to him, but a lot can be learned by careful questioning and observation. Parents should be asked about his use of toys (does he investigate what they will do and does he understand how they should be used? does he push a toy car along the floor or does he put it in his mouth?); his patterns of play (does he use toys in a limited stereotyped manner or does he develop their uses to make a game or story?); and his approach to new objects (does he investigate and explore things about the house – new toys or household equipment? how good is he at finding out how things work? how curious is he? how long does he persist in exploration?). The extent to which he can look after himself and help about the house is also informative (does he help clear the table or fetch things? can he dress or feed himself?). In observing the child himself, particular attention should be paid to the way he approaches a new situation; to the extent to which he is curious and interested in objects; to his skill in understanding how things work; to his constructional abilities and most of all to the degree of system and logic he uses in finding out how to use or manipulate objects, toys or implements.

Children's games involving meaningful use of objects and make-believe play also reflect a child's knowledge of verbal concepts or 'inner language', an important point in the assessment of children delayed in speech. By the age of eighteen months or so children should be able to use real objects such as a hair brush, spoon or cup in a way that clearly indicates that they have understood their use, and by their second birthday they should be able to do the same thing with miniature toys. The parent may be asked whether the child 'talks' into a toy telephone or just takes it apart. In the clinic the same functions may be assessed by handing the child objects such as a baby's brush and comb, a doll or a toy car and observing what he does with them. Imaginative play should be progressing during the third and fourth years and the parent should be asked when the child plays at 'tea-parties', 'mothers and fathers', 'school' or dressing and undressing dolls. Does he use toy cars for racing or driving into a garage or does he just push them to and fro? How far are toys used in a way which implies a story or sequence of events? How far does the child put meaning into his drawings?

Imitation plays a role in the growth of language and the parents should be asked about imitative games such as 'peek-a-boo', 'pat-a-cake', 'ring-o-roses' and whether he waves 'good-bye' or tries to copy his mother's actions in dusting or using the vacuum cleaner.

Quite apart from reflecting language development and intellectual skills, play is a rich source of data on the child's feelings and thoughts and on his social relationships.[113] Particularly at this age, a child's fantasy play may closely reflect his current concerns and anxieties. It is not that what occurs in his play actually happened at home or at nursery school, but rather that his wishes, his fears and his attitudes are often reflected in the imaginary situations he portrays in his play. Interpretation of these requires some knowledge of the child and it is important that the clinician does not leap to conclusions too quickly on the basis of *his* fantasies rather than those of the child. Even so, much can be learned by observation of fantasy play and, with an adult he trusts, a child may come to express his feelings fairly overtly, using the convention of putting his thoughts into the characters in the game. Young children do not usually talk about their emotions directly in the way that an adult may and more indirect methods must be used in assessment. Because they are indirect, of course, caution as well as skill is required in drawing appropriate conclusions.

The degree to which a child has moved from solitary play to parallel play to cooperative play tells the clinician about progress in social development. The *manner* and *style* of interaction with other children indicate the quality of relationships, and a careful note of the *timing* of interactions with other children (or with adults) may be informative on the various factors which impede or facilitate positive interaction, together with those that lead to clashes and distress.

Identification

As they approach school age, children increasingly *identify* with other people, particularly with parents but also with older brothers or sisters and sometimes even with people outside the home. This is a poorly understood process by which the child comes to think, feel and behave as though someone else's characteristics belonged to him. He gets pleasure from the other person's successes, shares his misery and learns to value the same things. This is not usually a conscious process but the child may express what is happening by proudly stating '*I'm* like daddy' or '*I'm* like mummy'.

It is not an easy process to study, but experimental evidence suggests that identification is most marked with respect to persons who appear to the child as powerful and competent and who share a warm loving relationship with him.[3] What seems to happen is that the child perceives similarities with the other person and learns that the other person has privileges, skills and opportunities which he does not have but would like. He seems to behave as if he believed that acting like the person would bring the desired privileges and qualities. In this way there develops a vicarious sharing of emotions. At first the child imitates particular actions and habits of the person, but gradually these become generalized, automatic and part of his own personality. The process is clearly likely to be influenced by the values other people put on these behaviours and the way they respond to him when he tries to emulate someone. To what extent this process can be understood as a generalized form of imitation influenced by whatever rewards are given in response to it and to what extent it must be thought of as a rather different process involving other mechanisms, is quite uncertain at the moment. However, that it occurs is not in doubt. Children will usually identify to some extent with both parents and often with other people too, but in most instances identification tends to be particularly strong with the same-sexed parent.

As the child who strives to be like his parent comes to identify with many of his actions and behaviours so also will he gradually absorb parental moral standards, behaviours and prohibitions. This is a process which becomes established during the school years (see below) but it has its origins during the pre-school period, so that Erikson has called this the stage of initiative and guilt.[52] Freud regarded the development of conscience as a product of identification, and the very limited evidence which is available suggests that this is the case to an important extent, although obviously many other things are likely to influence it. It should be added that of course neither identification nor conscience can be regarded as present or absent – they are features which develop and must be considered in terms of degree and type.

Psychosexual development

Psychosexual development involves several different features.[154] First, there is the matter of gender role (that is the child's identification of himself as male or female). This is usually well established by age three to four years, by which age most children know whether they are a boy or a girl. However, it takes a little longer to reliably recognize other people's sex and longer still to sort out the physical basis of sex differences. Both biological and psychological factors are thought to influence gender role. Recent studies suggest that the circulating sex hormones during the period of growth in the womb play an important part, and other work indicates that the way the child is brought up can also be crucial.

What sex children would like to be is another matter. Although even by age three years there is a strong tendency for children to show a same-sex preference, this is not synonymous with gender role, especially in girls. Boys develop a same-sex preference both earlier and more consistently than girls, a substantial minority of whom continue to prefer the boy's role. Presumably this is a result of the greater power and prestige afforded to males in our society.

Sex-role standards are a related phenomenon. These refer to sex differences in children's behaviour and attitudes. To some extent these are biologically determined (see chapter 3), but they also involve learning the sex-role standards set by society. Sex differences in attitudes, choice of games and other activities is already marked by four to five years, but differences continue to increase up to eight or nine years of age. Because these preferences are in part defined by society, there can be no 'right' and 'wrong' way for a child of either sex to behave and the range of variation is wide. Many boys enjoy some girlish activities and many girls take pleasure in boys' pursuits. In itself this is a matter of no concern, but there are a few children who identify so strongly and pervasively with the opposite sex that they are likely to be teased and ostracized to an extent that brings misery. In these cases help may be required.

By age four to six years children are generally showing a good deal of curiosity about sex and there is an obvious genital interest in many children's games at this time. Games involving undressing or sexual exploration are common and normal and masturbation is quite frequent. Psychoanalytic theory maintains that anxiety about castration (in boys that they will be and in girls that they have been castrated) and sexual rivalry with the same-sexed parent (the Oedipus complex) are both universal and critical to later development. These views have proved rather difficult to test. Castration anxiety undoubtedly occurs, probably more in boys than in girls, but it seems doubtful whether it is universal and its importance for development is even more doubtful. Children do tend to become attached to the opposite-sexed parent for a while and some go through a phase in which there is some antipathy to the same-sexed parent. Whether this is based on feelings of sexual rivalry is quite unknown; the significance for later development is equally uncertain and the Oedipus complex seems to be far from universal, being dependent to a considerable extent on family circumstances and attitudes rather than innate predisposition.

Emotions

Emotional responses are characteristically intense and labile during the preschool period.[19, 87] Exuberant joy and excitement can quickly turn to impatience and anger following frustration. The child's expression of emotion is usually uninhibited at this time, so that he may leap about in pleasure or kick on the floor in temper. He has not yet learned socially acceptable ways of expressing his displeasure and often he may bite, scratch or kick in anger. Such physical expressions of anger are more common in boys than in girls. However, anger in young children has a rather different quality to that shown by older children. It is usually an explosive, non-adaptive, short-lived response to some immediate stimulus. Quarrels and conflicts between young children are more frequent and generally develop as a result of conflict over some possession. Calculated and planned retaliation only develops later, as children become increasingly able to direct their energy towards some goal. The differences of opinion and clashes over planned play become important as sources of quarrel in the later preschool years.

Competition with other children in activities or skills is infrequent in two to three year olds, although rivalry for the attention of an adult, particularly a parent, exists as is evident from what happens between brothers and sisters. Sibling rivalry probably reaches a peak about two to four years. Children of a year to eighteen months show much less concern over the arrival of another baby in the family (although clashes may arise when they are older), and children over four years are sufficiently old to look after the baby to some extent, and so not be put in a position of direct rivalry. Whether rivalry in fact develops will of course depend as much on how the parents deal with the situation as on what age the child is. If the older child can be given some privileges and responsibilities and if the household can be so arranged that he does not lose out on parental attention as a result of the new arrival, rivalry is likely to be less (although the factors influencing sibling rivalry have not been much studied).

Resistance and negativism are most marked in the eighteen-month to two-and-a-half-years age-period and gradually diminish during the later preschool period, as children learn better both what they are capable of and what other people will accept. Temper tantrums follow a similar developmental course with outbursts usually less frequent and more controlled by the time children reach school. It is characteristic then that tantrums are much more liable to occur in the family setting than they are at school or elsewhere. This can be particularly infuriating to parents, who may feel that the child is only naughty to get at them. Certainly children can and do act deliberately to provoke parents, but part of the explanation is that in a new setting a child is liable to respond by developing new age-appropriate ways of responding, whereas at home old habits may reappear at times of stress. Also children are likely to feel the need for more constraints and inhibition away from home, whereas they feel free to behave as they feel in the family.

Fears of animals increase at first during the preschool years, but are then gradually replaced by fears of imaginary dangers (ghosts and the like), with nightmares reaching a peak about four to six years. Fears, particularly of animals and of storms, are often learned from parents, but fears also develop through unpleasant happenings (falling into the water or a large playful dog jumping up on the child) and, especially later, from the workings of the child's imagination. Young children are often apprehensive in new situations if placed there on their own, but the presence of a familiar adult to whom the child is attached goes a long way to removing this anxiety.

Problems

The most common problems facing the psychiatrist in this age period are temper tantrums, disobedience, aggression and over-activity. Often these are behaviours which would be normal in a slightly younger child but which have persisted because the child's temperamental characteristics have made him more difficult than other children to deal with, because the parents have expected too much of a young child, because they have mishandled the difficulties or sometimes because physical factors have delayed development or made the child less adaptable.

Fears and worries, often associated with sleeping difficulties or feeding problems, are also quite common. Children may refuse to eat or show extreme fads. Others have nightmares or an inability to go to sleep unless the mother stays in the room. A fear of dogs often comes to attention during the fifth year, because parents are concerned that the fear is going to prevent the child walking to school.

Delays in development are the other major group of disorders leading to referral in the preschool period. The concern may be in the child's general failure to make normal progress or it may lie in specific delays such as those involving speech or language. A rare but important disorder associated with severe language delay and a failure in social development is infantile autism.

Middle childhood
Latency

Many of the trends noted in the preschool period continue during the school years, but there are also important new aspects of development. Freud regarded the middle years of childhood as a *latency period* in which sexual development came to a halt, and, following this, people have sometimes tended to consider the five- to ten-year age-period as a quiescent interim phase in which not much happened.[58] In fact Freud was clearly wrong about sexual latency, as it is a period of *increasing* sex interests.[154] Sex talk and games with a sexual component are frequent, but often they are concealed from adults. Some children even develop immature heterosexual love relationships, although these usually remain largely or entirely in fantasy. In middle childhood children come to play almost exclusively with their own sex,[29] but chasing games such as kiss-chase or provocative teasing make it very evident that heterosexual interests are still active and lively although they have been rechannelled. In some sexually permissive cultures even frank sex play and love-making may be common during middle childhood, although this would be very much a minority activity at this age in our own culture. In boys masturbation gradually increases in frequency, although a rapid rise does not take place until puberty. Homosexual play (which mostly consists of mutual handling of genitals) also shows a gradual rise during childhood.

It is also untrue to say that there are no major changes in development during the middle years of childhood. In fact there is a host of changes, particularly in mental functioning and in social competence, and Erikson[52] has called this the stage of industry versus inferiority because it is the time when most of all the child develops (or fails to develop) mastery of his environment.

Mental skills

Piaget has written most extensively on the various phases of mental development. He regards age seven years or thereabouts as the turning point from 'pre-operational' to 'operational' thinking.[201] During the two and a half years up to seven there is an intuitive stage in which children begin to give reasons for what they do and to develop concepts. But they do this in a way which tends to be dominated by what they can see before them rather than by a set of principles. Then, with the beginning of what Piaget calls 'operational' thinking, children start to learn and to use more general rules. They are not so easily fooled by immediate impressions, because they have a firm concept of what should be. This is not a sudden shift and the age of transition shows considerable variation. Nevertheless some time about seven years children develop skills in appreciating serial relationships (which are essential for mathematics), in holding a mental image of routes and directions and in appreciating the invariance of weight and number despite changes in external appearance.

A knowledge of what a child can and cannot accomplish in these tasks is vital in planning a school curriculum. But it is also essential to know why he can or cannot accomplish something, and in this respect wrong conclusions and implications seem to have been drawn from Piaget's accurate observations. Conservation and serial relationships are complex issues and recent work by Bruner,[25] Bryant[26] and others has cast doubt on whether they can reasonably be regarded as specific skills in their own right which develop at a particular time when the child reaches the appropriate degree of biological maturation. Whereas maturation is certainly necessary, so is experience. Tasks in a familiar setting are easier than those in an unfamiliar setting and some sorts of experience facilitate one sort of mental operation and some another. Memory is also important, and it now seems that some tasks are failed simply because the child has to hold too many things in his mind at once rather than because he does not understand serial relationships or some other concept. Also for some tasks a child's language competence may make a big difference, as appreciation of verbal concepts aids learning in some circumstances. We are still only just beginning to learn how these several variables work together to produce particular skills, but already it is clear that some of our earlier ideas based on Piaget's stages need revision.

In later childhood the child's ability to develop hypotheses, to classify objects and to make abstractions increases markedly in what Piaget called the period of 'formal operations'. In association with these advancing mental skills the child's competence in problem-solving increases proportionately.

Conscience formation

In keeping with his advancing mental development, the child is better able to conceptualize right and wrong. In the preschool period he tends to obey immediate specific instructions in which he stops doing something when smacked or told to desist. Behaviour control is dependent on immediate consequences. After a while he learns that a particular action is not allowed, so that he refrains from doing it even when not told specifically on that occasion. Somewhat later he is able to generalize the prohibition in the form of a rule applying to a class of actions (such as not snatching other children's toys or not shouting during meal-times). At first these rules are laid down according to parent or teacher approval, but eventually there comes a higher-order morality based on the child's own concepts of what is right and wrong. As this happens, a rigid and inflexible notion of right and wrong based on adult authority develops into a set of standards based on principles of conscience which are applied with regard to context and motivation.

Obviously full development of conscience requires certain mental skills and as such it closely parallels mental development. However, as already noted, the adoption of personal standards and the internalization of rules is also based in part on a process of identification, and what sort of conscience develops will depend to a considerable extent on the nature of family relationships and interaction. In the first place the likelihood of a child developing a set of standards from his parents will be influenced by the extent to which he can perceive coherent principles behind the way they act. In this connection, although both are important, what they do probably takes precedence over what they say. If they are arbitrary and inconsistent in the way they behave, this will be the model he is given to follow. In detail too what they do and do not regard as important will have an impact. If the parents do not care about honesty, it is less likely that the child will place much emphasis on this quality. Similarly, the extent to which importance is placed on what *should* be done rather than what should *not* will influence the kind of conscience the child develops. But it is not only the model they present, it is also the behaviours in the child which they praise and punish which help shape conscience. Incorporation of parental standards (with modification) is more likely when there is a good relationship with the child and, probably, when the methods of discipline used convey the message that what the child does really matters to the parent because *he* matters. Arbitrary imposition of external prohibitions will not have the same effect. Conversely an excessively harsh set of standards, leading to frequently expressed disapproval and disappointment in the child as a person may lead to an anxious, unconfident, guilt-ridden child if he identifies with his parents, or to rejection of what they stand for if he does not.

The evidence is meagre on exactly how conscience develops and on how child rearing may influence children's moral standards. Certainly there can be no single 'right' way, because both children and parents differ in what they would regard as right. In the past, research has mainly focused on methods of discipline (whether smacking is better than withdrawal of privileges, etc.), but this now seems the wrong point for attention. Within quite a broad range the precise method of discipline used is not very important, although its consistency is. Firm findings are lacking, but it seems more likely that the crucial variable will lie in the strength and quality of the parent–child relationship, in the parental model of behaviour and in the particular behaviours of the child which the parent encourages or praises or in those which he ignores or punishes.

Friendships

During the early school years there is increasing sex-role differentiation in terms of sex-linked styles of behaviour and also games, activities and hobbies. Boys develop an acute sense of what is 'girlish' and 'cissy' and, to a lesser extent, girls become aware of what is acceptably feminine and what is tomboy behaviour.

Friendships are becoming more intense during this age-period although, also, many prove quite transitory. Children learn that group activities may be fun and newcomers to a group make efforts to join in and behave similarly. At first children are not very good at this, and one of the important tasks of the middle school years is learning how to make friends and how to get along with a varied group of children. Good social relationships require social skills, and like other skills they have to be learned. The changing pattern of friendships in early childhood is partly due to this need to try out new social skills and partly to fluctuations and alterations in children's interests and activities. Among older children interests become more stable and friendships become more enduring. However, this process seems to be influenced not only by the child's experiences with his friends, but also by the attachments and persisting relationships he has earlier formed in the family. Because they come first they help set a pattern. Also it seems that to some extent the *ability* to form close friendships is determined by the bonds the child develops in the first five years (although the evidence on this point is circumstantial and preliminary).

Popularity is determined by a complex set of factors including intelligence, sports ability (at least in boys), physical maturity and a variety of personality features.[69] These vary with age, sex and social circumstances. Children can be helped to make friends by an increase of their skills in the activities valued in the groups they want to join and by specific help with social skills as such. Also, however, studies have shown that adults can influence relationships between children by their use of approval, by getting children to work together for a common purpose and by altering the structure of the setting in which children meet[30] (see chapter 5).

Peer-group identification increases markedly during middle childhood. The activities of boys and girls, their style of talk and what they wear become progressively more influenced by the norms set in the group of children with whom they identify. It is a time of great conformity, but increasingly it is conformity to peer-group standards rather than to adult ones.

Perhaps most of all this age-period is characterized by children's increasing exposure, and response, to influences outside the home. School provides an important learning experience for social skills of all kinds as well as for scholastic achievement. Teachers often play a large part in setting standards and developing interests, although the extent to which they do so will depend on the sort of relationships they form with their pupils, on the kinds of contacts they have with them in and outside the classroom. Other adults too come to occupy a more important role than they did in the preschool years.

Together with the child's increasing intellectual competence, bodily strength and coordination there is a growing striving for achievement. Whereas in infancy a child's self-concept was largely determined by parental responses, now it is much influenced by comparisons with other children and by peer-group approval or disapproval. Competition both with other children and with his own set of goals is much more important than it was when he was younger. The child's strivings may centre on intellectual performance, on verbal skills, on athletic prowess or on other pursuits according to his individual capacities, temperament and circumstances. This concern with mastery, with adequacy and with competence is often accompanied too by feelings of doubt and inferiority which may be increased or dispelled according to the reaction he encounters from others in response to his successes and failures.

Emotions

Although school-age children show much less fear of actual objects and experiences than they did when they were younger, fears of imaginary things remain important.[87] Also during middle childhood children become more aware of death and what it means. Some children become quite preoccupied with the idea and develop concerns that their parents may die. Youngsters also become more shy and inhibited as they become more aware of social situations and more concerned about other people's reactions to them. Self-consciousness becomes more pronounced.

When children first start school, some remain so anxious and aware of themselves that they will only whisper when called upon to speak in class and for a while a few will not speak at all. In the great majority of children this is a passing phase of no great moment, but in a very few it may become a more persistent problem.

Probably most children have times when they are reluctant to go to school and many dig in their heels and refuse to go, saying they feel sick or complaining that they are not well. This is particularly common when children first start school, but, if sensibly handled with understanding and firmness, the difficulties soon settle down in most children. However, in a few the problem can become quite entrenched (see chapter 6). The anxiety over going to school stems from many causes, but fear of leaving mother and fear of some activity at school are the two most common.

Children can become unhappy and miserable at this age and sometimes these feelings may be prolonged. More usually, however, the feelings are tied to specific situations and are generally more labile and transient than the moods which develop in older children.

Emotions include essential bodily reactions, such as increase in heart rate, muscle tension, sweating and outpouring of intestinal juices. It is these that lead to headache or feelings of sickness with fear. If children get little sympathy when they say that they are worried, but the complaint of sickness gets a better reception, the way is laid for the child to learn to respond to stress with bodily symptoms.

Tics and obsessions may develop as a means of allaying anxiety. Most people have some slight odd movement they make when they are feeling worried or ill at ease and children often come to blink their eyes or twitch their face at times of tension. It cannot be assumed that the presence of tics necessarily indicates anxiety, but often it does. In most cases it is better to deal with the anxiety rather than focus on the tic itself.

Many children in the middle school years develop the habit

of walking in straight lines, touching lamp-posts or doing something in a special way to avoid some supposed dread consequence. In most children this amounts to little more than a game and it is of no clinical significance. However, very occasionally these obsessions or compulsions may become a maladaptive way of coping with worries or conflicts.

Adolescence

Most obviously adolescence is signalled by the onset of puberty with its associated growth spurt and development of secondary sexual characteristics (facial hair, swelling of the breasts, etc.).[186] In girls puberty begins some two years earlier and extends over a slightly shorter period (three to four years rather than four to five years) than in boys. The production of androgens (male hormones) increases in both sexes at about eight to ten years with a further, much sharper rise in adolescence, this latter rise being much more marked in boys. The excretion of oestrogens gradually rises in both sexes from about age seven years with a very large and sharp further increase in girls during adolescence. In both sexes it is the androgens which have the most effect on sexual drive and energy, and accordingly adolescence is a period of greatly increased libido, especially in boys.

Timing of puberty

There are several psychological correlates of the age at which children reach puberty. One of the most puzzling is the fact that early maturers have, on average, a slightly higher level of intelligence than do late-maturing children. The difference is not due to an intellectual 'spurt' at puberty, because the advantage is evident in the early maturers well before they reach puberty and persists until at least fifteen years (it is not known whether it persists into adult life). However, there are reasons for supposing that the apparent advantage in intellect shown by early maturers may be an artefact due to an association between late puberty and large family size[48] (large family size is known to be associated with lower levels of verbal intelligence – see chapter 4).

Of more direct relevance to the psychiatrist is the observation in some American studies that early-maturing boys have a slight advantage in personality.[106] They were reported as more popular, more relaxed, more good natured and generally more poised. In this country Schofield found that early-maturing boys tended also to have more sexual experience.[171] It is of interest that this advantage in personality was not found with early-maturing girls. The explanation is almost certainly social and psychological rather than biological. Early-maturing boys tend to be more muscular and part of their advantage may lie in the social benefits in a peer group of being strong and good at sport. That strength and athletic prowess are not so important in determining a girl's popularity may explain why early puberty does not have the same psychological advantage in girls that it does in boys. A child's physique plays an active part in determining how other people react to him, and the mature boy of manly appearance may be better accepted by adults too than is his childish-looking friend who has yet to reach puberty. In this connection it is worth noting in passing that popularity is also influenced by facial appearance and even by name. Children with unattractive features or with peculiar names tend to be less popular and may even have more emotional difficulties. Sexuality is very important to adolescents and much talk centres around the topic. As a consequence, the very late-maturing boy may well have many anxieties about his manhood and suffer accordingly.

Psychosexual development

The way in which sexual drive is manifested during adolescence is, of course, much influenced by sociocultural and familial expectations and restrictions. However, in most societies masturbation is an almost universal occurrence in boys, although it is less common in girls. Intense attachments or 'crushes' on someone of the same sex occur fairly commonly as a transient phase in both boys and girls, but overt homosexual activities are less common. Such activities are considerably more frequent in boarding schools than in day schools and it appears that the development of homosexual behaviour is much influenced by the social setting and by the presence or absence of heterosexual opportunities. However, it is doubtful whether this transient phase of homosexual activity has any bearing at all on persisting adult homosexuality.

During and after adolescence there is a very marked upsurge in heterosexual interests and activity in both sexes, this increase beginning in girls before it does in boys, in keeping with their earlier onset of puberty. Schofield's English study of teen-agers[171] showed that, in most youngsters, dating and kissing begin between thirteen years and sixteen years, but a quarter of the boys and almost a third of the girls had had their first date by the age of thirteen. Deep kissing and breast fondling begin somewhat later, but by seventeen years the majority of adolescents have had these experiences. At the time of Schofield's study, a decade ago, by age eighteen years only a third of boys and a sixth of girls had had sexual intercourse. There are differences between the sexes in their approach to sexual relationships. The boys have more sexual partners (implying a small core of promiscuous girls) but the girls more often have an enduring sexual association. Attitudes to sex also differ. Girls tend to look for a romantic relationship, while boys are more likely to seek a sexual adventure.

Emotions

Traditionally adolescence is supposed to be a period of great inner turmoil and emotional difficulties. The psychiatric significance of this has often been exaggerated and it would be wrong to suppose that most adolescents show emotional disorders. They do not. Nevertheless it is true that adolescents tend to feel things particularly deeply and marked mood-swings are common during the teens. A large-scale study of fourteen year olds living on the Isle of Wight found that nearly half reported that at times they felt so miserable that they cried or that they wanted to get away from everybody and everything.[162] About a quarter sometimes felt that people were looking at them or talking about them or laughing at them. Feelings of self-depreciation and worthlessness were less common, but even so about a fifth said that they felt that what happened to them was less important than what happened to other people or that they didn't matter very much. Approximately one adolescent in twelve admitted to occasional suicidal ideas, although only rarely had these been at all persistent. An American study by Masterson[110] also found that anxiety and depression were common in ordinary adolescents.

In short, 'inner turmoil', as represented by feelings of misery, self-depreciation and ideas of being laughed at are quite common in fourteen year olds. These feelings cause appreciable personal suffering to the adolescent at the time, but usually they do not last and often they are unnoticed by adults. Although common, it should nevertheless be emphasized that about half the adolescents in this age group did *not* report feelings of this kind.

Most teenagers are generally happy individuals, but, compared to earlier childhood, moodiness and periods of misery are more frequent. Serious depression is still quite infrequent, but it becomes increasingly common during adolescence and disorders of this kind are very troublesome to some young people. Suicide is still very uncommon, but it is decidedly more frequent than before puberty, when it is exceedingly rare.

School phobias are very common in early childhood, but at that age they are in keeping with normal developmental trends and the outlook is usually very good as most clear up completely. During the middle years of childhood this problem becomes less common, but during adolescence it reappears in a slightly different form. Whereas school refusal in the young child is often an isolated fear, in the adolescent it is more often part of a widespread emotional disorder and the prognosis is accordingly less favourable.

Social phobias become more frequent after puberty. Many youngsters become more self-conscious and more aware of defects in their appearance and behaviour. This may sometimes be associated with shyness and fear of meeting people or going to parties. Usually these feelings are not so marked as to seriously interfere with social life but in a few there may be paralysing social anxiety, so that there is withdrawal from most group activities. A fear of open or of closed spaces (agoraphobia or claustrophobia), which is rare in childhood, may first appear in adolescence. More than other sorts of fears (which are often isolated symptoms in normal individuals), this type of fear is more likely to be associated with more generalized psychiatric symptoms.

Friendships

Friendships are particularly important during adolescence and, compared to both younger and older people, teenagers are very good at making friends.[30] It is a time of life when unusually close friendships develop and young people share their deeper feelings in a way which is less usual at other points in the life cycle. Friendships made at this time, especially in late adolescence, can be particularly lasting, although a lot will depend on how interests change as the youth passes into adult life. To some extent the sexes differ in their pattern of friendship in that girls' relationships tend to be deeper, more dependent and more subject to jealousy than are those of boys.

Groups and cliques become more prominent during the teenage period. At first the pattern tends to be that of isolated unisexual cliques, but these then tend to coalesce to form larger 'sets' or 'crowds' of people who do things together. Sometimes these may take the form of 'gangs' with a leader, but usually the structure is more informal and changing. In early adolescence the 'crowds' are most often composed of either boys or girls, but during adolescence mixed groups become much more common. Later there is increasing pairing off, so that the crowd comes to consist of only loosely associated groups of couples.

Parent–child alienation

It has sometimes been claimed that the peer group achieves such importance during the teenage period that adolescents come to constitute a sub-culture of their own almost cut off from adult society. This is a picturesque notion, but false so far as the majority of teenagers are concerned. Several studies have indicated that, at least up to age sixteen years, most adolescents continue to trust and respect their parents, are upset by parental disapproval and on the whole follow parental guidance with respect to major issues. The Isle of Wight study of fourteen year olds[162] found that only a tiny minority of adolescents tended to withdraw from their families, and very few parents reported that they had any difficulties 'getting through' to their children, who continued to discuss things with their parents as they did when younger. It may be concluded that alienation from parents is *not* common in fourteen year olds. Most young teenagers continue to be influenced by their parents and get on quite well with them. Most young adolescents are not particularly critical of their parents and few reject them.

If this is so, and the research findings appear well based, why are views of adolescent alienation and rebellion so strongly held by many people? The explanations are several. In the first place alienation from families is much more common in teenagers with psychiatric disorder, so that the youngsters seen by psychiatrists at clinics are atypical in this respect. It is often thought that alienation arising in adolescence causes the disorder, but the Isle of Wight findings suggest that this is not usually the case. When there is parent–child alienation, it has usually started during early or middle childhood well before adolescence. Also alienation was found to be as common in disorders arising before age nine or ten years as in those with an onset in adolescence. Usually alienation is part of or due to psychiatric disorder, rather than the other way round. When alienation acts as a causal influence, it usually does so in the pre-adolescent years.

In the second place, although parent–child alienation appears uncommon in the early and mid-teens, this is a period when children's leisure activities less often involve the family and when disagreements about clothes, hair, going out and similar issues are quite frequent. Some of these disagreements may get quite heated, many adolescents would like their parents to be less strict and regard their parents as 'old-fashioned'. These disputes loom large in many adults' eyes and certainly they can generate friction and tension. Nevertheless research findings suggest that, in spite of vigorous disputes over some disciplinary issues, the majority of adolescents share with their parents a common core of values and respect the need for restrictions and control.

Thirdly, although the evidence is meagre, it appears that during the *late* teens more adolescents may resist parental discipline and assert their right to make their own decisions. Most studies of late adolescence concern youngsters still in full-time education, who constitute a small minority group in this country. It may well be that parent–child disputes achieve a greater intensity and significance when youngsters are still in a dependent position at an age when they have reached maturity and most of their age-group have been earning their living for some time.

Fourthly, perhaps more often, particularly in the intellectually less well endowed, alienation from school increases considerably and the last year of school is often a most difficult one for both the teacher and the adolescent. The youngster often feels that formal school learning is no longer relevant to what he wants to do and he is anxious to leave and get a job, both because it brings money and because it signals independence. Absenteeism is particularly high in the last year of schooling and teachers face the dispiriting task of having to try to teach adolescents who see no point in school learning.

Such clashes, conflicts and turmoil as do develop in adolescence seem to bear no very close relationship to biological maturity, they are said to be less frequent in non-industrial societies and it appears that to some extent the alienation is a cultural phenomenon related to the long period of studentship, the deferment of adult roles and the considerable interval between sexual maturity and adult status in western society. Also, of course, as already noted, in some youngsters the alienation is a reflection of psychiatric disorder.

Each generation tends to feel that the next is worse, and expresses concern over the 'generation gap' between the values they hold as parents and those expressed by their offspring. This is a real enough phenomenon, but it is easy to exaggerate its extent or importance. Most young people continue to share quite good relationships with their parents in spite of an increasing divergence of interests and activities.

Idealism and Identity

Erikson[52] has described adolescence as the period in which the main psychological task is to establish a personal identity. Of course during the middle childhood years there will have been a gradual and regular progression in youngsters' development of both a personal conscience and a view of their own individuality and identity. However, in our society this process tends to be both highlighted and intensified during the teenage years. Youngsters become increasingly concerned with how they appear in the eyes of others and how this compares with the way they feel they actually are. While they are still very reliant on other people's views and ideals, it is often a time of questioning and doubt as the adolescents strive to determine their own position with respect to the crises they face. Youngsters in their middle and late teens are more liable to assert their independence to do as *they* think fit, and parents frequently find it a difficult task to provide the guidance, control and support needed by their adolescent children, and also to allow sufficient autonomy for them to learn by their own mistakes and to establish their own standards. Studies, mostly of a circumstantial kind, suggest that this process of identity formation is aided by an affectionate, responsive, parent–child relationship and by an adequate model of sex-role behaviour as provided by the same-sexed parent.

Probably at no other time in life is the average person more likely to be concerned with the problems of moral values and standards than during adolescence. It is often a period of intense idealism and this may well include a rejection of many of society's norms and standards. In some cases the idealism may include an element of rebellion against home, but more frequently the sociopolitical activism of youth is rather an extension and development of their parents' own idealism. Studies of American 'hippies' and student activists[23, 55, 93] show that they tend to come from privileged, professional families in which the parents have presented permissive, liberal or socialist views with a strong humanitarian concern for the plight of others, but with less emphasis on personal self-control. In short it appears that activists are often implementing the values of their socially conscious parents, although they often do so in ways that their parents would not approve of. In addition to the activists, there are also socially alienated youngsters who have rejected values on a much more widespread scale. Although they share many of the same family-background features as the activists, they are probably more likely to show personal psychological disturbance.

While this idealism is a prominent feature in some adolescents, it is necessary to recognize that only a tiny minority of adolescents are activists and protesters. Like their parents, most are rather conforming. The main difference from earlier childhood is that the standards to which they conform to a greater extent tend to be set by their peers rather than by their parents.

Psychiatric disorders arising in adolescence

Delinquency and troublesome behaviour is associated in most people's minds with the adolescent age-period, and of course this is when youths most often come before the Courts. However, it is important to keep the problem in perspective. Although minor examples of 'nicking' things are quite common, serious and persistent antisocial behaviour occurs in only a small proportion of young people. Delinquency is many times more frequent in boys than it is in girls and it is much more common in big cities than it is in non-industrial towns or in the countryside. Furthermore, although trouble with the law may become overt only in adolescence, it is evident from long-term studies that future delinquents differ in their behaviour and personality characteristics from other children even in the early school years. The growth of delinquency may be seen in adolescence but, to a considerable extent, the roots lie in early and middle childhood.

It is not delinquency, so much as depression, which is characteristic of the disorders arising for the first time in adolescence. Although both emotional and conduct disturbances may begin during the teenage period, as during earlier childhood, the main difference is that, whereas depressive conditions are not very common in young children, they are much more frequent in adolescents (as they are in adults).

However, the main shift that occurs in adolescence is not so much in the type of disorder as in its correlates. Conduct disturbances beginning in the pre-adolescent years are strongly associated with reading retardation and other types of scholastic failure, whereas this seems not to be the case at all with such conditions arising for the first time after age ten years.[162] Educational failure has its main impact in younger children. Also child psychiatric disorders are quite strongly associated with indicators of family difficulties, such as maternal neurosis, marital discord, parental irritability and broken homes. These factors show some association with psychiatric problems beginning in adolescence, but the association is rather weaker, suggesting that the causes of adolescent disorders may be somewhat different from those conditions which begin at an earlier stage in development. The causal factors which are specially important in adolescence are not properly understood, but presumably some of the biological and psychological changes associated with this stage of development play a part.

3 Individual Differences

Ruth was a lively, responsive and easy baby who quickly settled into a regular routine of feeding and sleeping. She was a jolly toddler who chortled happily when played with and who was a richly rewarding infant for her mother. Rosemary was quite different. She was restless and irritable as a baby and her mother never knew when she would be asleep and when awake. She continued to demand feeds at irregular hours throughout the night, and during the day she was unresponsive and frequently tearful. Mother got few rewards from looking after her and the process of mothering was difficult and stressful.

Children differ one from another. That is very evident to anyone who observes children, but surprisingly it is only relatively recently that this fact has received much attention in either studies of child development or in ordinary clinical practice.[12] Of course the knowledge that there are marked individual differences between children does not help very much in treating children with problems, unless evidence is also available that the differences are *relevant* to the development of disorder, and unless it is known *how* the differences are caused and *how* they influence development. So far there have been only a few studies designed to answer these questions but enough information is already available to indicate that the issue of individual differences is of considerable practical, as well as theoretical, importance.

Sex Differences
Perhaps the most conspicuous difference between children concerns their sex. The difference between boys and girls is so obvious physically as to be scarcely worth stating. Nevertheless the psychological importance of sex differences has only been

properly appreciated in the last few years and even now we have much to learn about the nature of these differences. What is known, however, is that sex differences have implications for development extending far beyond psychosexual development and the sex characteristics themselves.[151]

One of the best documented differences concerns the rate of physical development. Girls mature well in advance of boys. The difference, due to the Y chromosome (as shown by studies of children with chromosome anomalies), is as much as two weeks at birth, is almost one year at the time of starting school and is some eighteen months to two years by puberty.

Although boys are larger than girls at most ages and stronger in muscle power, there is some evidence that they are more vulnerable to almost any kind of physical hazard. Boys suffer more from the effects of complications during the birth process; they more often get and more often die from infection in childhood, and they are more likely to suffer impairment of growth after radiation as shown following Hiroshima, Nagasaki and the Marshall Islands disaster. Men also die at a younger age than do women.

It has sometimes been thought that this sex difference might be due to the supposedly greater pressures and strains which our culture lays upon male shoulders. That this is unlikely was neatly shown by a comparison of Roman Catholic Brothers and Sisters who had entered a religious community in early adult life and who were engaged in teaching or administration. Although the men and women led closely similar lives, the women outlived the men by several years, as they do in the general population. It could be added that this male vulnerability seems also to extend to other species. One study showed that male rats had greater deficits following malnutrition than did female rats. However much it may offend the male ego, it is clear that biologically speaking the male is the weaker sex. Why this should be so is not known. The sex difference in maturation may be one factor (because immature organisms are more susceptible to damage and the male is immature for longer). But this cannot be the whole story, as the vulnerability extends across the whole life span. As if to compensate for this biological weakness of the male, there are about 125 boys conceived for every 100 girls.

Psychiatric disorder is considerably commoner in boys than it is in girls. This well-established finding raises the question of why this should be so. Psychoanalytic theory offers no adequate explanation and, as the Women's Liberation writers have forcefully (and correctly) pointed out, Freud's view of women was heavily influenced by the cultural prejudices on the inferiority of women prevalent at the time. Behaviourists have seen much deviant behaviour in terms of faulty conditioning, but there are no marked sex differences in responses to conditioning. Autonomic responses to stress (such as changes in heart rate and amount of sweating) vary somewhat according to sex but not in a manner which allows any ready explanation for the sex difference in rates of psychiatric disorder. The same applies to explanations in terms of possible sex differences in suggestibility and imitation.

Three other explanations appear more likely to have substance, although none has adequate supporting evidence. First, there is the possibility that boys are constitutionally more vulnerable to psychological stresses just as they are more susceptible to physical stresses. Little is known on this point, but there is some suggestion that boys may be generally more prone to suffer from some types of psychological hazard. For example, this seems to be so in the case of family discord and disharmony. Boys are probably more affected by unpleasant separation experiences[152] and there is some evidence to suggest that this male susceptibility may extend to other species, in that several studies have found the male more often adversely affected by stressful separation experiences and various forms of privation.[156] In adults, too, men appear to succumb more easily to the stresses associated with bereavement and natural disasters. However, there are exceptions (girls seem just as likely to be harmed by a poor-quality, institutional upbringing), and there is no evidence on whether any vulnerability that does exist is inborn or acquired. The matter deserves further study.

A second explanation is that the sex differences in psychiatric disorder are at least in part, due to sex differences in tempera-

ment or styles of behaviour. There are good reasons for supposing that temperament plays an important part in the genesis
of psychiatric disorder (see below) and sex differences in temperamental attributes have been demonstrated from infancy
onwards.[82] For example, baby girls are more sensitive and responsive than are baby boys to a variety of stimuli, especially
those concerning the mouth or the skin generally. On the other
hand, one-year-old male infants show greater independence,
more gross motor activity and greater vigour in their play than
do female infants. Pre-school boys are more aggressive than
girls and this is so even when possibilities of mild brain damage
have been ruled out (this is necessary because damage is commoner in boys). There is more rough-and-tumble play in boys
aged three to five years and older, and boys tend to be more
impulsive. The sex difference in assertiveness, vigour and aggression appears to have its roots in biological differences. The
main evidence in favour of a biological explanation comes
from four sources. First, the differences are found in a wide
range of animal species – not just in man. Second, the
differences are present from very early in life. Third, female
monkeys masculinized by the injection of male sex hormones to
the mothers during pregnancy showed greater rough-and-
tumble and chasing play than did normal females. A study in
humans (where the excess male hormone during pregnancy came
from glandular disease or hormone treatment) also found an
apparently increased tendency to tomboyish behaviour in the
girls.[154] Finally, an additional Y (male) chromosome seems to
be associated with a somewhat increased tendency to aggressive
behaviour.[120] Although the exact mechanisms remain uncertain, there seems little doubt that there are biologically determined sex differences in styles of behaviour which are present
from early infancy.

But this conclusion probably applies mainly to assertiveness,
vigour and aggression and not to the wide range of other behaviours in which the sexes differ. Girls and women have
usually been found to be more dependent, conforming, conservative, sympathetic, emotional, anxious, tearful, interested
in people and more fastidious. These attributes generally

appear rather later in childho
school age onwards; they are not
(for example, male rats are mor
neither hormones nor chromoso
tematic influence on those behav
probable that social and cultural
role in determining these sex diffe

There are well-demonstrated di
towards the two sexes and in the s
women.[151] Even in the infancy per
handled and talked to differently b
whole there is more mother–daughter interaction. Probably the
sex differences in parental behaviours are partially secondary to
infant characteristics, as non-human primates also differ in the
way they treat male and female infants. However, this explanation is likely to be less important in the rather larger sex
differences in interaction found when the children grow older.
Increasingly, parental expectations as to how boys and girls
should behave determine how they respond to their children,
which behaviours they encourage and which they discourage.
These differences in expectation are also very influential
during schooling, both as regards behaviour and academic
achievement.

As well as these overt variations in parental and teacher behaviour related to cultural stereotypes of how a normal boy and
a normal girl should behave, there are widespread and
influential attitudes which act to place the female in an inferior
social position. Indeed in most cultures the inferiority of the
female is taken for granted; because she is assumed to be inferior, social pressures may make her so. The Bible is quite
clear that man is the basic model, women being just an after-
thought created from one of man's ribs, and in the Christian
church, even today, women are allowed only an inferior position. Arabs commiserate when a woman gives birth to a
daughter, and orthodox Jewish men give thanks in their prayers
that they were not born a woman.

In the English language masculinity is taken to mean virile,
vigorous, powerful, in contrast to feminine which is used as an

simplicity, inferiority, weakness'. These views
influence both teaching and literature in surprising
example, a modern method of teaching English
ar explicitly utilizes these stereotypes in labelling parts
peech, and even the heroes in children's stories are more
han twice as likely to be male as female. In nearly all societies
women tend to occupy a subordinate position. Often they are
discouraged from taking a job outside the home and, if men do
allow them to work, they are frequently expected to take
simpler, less arduous, more lowly paid jobs. Although the pattern in our culture is changing and variable, in marriage too
women frequently have to take second place in decision-making
and in other aspects of dominance and control. They often pay
the bills, but they less often control the purse strings. Perhaps
most important of all, as well as bearing children, they usually
have to take the main responsibility in child-rearing.

The starting point for this discussion was the greater frequency of psychiatric disorders in boys, whereas the evidence
suggests that the social influences impede the female, not the
male. On the face of it, this suggests that sex-linked social
influences are unimportant with respect to psychiatric disorder.
However, it is probably relevant that the social discrimination
against women increases in later childhood and adolescence and
reaches a peak in adult life. This is paralleled by a reversal of
the sex ratio in psychiatric disorders during late adolescence.
Before adolescence, disorders predominate in boys whereas
after adolescence they predominate in women. Neurotic and
depressive disorders are especially common in women, the rate
being very much higher than in men. Part of the explanation
probably lies in social influences.

Of course there are biological differences too which are important, and there may be genetic reasons which account in part
for the increased rate of disorder in women. The most important biological factor so far as adolescents are concerned is the
menstrual cycle. It is widely recognized that there is often some
emotional upset and increased irritability during the few days
immediately preceding and during the menstrual period. What
are less appreciated are the consequences. Dalton[45] has shown

that accidents, crimes and psychiatric disturbance are commoner during this stage of the menstrual cycle and that girls taking exams at that time do less well. This is a handicap obviously not shared by the boys. In women there are also physical stresses associated with child-birth, and psychiatric disturbances are more frequent during the period just after delivery. On the other hand there are also social factors which are relevant. One example is provided by the effects of marriage.[151] In men the married state acts as some sort of safeguard against physical and mental ill-health. Married men have less illness, a lower death rate and report themselves as happier than single, widowed or divorced men. The position for the female is quite different. The married women do not have the advantages shown by the married men and in some respects single women appear better off. It seems probable that adverse social influences placing the women in an inferior position may be partially responsible for the fact that neurotic and depressive disorders become much commoner in the female during and after adolescence.

Temperamental attributes

Quite apart from sex differences, children also differ markedly in their temperamental attributes right from the time of birth.[12] This has been shown to apply to a wide range of characteristics. For example, Bridger and Birns[20] found consistent individual differences in the way babies' heart rates changed in response to being touched, and in their response to various attempts at pacifying after stress stimuli. Other studies have shown differences in mouthing behaviour, in patterns of startle response and in conditioning. Important differences also exist in children's *styles* of behaviour – that is, in *how* they do things rather than *what* they do. The New York longitudinal study by Thomas and his colleagues[35, 188] has done much to increase our understanding of these behavioural differences. They have shown that infants consistently and reliably vary in such features as their level of activity or energy output, in the regularity of their various biological cycles (sleeping/waking, hunger/satiety, patterns of elimination, etc.), in their adaptability (that is, how easily their behaviour changes in response to altered circumstances), in the intensity of their emotional responses (i.e. whether they show pleasure by roaring with laughter or just smiling quietly, or displeasure by screaming or just whimpering) and in whether they tend to approach or withdraw from new situations or new people. Children's styles of behaviour as assessed in this way tend to remain fairly consistent over a year or so, but the characteristics are by no means fixed and marked changes take place over a longer time-period.

Association with disorder

The importance of these temperamental attributes for later development has been shown in three rather different studies. The New York group studied these attributes in a longitudinal study of children from predominantly professional middle-class families.[188] Comparisons were made between the characteristics of the third of the children who developed some kind of (mostly mild) behavioural disturbance and the remainder of the children who showed no difficulties of any kind. It was found that even as early as the second year of life, and before symptoms of disorder were evident, the children who were later to develop behavioural difficulties showed different temperamental characteristics.[160] Children with markedly irregular patterns of functioning (as shown for example in the fact that they woke and went to sleep at unpredictable times), who were slow to adapt to novel circumstances, whose emotional responses were usually of high intensity and whose predominant mood was negative (miserable or irritable rather than contented or placid) were the children most likely to come to psychiatric notice later because of behavioural difficulties. Over two thirds of the children with all four of these 'difficult' attributes developed problems and it was quite clear that there was an important association between children's styles of behaviour in early childhood and the risk of developing behavioural problems when they were older.

Rather similar attributes were studied by Graham and his associates[68] in a group of children of predominantly working-class

London families in which one parent was under psychiatric care. It is striking that in this very different group of families, much the same characteristics were associated with a high risk of the children developing psychiatric disorder in middle childhood (the disorders in this sample were more severe than in the New York study). The children most likely to show disorder a year later were those with markedly irregular sleeping, eating and bowel habits, whose behaviour lacked malleability, in that it was difficult to change and who were less fastidious, being more tolerant of mess and dirt than most children (a variable not examined in the New York study). There was also some indication that, as in the New York investigation, the children with disorder at home showed more negative mood and greater intensity of emotional expression.

Richards and Bernal[136] have undertaken a detailed longitudinal study of some 100 children from birth to school age. Particular attention was paid to sleep problems, which are commonly attributable to parental mishandling. Their findings suggest that this view is often incorrect. The group of children with sleep difficulties at fourteen months differed right from birth in being slower to begin crying and regular breathing, in being more fussy and irritable in the first week of life and in sleeping for shorter periods right from the beginning. Although quite differently measured, these characteristics are similar to those found important in the other two studies.

All three investigations demonstrated that a child's own temperamental characteristics have an important association with the later development of emotional and behavioural disorders. The fact that the studies involved such different groups of families and yet produced such similar findings indicates that the effects found are likely to be of general importance. It seems that emotionally intense children, slow to adapt to new situations, whose behaviour is difficult to change, with irregular sleeping, eating and bowel habits, who tend to be irritable and negative in mood and who are unusually tolerant of messiness and disorder have an increased risk of psychiatric problems during childhood.

Conversely the easy, adaptable, regular child of positive

mood is much less likely to develop behavioural problems. Of course, although some characteristics may always put the child at risk, many may be good or bad, according to circumstances. For example, in these studies the child's activity level was not a particularly important variable. But, in a study of institutional infants under five months of age, Schaffer[169] found that the most active infants were the ones who showed the least developmental retardation. In these circumstances a high-activity level proved to be a protective factor in an environment which provided little stimulation.

The New York study showed the importance of temperamental differences in a group of children who were not subject to any unusual stresses; Graham's study did so in a group experiencing the chronic stresses associated with parental illness and sometimes marital discord. Stacey and her colleagues[182] have also produced findings which suggest the importance of individual differences in relation to the acute stress of admission to hospital. They report that children said to make poor relationships with adults or with other children and to be socially inhibited, uncommunicative and aggressive were the ones most likely to be disturbed by admission.

Temperamental characteristics have also been shown to be important with respect to both reading difficulties and delinquency. Several studies have indicated that children who show restlessness, poor concentration and impulsiveness are more likely to have difficulties than other children in learning to read. The same characteristics, especially impulsiveness, together with aggressiveness and insensitivity to the feelings of others (as measured rather later in childhood), have been linked with delinquency.

Origin of characteristics

These studies indicate the psychiatric importance of individual differences in children's temperamental attributes, but they do not show the *origin* of the attributes, nor do they demonstrate *how* they influence development. The attributes are known to have a strong genetic component and also they may be modified by damage to the brain (see below), but it would be quite misleading to regard them as entirely 'constitutional'. Like any other human characteristics they are also influenced by the child's life-experiences, so that the attributes are the result of a complex and continuing interaction between genetic influences, other biological forces and many environmental variables.

Sometimes people give a figure for how much of an attribute is due to heredity. For example, it is often said that intelligence is eighty per cent due to heredity. However, figures of this kind do not have much meaning.[21] The first point is that the amount of variation attributable to genetic factors is necessarily modified according to environmental circumstances. In the theoretical situation in which everyone experiences precisely the same environment *all* differences will be due to genetic factors. Conversely, in a group of individuals who are genetically identical, all differences must be due to environmental or other nongenetic influences. These are only theoretical situations, but applying the argument to real life it follows that where environmental circumstances experienced by individuals are extremely different, the influence of genetic factors in accounting for individual differences will necessarily be less than when environmental circumstances are closely similar.

A second, and closely related, point is that genetic and environmental factors interact and cannot be considered to be independent of each other. This is most easily illustrated by Cooper and Zubek's study of rats.[39] It is possible to selectively breed rats who are very good or very bad at solving mazes. Over the course of several generations two groups were obtained which in ordinary laboratory conditions scarcely overlapped in this respect. Maze-learning was shown to have a very strong genetic component (as has human intelligence and personality). But the interesting finding was that the difference between the genetically superior and the genetically inferior group did not apply in very deprived or very stimulating environments. In the deprived environment, both performed equally poorly and the superior genetic endowment of the one group made no difference. In the stimulating environment both did well. The genetically superior group did rather better, but the difference between the groups was far less than in ordinary laboratory living conditions. Of course, these were rats, the task was the highly specific one of maze-learning and there are limitations on the findings due to the methods used in the study. We do not know how far this kind of genetic–environment interaction also applies to humans, but it seems likely that much the same occurs to some degree.

A third point is that environmental variables may actually *change* the biological constitution. This can only be demonstrated convincingly with very abnormal environmental circumstances. For example, rearing very young animals in the absence of patterned vision may lead to dysfunction of the visual cortex in the brain,[137] and some studies with rats suggest that stimulation may lead to changes in brain chemistry.[145] Very recent work has shown that in the cat the way cortical cells respond to vertical or horizontal stripes is determined by visual experiences in early life.[16] The findings suggest that the development of the brain is influenced not only by damage but also by life experiences not involving injury of any kind. It is not known how far phenomena of this kind occur in the more ordinary circumstances of real life. It is unlikely that there are such dramatic effects on development, but it is evident that the constitution and the environment cannot be considered as independent.

A fourth point is that there may be strong associations between a characteristic in early life and a behaviour some years later without the characteristic itself persisting in the same form. This is illustrated by the New York findings on temperamental attributes,[160, 188] already mentioned. The attributes as measured in the second year of life correlated only weakly with the same attributes three years later, *but* the early attributes did predict behavioural disorder three years later. The finding suggests that disorder did *not* develop as a direct result of the persistence of an unusual temperamental attribute, but rather that disorder resulted from some train of events set in motion by the attribute or something associated with it.

It is considerations of this kind which have led many people to shift from a 'trajectory' view of development to an 'interactive' view. At one time the former held sway and it still has its proponents. According to this view, a child's innate disposition thrusts him forth on a trajectory of development determined by his innate qualities. The environment may retard or facilitate this progression but the limits within which development can take place is set by the basic hereditary constitution. The 'real' personality is determined genetically, although of course a deficient or distorted development may prevent its full potential being realized. This view is most clearly expressed by the proponents of 'innate' intelligence who regard it somewhat in terms of a rocket buffeted by environmental cross-winds and air-currents but not fundamentally altered by them. Measurement of this innate core represented by the rocket can only be indirect but it is supposed that the core has a reality.

There is something in this view that the biological endowment sets limits, in the sense that it regulates probabilities. A child born with very poor physical coordination is most unlikely to be a champion gymnast and a child with a very poor intellectual endowment is unlikely to become an outstanding mathematician. But these are probabilities, not certainties, and the 'trajectory' or 'fixed potential' view of development does not fit well with some of the facts, in that it does not take account of the changes induced by interaction with the environment. In this respect it probably implies a wrong view of what actually happens. A more appropriate analogy may be that of a river given powerful impetus by its source of origin in a large mountain lake. The lake provides the river with its main source of water but the constituents of the river become altered and modified by the minerals in the river bed over which it flows, the pollution it encounters at various points and the additional impetus provided by the multiple tiny streams which join it on its way to the sea. There is continuity throughout the whole of the course and without the lake of origin there would be nothing. But equally the interactions occurring at each stage slightly alter the river, so that each new encounter is influenced by the last.

Probably the course of development may take place somewhat on these very general lines. Genetic endowment provides the main determinant in most cases, but its force will vary with the strength, nature and variety of environmental circumstances encountered, and at each point in development interactions are leading to changes which will influence the next interaction.

How temperamental differences influence development

Taking this view of development, the next step is to specify the nature of the interactions which occur with respect to temperamental attributes. Only very limited evidence is available on this topic, but several modes of interaction may be suggested.

(a) Effect on others.

Although most studies of parent–child interaction have assumed that it is parents who influence children, several studies in recent years have shown that the converse also occurs. The characteristics of the children help shape parental behaviour. This has been shown in a variety of ways. For example, Levy[104] found in a study of nursing mothers that each mother's behaviour towards her infant was considerably influenced by what state the baby was in when brought for feeding – whether awake or asleep, placid or irritable. Yarrow[203] found that the maternal behaviour of a foster mother was altered by the attributes of the infants placed in her home. Different infants elicited different maternal behaviour. The amount of stimulation and comfort the foster mother provided varied with the infant's activity level. Recently Campbell[28] has also shown that active infants in a neonatal nursery get more attention from the nurses than do the inactive infants (an observation which helps to explain Schaffer's finding that the more active infants were less affected by a depriving environment – because they elicited stimulation they were less deprived). Osofsky[123] manipulated the extent to which children exhibited dependent behaviour by varying the level of difficulty of the laboratory tasks they had to perform. She found that when the children were being dependent their mothers interacted more with them, both verbally and physically, and displayed more controlling behaviour. Studies of families with a congenitally handicapped child have also shown that this is associated with different parental behaviour.[44] In short, the characteristics of children have been found to *elicit* different behaviours from other people. So far, this effect has been studied to only a very limited extent and the specificities of the effects of different temperamental attributes are not known.

Nevertheless it is not difficult to see how the attributes associated with later disorder might have effects on parents. The highly irregular child who never settles to a steady sleeping or eating routine poses particular problems for his mother who will find it difficult to arrange her life just because her child is so unpredictable. The malleable child who easily adapts to changes and new situations is likely to be very much easier to bring up than his non-adaptable brother whose behaviour is so tiresomely difficult to alter. Because children with these attributes are so difficult to rear, they may well arouse more irritation and the parents may come to expect problems because they have occurred before. Such expectations may become self-fulfilling through their effect on the child, and so a vicious circle is created.

Some children are much easier to love than others because they are lively, responsive and interesting. More of an effort may be required to love a passive, inert and unresponsive infant who seems to 'give nothing back'. Parental behaviour is not merely instinctive. Parents need the child to look at them, to cuddle, to smile and to respond to their overtures and if, for any reasons, the child does not do that, being a parent may be more of an effort. This is illustrated, for example, by the Klaus and Leiderman studies[94, 100, 101] which showed that mothers of small premature babies who were separated from them in the first few weeks of life (because they were in an incubator or an intensive care nursery) tended to be less confident and less attentive to their babies. This effect probably arose in part from the fragile, rather unresponsive nature of very premature babies and partly from the lack of contact with the baby during the early period when mothering skills should be developing. It is noteworthy that battered babies are more likely than other children to have been weakly, handicapped or premature babies. The parents may have battered because of their own problems but, in part, it was that particular child (rather than his brother) who was battered because of what sort of child he was.

It is not, of course, a simple matter of some children being difficult and some easy. It is also a question of interaction with parental attributes. Although there are some children whom nearly all parents would find rewarding and easy, and some who would pose problems to practically anyone, there are many whose characteristics lead to less consistent responses. Some parents like a lively, active, mischievous child but others may find him wearing and prefer a quieter, passive, inactive youngster. Accordingly, in assessing parent–child interaction in clinical practice, it is necessary to determine how each responds to the other and which attributes *they* find rewarding and which aggravating. These will not necessarily be the same in all families.

The ways in which children's temperamental attributes may influence parent–child interaction and the ways in which development will vary according to the parental response may be illustrated by considering two children with similar temperamental characteristics.

Sam had been a difficult child right from infancy. As a baby he slept badly and never settled into a regular sleeping pattern, he cried a lot of the time and was upset by any changes. He vomited frequently, was very difficult to feed and had frequent breath-holding attacks in the first few months. Sam had always seemed odd, there were frequent tantrums as a toddler, he was very wearing to look after and subsequently it turned out that he had mild mental retardation. Mother was a very warm, placid, easy-going person who coped very sensibly with Sam's various problems. Father was a friendly out-going person whose only problem lay in recurrent backache. The marriage was harmonious and happy. Both parents found Sam's crying, tantrums and waking at night in his first year very trying, but they remained fond of him and together found ways of coping with the difficulties. As Sam grew older it was evident that he was a very anxious boy, who found it difficult to get on with other children and who readily developed fears. There had been periods of great anxiety when mother went out, of refusing school, of refusing to go to new places, of panic in crowds, of screaming when taken to the doctor and of fear of buses. On each occasion his parents responded with firm and understanding encouragement and none of the problems persisted. When seen at age ten years, he was still a very anxious boy who frequently sought reassurance and who tended to cry if faced with any new situation. There was some jealousy of his younger brother and he preferred the company of younger children. Nevertheless he had learned to cope with all the things he had been afraid of and there were no more than trivial psychiatric problems.

Without any doubt Sam had been an exceptionally difficult baby whose temperamental features of irregularity, non-adaptability, negative mood and high intensity of emotional expression were just those which might have been expected to lead to psychiatric disorder. They had indeed led to his being a rather sensitive, anxious child and throughout childhood he had shown many behaviours which might well have constituted the beginnings of a serious psychiatric problem. The fact that no important disorder developed was due to the warm, firm, consistent and thoughtful way his parents dealt with his difficulties. Temperamentally he was a vulnerable child but he was fortunate in the life circumstances he encountered.

Toby, the child referred to in chapter 1 (see page 14), was very similar in infancy. Like Sam, he slept poorly and did not develop a regular sleeping pattern. He cried frequently, adapted poorly to any changes and appeared anxious and fearful from the outset. He too had feeding problems in infancy and was later found to have a level of intelligence at the bottom end of the normal range. However, the parental reaction was quite different from that which Sam experienced. Father was infuriated by Toby's tears and tempers and used to hit him whenever he cried. As Toby grew older he began to provoke his father more and the father–child relationship deteriorated to the point of hostility. Mother was fond of Toby but she tended to respond to his fears by becoming increasingly worried and panicky herself so that she was unable to help him. She had several phobias of her own and later became depressed. The end result was that Toby's difficulties increased greatly and, when seen at age ten years, he was a severely handicapped boy with a gross and incapacitating emotional disorder. Like Sam, Toby was a temperamentally vulnerable child. The outcome was different largely because with Sam the parental response served to diminish the problems, whereas with Toby the temperamental difficulties served to initiate a vicious circle of maladaptive parent–child interaction.

The focus of this discussion so far has been on parent–child interaction, but exactly the same kinds of mechanisms may be seen in children's effect on their peers, on teachers and on other people. Popularity (and unpopularity) has been mainly studied through sociometric techniques in which children are asked to specify (for example) the three classmates whom they would most like to sit next to or with whom they would most like to play or whom they would most like as group leaders.[69] These studies have shown that popular children tend to be of above average intelligence and educational achievement (for their class), to have good athletic ability and to have an attractive appearance. Personality characteristics leading to popularity vary somewhat with age, sex and social group, but social skills and sociability always rate high, and cooperativeness, helpfulness, kindness, generosity and sensitivity to others often appear relevant. Similarity of interests is also important. Some of these attributes are relatively unalterable, but some are open to change, and children may sometimes be helped in their social adjustment by development of the social, scholastic or athletic skills which rank as important in the social group they wish to join.

(b) Range of experiences.

Another way in which temperamental attributes may operate is in shaping other types of life experiences. What children do is determined in part by what they are like. For example, an active, exploratory child is likely to have many more adventures and more social experiences than his inactive and passive brother. The first child will learn by trying out new things and will encounter new situations not experienced by the second child. His behaviour in later childhood will have been shaped not only by what sort of child he is, but also by what sort of things he has done and the latter depends to some extent on the former. The friendly, approaching child will meet more people and make more friends than a timid withdrawing child. Because of this he may adapt more easily to a separation experience which places him in the care of a strange adult. The experience may be less stressful to him because he generally has a positive approach to new people, and because he thereby gets more attention, but also because he has met more people before, is more used to meeting people, and therefore the situation is less strange to him.

(c) Effective environment.

A third mode of operation of temperamental attributes is their influence on what is an *effective* environment for the child. The distinction between an *objective* and *effective* environment is most easily appreciated by considering some gross handicap such as deafness. A home filled with lively conversational interchange objectively constitutes a richly stimulating linguistic environment, but, to the deaf child, effectively it is a barren environment because he cannot hear what is said. The same sort of thing, in lesser degree, may be seen with the variation in temperamental attributes. For example, children vary greatly in their distractibility by extraneous stimuli. In a school classroom situated next to the railroad, some children will not notice the noise of passing trains, whereas others will be constantly startled and interrupted in whatever they are doing whenever an engine goes by. To some extent this will be a function of how engrossed they are in their work, but also to some extent it will be a reflection of a more pervasive temperamental attribute.

The New York longitudinal study showed how normal children vary in their threshold to sensory stimuli – some are very sensitive and some very insensitive. This temperamental difference will result in their feeling the environment in rather different ways. The world will not be the same for them.

(d) Competence.

What children are capable of and what they achieve will also have a major influence on their lives. Both intellectual competence and adaptability are likely to help determine how children respond to various sorts of stressful experiences. The child who knows what to do in an emergency or who can cope during times of stress or limited resources may be less likely to succumb to the difficulties he faces. Adaptability will be important in so far as changed circumstances may be less stressful for a child who can accommodate himself to the new situations he encounters. Just as many old people find changes very stressful because they have become rigid and routinized in their habits and because they no longer have the skills to cope with a novel environment, so the child who lacks malleability and competence will also find changes stressful.

In the school situation the child who is good at his work is in a favoured position because the work is less of a struggle, because life consists of a series of successes instead of failures, and because the teachers will probably view him more positively. The child who falls behind in his school work is at a serious disadvantage for the obverse of the same reasons. Many studies have shown that behavioural problems are very much more common in children who are behind in their reading[167] (see chapter 8). There are probably several reasons for this association, but one of them is that educational failure leads to such opprobrium that the child becomes disenchanted with school, finds the whole thing a negative experience and reacts adversely to this painful situation.

Athletic prowess is important both because of the pleasure given by success in any field of activities and because of its relevance to popularity with other children, as already noted.

Social skills are probably the most crucial of all, in view of the importance of interaction with other people as a source of learning and of pleasure. In part these skills are based on temperamental attributes – some children are 'naturally' outgoing whereas others are not – and in part they rely on appropriate learning experiences.

(e) Vulnerability.

Finally, in this connection, there is the rather imprecise concept of 'vulnerability', already discussed with respect to sex differences. How far vulnerability is singly an overall measure based on the mechanisms considered above, and how far it involves other modes of action, remains uncertain. Certainly it is a well-established observation that there are large individual differences in children's responses to privation and stress. We still know relatively little about what these differences are due to and how they operate, but it is an issue which requires much greater understanding if we are to devise really effective ways of treating child psychiatric disorder.

Chronic physical illness

Systematic surveys have shown that children with a chronic physical illness (such as asthma, diabetes or heart disease) tend to have a slightly higher rate of emotional and behavioural problems and a slightly higher rate of reading difficulties than do other children.[166] This increase is almost certainly not due to any direct effects of the illness itself, but is rather due to the special difficulties faced by children with chronic physical disorders. A handicapped child may be unable to engage in many normal children's activities (because of his physical restrictions) and as a result may be cut off from important formative experiences. As a consequence there may be effects on the way the child views himself, that is, on his self-image. Attitudes to self have an important impact on behaviour. The child who sees himself with confidence as a competent, successful person is more likely to succeed just because of the effect of this attitude on the way he sets about the task. Because of his restrictions and incapacities, the child with a physical handicap may come to see himself as a person of little worth whose actions do not matter. Alternatively the reverse may happen with the child becoming totally absorbed in his own health and treatment, so that little time is left for other things or for consideration of other people.

The attitudes and behaviour of the child's parents are equally important in this connection. Some may find it difficult to remain receptive to a child whose disability arouses guilt or repugnance (this applies particularly to those with congenital defects or deformities) and sometimes parents may overcompensate for these feelings by becoming unduly protective or overattentive and smothering. Children with physical defects may need some protection and support, but equally, like other children, they need to learn to be independent and able to do things for themselves.

The Isle of Wight study showed that children with chronic physical disorders also have increased reading difficulties in spite of normal intelligence.[166] It was found that reading difficulties were more common in children who had missed a lot of school and it appeared that this was one reason for the scholastic problems. It was not that the children had had one prolonged absence from school. Most children can compensate for that without too much difficulty. Rather it seemed to be the effect of repeated short absences with all that that means in terms of discouragement and lowering of morale and confidence. The effect on children's attitudes to work may well be as important as the actual amount of school time missed.

Of course, as the authors of the Isle of Wight study pointed out, most handicapped children weather these difficulties without any trouble, they have a normal self-image and are brought up by responsive and well-balanced parents. The point is simply that handicapped children face special difficulties in adaptation and these difficulties occasionally lead to educational and emotional problems.

Brain disorders

Whereas children with chronic physical disorders, such as asthma or diabetes, which do not involve the brain have a *slightly* increased rate of emotional and educational problems, children with damage or disturbance of brain function have *much* increased problems.[161] Thus the Isle of Wight survey found that children with cerebral palsy, epilepsy and other similar conditions were three or four times as likely as other children to have such problems. Of course this still means that some two thirds of children with brain disorders do *not* have any psychiatric problems, but about a third do and that constitutes a much increased risk.

If these children are to be properly helped, it is necessary to know *why* and *how* they develop emotional and behavioural problems. The first question is clearly whether the problems *directly* result from the damage to the brain – and the answer is that usually they do *not*. Of course there are certain disabilities which do result fairly directly from brain injury. For example, damage to the brain may result in some impairment of intelligence (although often it does not), it may occasionally lead to specific difficulties in speaking (just as it may lead to specific difficulties in coordination or movement) and it may impede concentration. But brain damage does not lead to a typical or different form of emotional or behavioural disturbance. Children with brain disorders show much the same range of problems shown by any other group of children – including anxiety and fears, overactivity and aggression, difficulty in getting on with other children, misery and antisocial behaviour. It has sometimes been thought that there is a special type of behaviour disorder typical of the brain-damaged child – so that psychiatrists have sometimes talked of the 'brain-damage syndrome' or the 'syndrome of minimal brain damage'. This description has usually been used for very overactive children. However, research in the last few years has shown this concept to be mistaken and misleading.[161, 176] Most overactive children do not have brain damage and most brain-damaged children are not overactive. It is not that the problems in the child with cerebral palsy or epilepsy are different; it is just that they are much more frequent.

The question is why? To answer that question we need to find out what is different about the brain-damaged children who develop emotional or behavioural problems. How do they differ from other children with brain damage who are psychologically normal?

Several factors have been found to be important. Some of these relate to the brain damage itself, but many relate to factors which are also associated with psychiatric problems in children who have not had any kind of injury to the brain. Emotional and behavioural problems have been found to be more frequent when the damage affects both sides of the brain, suggesting that the *extent* of the damage is important. Among epileptic children disorder is more frequent in those children with psychomotor fits. These are a type of fit particularly associated with the temporal lobe, so this finding suggests that the *locus* of the damage may also be relevant. It appears that psychiatric difficulties may be more likely if the brain disorder involves fits or abnormal electrical activity of the brain, so that the *type* of the brain disorder is also important. In general it seems that abnormal brain activity is worse than lack of brain activity. A loss of function can often be compensated for, but if the damage causes disturbed function in the remaining brain this can be more troublesome.

These factors are all specific to the brain disorder, but in addition non-neurological factors play an important role. In the general population, below-average intelligence and severe reading difficulties are both strongly associated with a higher rate of psychiatric disorder. Exactly the same situation applies in the case of children with brain damage. In their case the low IQ and reading problems may derive from the injury to the brain, but it is probable that the mechanisms by which they are associated with emotional and behavioural problems are similar to those operating in normal children.

In the general population, neurosis in parents, marital discord and 'broken homes' are all strongly associated with the development of psychiatric problems in the children (see chapter 4). The same applies to children with cerebral palsy, epilepsy or other brain conditions. With respect to these variables, the brain-damaged child is much the same as any other child. The fact of brain damage makes him more susceptible, but it is the same kind of environmental stresses and disturbances to which he succumbs. Poor social conditions or low social status may also increase the psychiatric risk.

If these and other findings are used to consider the possible mechanisms by which brain damage leads to emotional or behavioural disturbance, it may be concluded that several different mechanisms may be operative. The damage to the brain may lead to specific or general cognitive deficits involving language, perception and coordination. These in turn will be associated with impaired intelligence and with reading difficulties. The means by which reading retardation may lead to psychiatric problems are far from fully understood, but one possible factor is the effect of educational failure. The child who

repeatedly fails in school and falls behind in his schola﹀
ments not only has the dispiriting experience of constantly ﹍﹍
but he is also likely to be repeatedly the recipient of opprobrium
from home and school. This may be especially likely if his reading difficulties are present in spite of normal intelligence. In
these circumstances he is likely to be urged time and again to 'try
harder', when he feels he is already trying as hard as he can. The
result of such discouragement may be either emotional upset or
rebellion according to the child's personality. If that were a
factor, it might be supposed that, in special schools with lower
standards and no competition with normal children, reading
difficulties should be less likely to be associated with psychiatric
problems. In the one study to examine that issue, that was just
what was found.[175]

Another mechanism involves temperamental attributes. Although not systematically studied, it is probable that children
with brain damage may be more likely to have those attributes
which are associated with a higher psychiatric risk – namely
irregularity of body functions, lack of malleability and impaired adaptability, impulsivity and poor concentration. By their
effect on other people, on the child's experiences and on his
ability to adjust to changing circumstances these attributes may
make emotional and behavioural disturbances more likely.

A third possibility involves society's reactions to the child's
handicap. It is known that there are community prejudices, particularly concerning epilepsy, but also involving other physical
disabilities. These exist because people do not understand and
are frightened by the disability, but they may lead to the development of attitudes towards the child which impede his psychological development. While this is not a major factor in the
development of psychiatric disorder in brain-damaged children,
it is one which requires attention.

The child's own attitudes towards his disability are also important and it is easy to see how a poor self-image may develop.
Also some aspects of brain disorders may be particularly frightening and upsetting. The sudden loss of consciousness which
occurs in an epileptic fit may be a very threatening experience to
a child, who never knows when his powers are going to be taken

an attack. The aura preceding some
                         .otor fits, may be very unpleasant,

                    are the things which we do to the child to
              .t which may have unfortunate adverse side-
                 .le, admission to hospital carries some stresses;
              disrupts education; and drugs and medicines
i..   excite the child in a way which interferes with his
psyc..   .d functioning. Recent work has also shown that
some con.nonly used drugs may interfere with learning to some
extent.

The upshot of all this is that the assessment of the brain-
damaged child with psychiatric problems needs to be just as
comprehensive as in any other child. The fact of brain damage
puts the child at an increased risk but it does not explain why
problems developed. Before a proper plan of treatment can be
made, it is necessary to determine for that particular child
which factors in him and in his environment led to the disorder
and which are now causing the problems to continue.

This may be illustrated most easily by considering three children, each of whom developed psychiatric problems after a
severe head injury, but in each of whom the mechanisms were
rather different.

Ernest had had a severe road accident at the age of six years, in
which he broke his leg and fractured his skull. He was unconscious
for a fortnight and could not speak for a month. Referral to the
clinic occurred some nine months later because he was asking point-
less questions repeatedly, was anxious and tearful, had many odd
mannerisms and was disobedient and difficult. The brain injury had
left him rather clumsy and as a result he had become worried and
lacking in confidence about whether he could cope with ordinary
tasks, such as getting dressed in the morning. During the year preceding Ernest's accident his mother had become increasingly depressed and this reached a peak with her suicidal attempt during the
months in which Ernest was recovering from his head injury. She
remained low spirited and found it difficult to cope with him, so that
she was alternately irritable and cross and then oversolicitous and
fussy to make up for her earlier temper. Father's job meant that he

was rarely home in an evening and so had very ┊
children. The marriage had been under strain fo┊
there were frequent arguments between the parents.┊

Ernest's head injury was of direct importance in┊
effect in causing loss of speech. The persistent ques┊
veloped during the period he was regaining speech a┊
many of the qualities of the questioning used by tod┊ in
order to practice and explore language as well as to gain information. Although irritating to his depressed mother, there was
nothing abnormal in the questioning itself, but later it came to
be used as a means of seeking reassurance. The accident was
also important in terms of Ernest's worries about his clumsiness
and lack of coordination. However, much the most important
factor was mother's depression and its effect on her relationship
with Ernest. Both the timing and the form of disorder suggested
that Ernest's anxiety, tempers and difficult behaviour were a
response to mother's tension, misery and inconsistency. This
formulation was subsequently confirmed when it became evident that Érnest's sister (who was not involved in the accident)
was responding in exactly the same way. Treatment involved
several elements. The social worker helped mother through casework to deal with her marital difficulties, to avoid involving
Ernest in the parental quarrels and to be both more consistent
and more effective in dealing with Ernest's tempers and fears.
Antidepressant tablets were also prescribed. The psychiatrist
saw the boy in psychotherapy both to discuss his reactions to his
injury and subsequent disability and to come to terms with the
family tensions and discord. It would have been helpful to have
involved father in treatment but he was unwilling to attend,
having by that time largely opted out of the family. Over the
course of the next six months Ernest improved greatly as
mother became less depressed and her difficulties in dealing
with him lessened. The marital conflict was not resolved although it impinged less on the children.

Peter also had a severe head injury as a result of a road accident,
but this occurred when he was aged seven years. He was in hospital
for nearly a year and for a long time he was like a baby – unable to

speak and unable to feed himself. His parents were told at that time that he would probably be 'mental' for the rest of his life. In the event this prognosis proved to be much too pessimistic as he made a good recovery, returning to school nine months later. He was referred to the clinic at thirteen years because of severe tempers and difficult behaviour at home and at school. His intelligence was low average but he was some four years behind in his reading. After the accident he had some fits during the first year. Although these ceased, he was left with a brain wave pattern on the EEG (brain wave test) which showed abnormal electrical activity. Both parents were stable, sensible people who had a warm and responsive relationship with Peter.

Although Peter's problems on referral – tempers and disobedience – were in many ways similar to Ernest's, the underlying mechanisms were quite different. In his case the head injury was of greater direct importance in its production of abnormal brain function (as shown by the EEG) and fits. This is the type of brain pathology especially associated with vulnerability to psychiatric disorder. The second causal factor lay in his severe reading retardation which had developed as a result of the brain damage. He received remedial help with his reading but his scholastic difficulties remained a matter of great worry and concern to him. The third factor lay in the family's response after the accident. Understandably his parents had been rather protective of him at first, as they expected a continuing handicap and it took some time for them to adjust to the fact that he was in fact left with very little physical disability. Treatment consisted of the social worker aiding the parents' understanding of Peter's difficulties and helping them deal with him as a basically normal boy rather than as an invalid to be protected. In psychotherapy Peter's feelings about his difficulties were discussed and he was helped to find more constructive ways of dealing with his problems. The family was a cohesive group and Peter's difficulties rapidly subsided, in spite of the continuing EEG abnormality, so that it was possible to stop treatment after about four months.

Margaret also came to the clinic during adolescence, several years after a very severe head injury. Her problem was that she had recently become miserable and depressed and had developed multiple aches and pains. After the accident she had been in hospital for many months with a severe paralysis, but ultimately she was left with just weakness of one arm, an inability to see to one side and slight clumsiness of gait. However, she had also become rather overweight. Margaret was able to look after herself in most things, but she had needed to make certain adjustments to do so – for example, she had to write in an awkward manner. Also there were some things, such as shoelaces and hair grips, which she could not manage. She had learned to cope with her physical problems by becoming very precise and controlled, but this now led to teasing. Her problems developed after puberty with an increasing concern about the effects of her disability on her appearance and on her attractiveness to boys. She became jealous of her pretty and petite older sister and she responded to her inner feelings of misery, self-depreciation and worthlessness by becoming sexually provocative as if to prove to herself that she really was loved and wanted. The family was happy and harmonious but Margaret's parents were upset by their inability to understand why she was behaving as she was.

In Margaret's case most of the difficulties stemmed from her attitude to her handicap and to the increasing problems this brought during adolescence. When younger she had enjoyed the spoiling she got at home as a result of her disability. Now she wanted more independence but was uncertain of her ability to cope. Adjustment had been easier when she was obviously crippled. Now the physical handicap was less, she felt the need to compete with the physically normal. With sexual maturity, her self-image became more important and she was increasingly aware of her clumsiness and fatness, and the implications these had regarding her sexual attractiveness.

The parents were seen by the social worker, who helped them to appreciate the nature of Margaret's uncertainties and doubts. As they did so, they became better able to help her. However, the main focus in treatment was psychotherapy with Margaret herself, in which the goals were to help her understand the nature of her doubts about herself and to enable her to find better ways of adapting to her mild physical limitations. She had been unable to resolve her difficulties partly because she did not really understand the nature of her own feelings and partly because she tended to deny her problems. When she could not easily accomplish things she maintained she did not want to do them. The therapist sought first to help Margaret feel free in talking about what she thought and soon she readily expressed guilt, doubt and resentments which she had hitherto kept to herself. The very fact of being able to do this with an understanding adult was helpful in itself. However, it was necessary for the therapist to go further in enabling Margaret to understand why and how she felt as she did. By means of encouraging responses, comments and the occasional question he facilitated self-exploration and ventilation of secret feelings. He used interpretations and suggestions to enable Margaret to build links between her feelings and actions. At the same time as he was assisting her to develop self-understanding he made sure that she used the understanding to work out constructive solutions to her problems.

Margaret spoke of her ambivalent feelings regarding help and control from her mother and her resentment at being different. This theme of ambivalence about receiving help kept recurring throughout treatment sessions. When she arrived on the wrong day for an appointment and was late for the next, the therapist made the interpretation that she was also ambivalent about help from the clinic. Margaret agreed and this led to a fruitful discussion on her mixed feelings concerning the need to accept help from others. Margaret also spoke about feeling that she needed to pay back a debt to her family for all the help they gave her after the accident and about her resentment that they could not give her a perfect recovery. The therapist suggested that Margaret might be worried about being imperfect 'inside' as well. Margaret took this up by speaking about her menstrual periods. She was conscious and pleased about emerging womanhood but embarrassed by her periods and anxious about growing up because she still wanted to be childish. This led to a discussion regarding Margaret's view of growing up as just taking on responsibility but not getting any rewards. Early in treatment Margaret got a boy friend. The fact that he saw her as desirable and attractive greatly boosted her morale but increased her sexual anxieties. Other girls laughed at her disability and she found that having boy friends (she had several during the course of treatment) both helped to compensate for the mockery and raised her prestige with the girls. Margaret's anxieties and mixed feelings were those experienced by many normal adolescents, but they were intensified by the self-doubts stemming from her physical disability.

Psychotherapy helped her to regain both a better self-image (in fact she was reasonably attractive in spite of her handicap) and more confidence in herself as a person. Margaret's depression lifted early in treatment, and over the course of the year during which she was seen she gradually developed a more secure self-identity. Her relationships with boys became more relaxed and she no longer felt the need to prove her attractiveness.

Missed physical disease

In all three children the physical disorder was obvious and the psychiatrist's main role in diagnosis was to understand the children's psychological reactions to their handicap. However, in other cases the physical disease is less obvious, so that an important element in differential diagnosis is the question of whether or not the child has some underlying medical illness. The psychiatrist must always be prepared to make a full medical assessment, as some somatic diseases masquerade as emotional or behavioural problems. Two rather different cases illustrate how this can arise.

Bruce was referred to the clinic when he was eight years because he was thought to have hysterical blindness which had begun eighteen months earlier. The trouble began with unreasonable tantrums and increasing stubbornness. Bruce shared his parents' bedroom and it was thought that he had witnessed sexual intercourse between them. His inability to see developed after a quarrel between his mother and grandmother, during a game in which his father was trying to teach him cricket, insisting that he 'keep his eye on the ball'. Bruce was seen by a paediatrician who found no physical abnormality and he was referred to another psychiatric clinic where he received weekly psychotherapy. During therapy it emerged that a blind man used to visit the home and that Bruce had been very impressed by how everyone was kind to him and gave him meals. Bruce continued to appear partially blind and, as his vision seemed to be getting worse, he was admitted to a children's psychiatric unit for further investigation. Examination of his eye still revealed no abnormality. Father was a hot-tempered, self-opinionated man, still very dependent on his own mother. He was firmly convinced that Bruce could really see. Mother was a more relaxed person but she was sexually frigid and the marriage was not a happy one.

There were many reasons for supposing that Bruce's blindness might be hysterical; there were family difficulties, there were stresses immediately preceding the onset of the blindness, and it was evident that Bruce thought that blindness was a means of bringing love and attention. However, Bruce had never shown any previous emotional disturbance and slowly progressive blindness is rarely hysterical. Accordingly he was carefully observed to determine if his behaviour gave any clues as to whether or not the blindness was psychogenic. It was noted that he continued to feel around for toys and food even when he was not aware of being observed and that he seemed to have to look out of the corner of his eyes to see things. As these findings appeared to indicate 'true' blindness, a further examination was made of his eyes. This showed a slight excess of pigment at the back of his eyes, which sometimes indicates a rare form of degeneration involving the brain and eyes. Unfortunately this tentative diagnosis was confirmed over the next year as Bruce became increasingly blind with more obvious abnormalities on examination of his eyes. He was transferred to a school for the blind but eventually had to be placed in a hospital for the mentally retarded, as his intelligence declined greatly and he developed epileptic fits.

Herbert first attended the clinic at age seven years with a diagnosis of possible autism. He was said to be not progressing mentally, was childish, concentrated poorly and was aggressive to other children. He was excitable and did not seem to understand what was said to him. There were various rigid routines he insisted on; he would spend hours doing and redoing jigsaw puzzles and he did not play well with other children. On the other hand he was very affectionate with his parents and always had been. His early development had been normal except that he had been markedly delayed in speech. When he did speak, his grammar was rather muddled and his pronunciation was poor and indistinct. When aged two and a half, he had been seen by an experienced audiologist who said that hearing seemed to be normal but that he should be retested within a year, as the testing had been difficult and was possibly unreliable. The family moved home soon after and no further testing was undertaken. His speech delay was first attributed to being brought up in a bilingual home (father spoke German and mother spoke English) and then to emotional disturbance. At interview Herbert was attentive, responsive and made a good relationship. He seemed keen to cooperate and he pointed to help convey meaning, but he often misunderstood what was said to him.

Herbert's behaviour was quite unlike that of an autistic child and several factors suggested the possibility of partial deafness. First, his speech was abnormal and its quality indicated the possibility that his production of sounds had been distorted by deafness. Second, his inability to understand seemed out of keeping with his language capacity and his degree of cooperation. Clinical testing showed a probable deafness particularly involving a loss of response to high-tone sounds. Expert audiological examination confirmed the diagnosis. His main care was transferred to audiological specialists, who fitted a hearing aid and arranged for special remedial help in school from a peripatetic teacher of the deaf. With the recognition of the true nature of his handicap Herbert's emotional difficulties soon improved and a year later he was reported to be well adjusted and doing better at school.

In both cases the children had been assessed early by experienced and competent medical specialists who made all the appropriate tests. However, at that stage the true nature of the physical disability was not apparent, a psychological 'label' was attached and for a while this inhibited further investigations. This was particularly unfortunate in the case of Herbert both because the original specialist had specified the need for further testing and because his condition was remediable. The cases emphasize the need for repeated reconsideration and re-assessment when the course of development suggests that the original diagnosis may have been mistaken, and also the need for psychiatrists to make an adequate medical appraisal of children referred to them.

Genetics

Doctors are often asked if a particular psychiatric problem in a child has been 'inherited'. The answer to this question is almost always no, in that very few disorders constitute single diseases which could be inherited as such. Of course there are a number of rarer conditions associated with mental retardation which are inherited directly. This applies, for example, to a number of the diseases associated with disorders in body chemistry (such as phenylketonuria). There are also several conditions due to chromosome anomalies, of which Down's syndrome or mongolism is the best known. But most disorders of behaviour or emotions are not of that kind. There are a few conditions, more characteristic of adulthood but which can occur in children, such as schizophrenia or manic-depressive psychosis, which have a strong hereditary component; but even these conditions are not directly inherited, in that non-genetic factors also play a part in the development and continuation of the disorders. The same applies to most of the behavioural disorders associated with chromosome peculiarities (see page 243).

Nevertheless it would be quite wrong to suppose that genetic factors are unimportant in development. On the contrary, twin studies show that genetic influences play a most important role in the determination of individual differences with respect to intelligence, neurotic tendencies and other personality variables.[179] As already noted genetic factors are very influential in the development of many temperamental attributes. But their effect is *not* to predestine a child to the inevitable development of any particular kind of behaviour. Rather there is an ongoing interaction with environmental influences which results in the eventual individual personality traits.

It is important to recognize that there are significant biological influences on a person's development and that these have a major impact in determining how children differ. It is no good expecting a child whose genetic endowment leads him towards extreme introversion to become an outgoing, ebullient extrovert. That is just not how he is made. The large differences in personality so often seen between children in the same family are due in considerable part to genetic influences. Each child gets his genes from his parents, but he does not get the same mixture as do his brothers and sisters. There has sometimes been a tendency to blame parents for all the shortcomings of their children, on the quite mistaken assumption that personality differences are largely or entirely due to upbringing. That is not so and many parents have suffered quite needless guilt on this account. Equally, however, it would be highly misleading to assume the converse. Children differ because of their genetic endowment and brain structure but also because of family and social influences. Some of these are discussed in the next two chapters.

4 Families

For a long time people have been aware of some of the unhappy childhood experiences which are associated with the development of emotional or behavioural problems. These
include things like broken homes, being brought up in an institution, the death of a parent, parental cruelty, very inconsistent
discipline, admission to hospital or an unloving or quarrelsome
home. This knowledge is important in providing pointers to children who are particularly liable to psychiatric disorder. However, if we are to provide effective help for these youngsters, it is
not enough to know which bad experiences are associated with
psychological problems. We must also know why they lead to
these problems, and *how* they have these unfortunate consequences. In short, it is necessary to understand the psychological mechanisms which are involved. We are rarely in a
position to undo bad experiences or to change a really bad
home situation into a really good one, but frequently we can
bring about some change in the right direction. To do this we
must know what are the key aspects which are crucial in leading
to emotional or behavioural problems. It should be emphasized
straight away that our understanding of the mechanisms
underlying family interactions remains very limited and much
has still to be learned. Nevertheless knowledge is available on
some of these issues and any psychiatric assessment must
include an appraisal of the likely mechanisms by which the
disorder arose. Accordingly, before discussing the several
family influences associated with psychiatric disorder in the
children, it is appropriate to first consider the various
roles performed by parents when bringing up their children.

Dimensions of parenthood
Provision of emotional bonds or relationships

The great importance of children developing emotional bonds
to other people has been noted when discussing child development. During the first two or three years of life the infant develops a series of attachments which are selective in that some
relationships become much more important to him than others.
These early bonds probably constitute the basis for later relationships and the child who has failed to make secure relationships in early childhood is likely to be at a considerable social
disadvantage when he is older. Generally the young child develops bonds with the individuals with whom he is in most
intense contact, so that in all ordinary circumstances these will
be members of his family, and especially his parents. The way
they interact with him and the extent to which they are responsive to his signals and his needs will help determine what
sort of relationships are formed during these early years. Of
course it should not be thought that it is only in early childhood
that bonds are important. On the contrary, family relationships
continue to be important right through childhood and into adult
life. The relationships change their form and, to some extent,
their function, but their importance persists.

A secure base

The existence of bonds is important not only through their role
in the development of later relationships but also through their
immediate effect in reducing the child's anxiety in new or stressful situations. In this way the family acts as a secure base from
which the child can test out new ways of exploring and responding to his environment. Similarly family members serve as a
source of comfort at times of stress and distress.

This dimension of parental functioning can easily be seen in
several different situations. For example, if you watch a mother
with her toddler in the park, a very characteristic pattern of
behaviour is evident. When she sits down on the park bench and
lets the child out of his push chair, at first the child stays close to
her. Then, gradually, he begins to make forays farther and far-

ther away from the bench. Each time, he will return for a moment as if to seek reassurance that she is still there and, having got the reassurance, off he goes again to explore further afield. Her presence constitutes the base which gives him his security to explore and wander. However, if apparent danger appears in the form of an overintrusive stranger or a lively dog, back he goes to his place of security. Paradoxically, the strength and security of the mother–child bond is probably shown as much by the child's willingness to move away from her when all is clear as by his rapid return when a threat is perceived. The insecure child will cling and fail to explore in this situation. The abnormally unattached child (a fortunately rare phenomenon) will wander but not return for comfort.

This use of attachments as a base for exploration and as a source of comfort at times of distress is not a particularly human phenomenon, as it is seen throughout the animal kingdom. Behaviour identical to that seen in the park can be observed with infant monkeys or with baby chicks.[18]

Another demonstration of the anxiety-reducing properties of parental presence occurs when children are admitted to hospital or when they go into strange and frightening situations.[156] Several studies have shown that children are much less worried and upset in these circumstances if a parent goes along with them. However, it is important to note that a similar beneficial effect is obtained if the child is accompanied by a brother or sister or friend. It seems that it is not the presence of the parent as such which is crucial but rather the presence of someone to whom the child is attached.

Models of behaviour and of attitudes

Children tend to copy other people's behaviour, and they are most likely to model themselves on those individuals with whom they have the closest relationships. In part this is a conscious attempt to behave in the same way as other people, in part it is unconscious imitation which is a feature of the process of identification, and in part the child's choice of ways of behaving will be governed by the range of behaviours he encounters in those closest to him. At a trivial level this can be seen (and indeed has been shown experimentally by Bandura and others[8]) in the mannerisms that children pick up. Children readily copy the peculiarities of gesture or gait or ways of speaking that are shown by their parents, by a specific friend, by a teacher or by the pop star whom they admire. This copying is more likely to occur with respect to people upon whom they depend and with whom they have a warm and loving relationship.

However, the importance of parental models of behaviour extends much further than the copying of mannerisms. The child's style of coping with stress will be influenced by the strategies that he sees employed by his parents. If they deal with difficulties by passive resignation or by maladaptive aggression, he is more likely to do so also. If dad shouts and swears when he is upset this constitutes an encouragement for the child to do likewise. If mum retires to bed with a headache at times of stress and tension this will make it more likely that the child, too, will learn to respond to difficulties in a hypochondriacal manner, using bodily complaints as a means of dealing with anxiety.

Interpersonal relationships are likely to be influenced in the same way. The marital relationship between the parents is the only model of a close relationship of which the child is likely to have intensive experience over a long period of time. His father's relationship with his mother will serve to an important extent as a model for the boy's own relationship with girls. If the model is one of warmth, mutual concern and respect he is more likely to develop similar relationships himself. If, on the other hand, he sees that his father treats his mother with contempt this may influence his heterosexual relationships accordingly.

In this connection it is important to note that parents teach children to behave in particular ways both by what they tell them to do (that is, by precept) and by what the child observes of the parents' own ways of behaving (that is, by percept). The child is most likely to follow the parents when the precept and percept are similar. However, it is not infrequent for a parent to say one thing and do another, to preach honesty but to cheat others, to demand self-control of the child but to exhibit temper, aggression and lack of control himself. In this situation various circumstances will influence whether the child follows the precept or his percept, but resentment and rebellion are most likely when he is expected to reach a higher standard than that which he sees followed by his parents.

Also the child may generalize the model of behaviour set by his parents in a way which leads to behaviour unacceptable to them. It is not uncommon for parents who are themselves unconventional, iconoclastic and anti-establishment to have adolescents who follow this model but extend the rebellion and rejection to include values which the parents hold dear. The youngsters have accepted the model of non-conformity and in doing so have included non-conformity to parental norms.

Of course children do not all follow the models of behaviour and the attitudes shown by their parents. Whether or not they do so will depend both on the other models with which they are presented (by friends, teachers, neighbours and other relatives) and on the quality of their relationship with their parents. If the relationship is bad they may come to reject all that the parent stands for. The same may apply if they see that the parents' behaviour leads only to trouble or rejection. It is in these ways that it sometimes happens that the children of alcoholics are teetotallers and the children of rigid abstainers are heavy drinkers.

Provision of life experiences

Parents are also extremely influential through being a source of necessary life experiences. For example, intelligence develops through experience as well as through heredity. Children learn by doing things – by manipulating toys and by playing games. The kind and amount of toys provided by parents and the extent to which they play with their children will help enhance or retard the child's intellectual development. Similarly the child's store of knowledge will be increased by the degree to which the parents provide the opportunities for the children to use libraries, to visit museums, to walk in the country and generally to have a rich and varied set of experiences which are made interesting, meaningful and exciting. Like the good teacher, the good parent must not only provide information but must also see to it that the circumstances and mode of transmission of information encourage the child to want to learn.

Talking with the young child is important for several reasons. First, it serves to aid the child's development of language and of verbal intelligence. Studies have shown that infants babble and vocalize more if they are read to, and speech development is advanced if, in play groups, special attention is paid to talking to children from poor homes. Second, conversation provides information and knowledge which is important to the child. Third, the way parents use talk will help determine how the child sees the value of spoken language. Bernstein[13] has pointed to the differences in the ways in which speech is used to communicate in different social classes. The linguistic codes employed by his parents will help shape the way the child uses language and this will have important educational consequences for him when he enters school.

It is usual to think of experience in relation to intellectual development and education, but also, of course, it plays a vital role in social and emotional development. The child who has been 'tied to his mother's apron strings' is likely to be much less able to cope with going to school or being admitted to hospital than is the child who is well used to playing with friends and staying with relatives in happy circumstances. Social skills have to be learned just as do other skills, and the child's experiences in being with and playing with other children will help determine how easy he finds it to make friends. Children used to a wide range of situations who have learned to cope with and enjoy many social experiences will adapt more easily and will be more likely to enjoy changes of environment or moves of house.

Discipline and the shaping of behaviour

Parents help shape the child's behaviour by means of their selective encouragement and discouragement of particular behaviours, by their discipline and by the amount of freedom which they allow. At least in the early years it is mainly from the parents that the child learns what he is supposed to do and what behaviours are forbidden. He will learn this by many different mechanisms, such as by what he is told and by the models of behaviour which he perceives. However, he will also learn patterns of behaviour by seeing how parents respond to his different actions: what he has to do to be told 'good boy' and what leads to his being smacked. In this connection the two chief elements are (a) the parental choice regarding the behaviours they want to encourage and discourage and (b) the efficiency of their discipline in bringing about the desired aim.

Parents obviously differ in the goals that they have for their children. There are well-known national, cultural and social variations in this respect.[119] Some families expect their children to be conforming and obedient, others value assertiveness and independence. Some demand that their children be self-reliant and able to take a major role in household responsibilities from an early age, while others prefer their children to be dependent for much longer. These choices regarding goals may play some part in determining characteristic styles of behaviour, but whether they constitute an important influence in leading to differences in rates of emotional or behavioural disorder is not known. The observation that, within New York, youngsters from Chinese families seem to have a lower delinquency rate than those from other minority groups might suggest such an effect. However, there are also other reasons why this might occur.

The importance of the 'efficiency' of disciplining techniques requires no emphasis. The limited amount that is known on this issue will be discussed below.

Communication network

Finally, the home provides a communications network by which the child can set his standards, establish his norms, develop his expectations and let his ideas grow. The conversations a child has with his parents and with his brothers and sisters are a very important means of his trying out his ideas and of working out his relationships with others. It is not just the words which are used, as communication also involves the transmission of feelings and attitudes by gesture, facial expression and posture. The child's development will be influenced by the extent to which there is good opportunity for free communications in the home, by the content of communications and by the clarity of communications. Homes where the parents provide conflicting messages or an excess of ambiguous communications are likely to be more difficult for the child although there is a shortage of evidence on this point.

These are by no means the only dimensions of parenthood, but they include the more important roles performed by parents in bringing up children. These can serve as a backcloth against which to consider the possible mechanisms underlying some of the family influences associated with child psychiatric disorder.

Child rearing and discipline

In the past, books dealing with child development have used a lot of space in discussing such issues as when to wean and to toilet train. Much of this concern stemmed from an old-fashioned psychoanalytic view of development in terms of oral, anal and latency stages. As we have seen (pages 64, 69, 86) this is a misleadingly simplified view of development, and research findings suggest that the timing of various aspects of infant care is of very little significance and that questions such as whether the child is breast fed or bottle fed and what method of toilet training is used are of little psychological importance.[27] That is not to say that the pattern of infant care is unimportant. Feeding and toilet training are vital parts of the child's day and the way the parent undertakes these activities is important. Thus feeding (whether by bottle or breast) provides a good opportunity to hold, talk to and respond to the infant. This interaction is necessary for optimal development, and it is not the same if the infant is just left with a propped-up bottle to feed himself. How the baby is looked after is of considerable significance, but it is the social and psychological context of the care which matters rather than its chronology or mechanics.

The subject of methods of discipline is equally unrewarding, for the most part, in spite of an immense body of research on this and other related aspects of child rearing. Much of this research has serious methodological and conceptual difficulties, as shown by Yarrow and her colleagues,[204] but so far as can be judged the findings are largely negative.[6] Within surprisingly broad limits it matters little what method of discipline is used or how severe is the punishment. Very severe or very lax discipline appears unsatisfactory in its effects, but there are few findings of any importance in the middle of the range, and there is little to choose between smacking, sending out of the room and reprimanding as punishments. On the other hand, while severity of punishment is not a major influence, frequency of punishment is more important. Boys who are constantly punished are likely to respond with aggression and antisocial behaviour. It is difficult to regard this as a straightforward effect of discipline, as very frequent punishment is often associated with rejection and hostility. It may be that it is the poor parent–child relationship which is as important in the genesis of behavioural disturbance as is the pattern of discipline.

Nevertheless consistency of discipline is most important. Marked inconsistency either between parents (dad is punitive and mum permissive, one says the lad can and the other says he can't) or within one parent's mode of discipline (punishment for staying out late one night but lack of concern the next) seems to be associated with a much-increased likelihood of aggressive or delinquent behaviour. The pattern of extremely lax discipline by mothers and rigidly overrestrictive discipline by fathers is particularly common in the families of delinquent boys. The evidence is less satisfactory on this point, but it is likely that inconsistency between how parents behave and how they tell their children to behave (i.e. hypocritical discipline!) may have a similar effect.

As judged by studies in the classroom and by experimental investigations, the way in which parents respond at the time to their children's good deeds and misdeeds is also likely to be of great importance. So far there have been very few studies in which parent–child interaction in the home has been observed for this purpose. However, the few pilot studies which have been conducted do suggest that the timing and character of parental responses can be very influential in shaping children's behaviour for better or worse.[88, 125, 126] The parents of problem children seem to differ from other parents in being less good at recognizing when and how to intervene, in giving less encouragement and praise for good behaviour, in responding erratically and inconsistently to bad behaviour and in giving a lot of attention (both positive and negative) when the child is misbehaving. Since much (but by no means all) disturbed behaviour has an attention-seeking element, the net effect is to encourage it by giving the child attention at these times. Often it would be better to ignore the misbehaviour, so that it no longer succeeded in gaining attention and hence would be more likely to subside. Conversely there is a failure to encourage the child when he is doing what he should be doing. As in the classroom, there is an awful tendency to feel 'thank goodness he's quiet for the moment – let's leave him be'. In fact what is needed at these times is parental interest, praise and encouragement for the child's positive behaviour. It's a very rare child who does nothing which is good or worthwhile, but all too often this gets overlooked in the preoccupation with his misdeeds. Frequently an improvement can be brought about simply by reversing this emphasis.

The effectiveness of discipline probably depends on many other factors as well. Firm knowledge is not yet available on what these are, but they probably include: the timing of parental responses (both rewards and punishments are much more effective when given immediately); the consistency and principles of disciplinary demands (children are likely to respond much better when they see the rules as reasonable and for a purpose); the quality of the parent–child relationship (parental approval and disapproval will have much more impact when the parent is loved and respected) and the balance of praise and punishment (a better response is more likely when there is a premium on praise and a minimum of prohibitions). The great importance of consistency has already been mentioned. It is better to have a few rules which are firmly applied than a mass of regulations haphazardly enforced.

Sometimes discipline tends to be thought of largely in terms of punishment, as if the main objective was the suppression of 'bad behaviour'. Of course it is not. In the first place, the enhancement of 'good' behaviour is at least as important as the reduction of 'wrongdoing', so that encouragement and praise are central. But even more crucial is the fact that the real objective is to enable the child to develop his own internal controls. It is necessary for him to gain his own set of values (which are not necessarily the same as those of his parents) in order for him to regulate his behaviour without remaining dependent on other people's rewards and punishments. For this to occur, the child should be able to discuss with his parents the reasons behind what is done, and as he grows older he should have the opportunity to participate in making family rules on things like who does the washing-up or what time to be in at night.

Parental constraint and overprotection

Related to the matter of discipline is the degree of autonomy and independence that the children are allowed. A quarter of a century ago Hewitt and Jenkins[77] in a study of clinic patients found that overinhibited, neurotic children were particularly likely to have been very constrained and restricted in their activities by their parents. Several other studies since that time have also shown some tendency for parental overcontrol and oversolicitude to be associated with emotional disturbance in the children. The pattern of overprotection and an unusual degree of mutual dependence between mother and child has been particularly described in relation to the problem of school refusal. Undoubtedly the pattern of parental constraint and overprotection is associated with some cases of emotional disturbance in children. However, many of the studies lacked adequate controls and it is not possible to determine the strength of this association or the frequency with which it is a factor in the development of children's problems.

On the other hand the classical study of maternal overprotection undertaken by David Levy[103] four decades ago has clearly demonstrated the different ways in which this form of parental behaviour may arise. Although lacking in statistical sophistication by present-day standards, his study still provides the best model of how to analyse the origins of any parental behaviour and how to plan methods of altering it. Because of its wide applicability in psychiatric practice, it is worth considering the study in some detail.

Levy took a group of children attending a psychiatric clinic and from within this group identified those children who had been subjected to marked maternal overprotection, as defined in terms of excessive contact with the child, prolongation of infantile care and prevention of independence. The excessive contact might be either physical or social. There was undue fondling and mothering, nearly a third of the children (all aged eight years plus) were still sleeping with their mothers, and the mother–child contact was so extensive as to exclude other relationships. The prolongation of infantile care was shown by dressing, bathing and feeding the child long after this was necessary and by excessive servicing of the child, being at his beck and call to get whatever he wanted. The prevention of independence was demonstrated by the child not being allowed to help in the house with washing-up, repairs and other chores; by restriction of his social contacts through determining whom he played with and through not allowing him out to play without permission; and by excessive guarding of the child, fighting his battles and encouraging him to come immediately for help if teased or unable to do something.

It will be noted that, in this definition, Levy placed a firm emphasis on what the mothers actually did with the child rather than on expressed attitudes. There is only a limited relationship between what people say they feel and what in fact they do. Secondly, Levy focused on the parents' behaviour with respect to one particular child rather than to children in general. This is necessary as parents do not behave in the same way to all of their children. Unfortunately these lessons have been ignored in many of the more recent studies which have used dubious questionnaire measures of general attitudes to child rearing. The one serious lack in the Levy investigation was the failure to study fathers. It is only since his study was undertaken that there has been a proper realization that the role of fathers is as important as that of mothers in relation to children's psychological development.

All the children subjected to marked overprotection had poor relationships with other children and the usual pattern was that of a child fearful of leaving his mother, slow to adapt to new situations and with difficulty getting to school. However, within this group there was a difference between those children who had permissive and indulgent mothers and those whose mothers were dominant, restrictive and disciplined. The indulged children were rebellious and defiant at home but less of a problem elsewhere, apart from their difficulty in making friends: in short the typical 'spoiled brat' syndrome. On the other hand the over-disciplined children were passive, submissive and dependent.

In Levy's study, just as in clinical practice, the next question was why the mothers behaved in this unhelpful way. The results showed that the excessive overprotection could arise in several ways. First, there were factors in the child. Compared with a control group, the overprotected children were more likely to have been born after various experiences which had threatened the possibility of a successful pregnancy. A quarter of the children had been born after long periods of sterility; in other cases there was a history of miscarriages, the death of the other children, or serious complications during the pregnancy. In short, there were reasons why the overprotected child should have been more valued than other children as a result of difficulties in conception or birth. Also, after the children had been born, the overprotected youngsters had an excess of chronic or life-threatening illnesses and three times as many operations as the controls. In these cases the illness had been a cause of reasonable overprotection at the time, the problem lay only in its continuation. These findings emphasize the child's role in shaping parental behaviour.

Second, there were factors in the mother's own childhood. Although the mothers were generally stable and active people, many of them had been brought up in homes which lacked warmth and love. They were determined to give their children what they themselves had lacked but rather 'overdid' it in developing an excessively solicitous and protective approach to the child. This emphasizes the fact that it is often necessary to look at the parents' own upbringing to discover why they are behaving in the way they do towards their children.

Third, there were factors in the marriage. The fathers were generally submissive men who took little part in the family life. In three quarters of the cases there was little social life shared between the husband and wife and in the same proportion there was sexual maladjustment. In these cases it seemed that the mother's marital relationship had to some extent been displaced on to the child. She was seeking in an overly close relationship with the child some compensation for what she missed in her husband.

Fourth, although deliberately excluded from Levy's study, overprotection may arise as a response to feelings of hostility and rejection. Sometimes, when people cannot face the reality of recognizing their own unpleasant feelings, such feelings are repressed and replaced by compensatory feelings of an opposite kind – a psychological defence known as reaction formation. When mothers unconsciously 'fight against' feelings of antagonism towards one of their children, they may respond by becoming overprotective and oversolicitous, as if to show themselves how much they really love the child. This is particularly likely to occur when feelings of love and hate co-exist and the parents cannot bring themselves to accept the possibility of hating someone they love. This kind of ambivalence is very common and in itself is perfectly normal. It is the response to the feelings which, in this case, is maladaptive.

Fifth, although also not included in Levy's series, overprotection may arise directly from some form of psychological disturbance in the mother which gives rise, as it were, to an abnormal 'need' for the child's dependency.

For example, Mrs Black was a chronic schizophrenic who insisted on sleeping with her son and who could not bear the thought of his growing up. Every night she went to sleep holding his hand and she showed in extreme degree the overprotective features described by Levy. In part this behaviour arose as a response to a rather unhappy marriage, but it also developed out of disturbances in her own thinking and psychic functioning. On occasions, when her illness got worse, she brought the child to the clinic, ostensibly to complain of his problems but actually to express near-delusional thoughts about him and covertly to ask for help for herself.

The variety of mechanisms by which overprotection (or any other maladaptive parental behaviour) may arise emphasizes the importance of a careful appraisal of all the possible factors before developing a hypothesis as to the origins of the behaviour.

The next step in Levy's study was to determine the best mode of treatment. He looked at three different approaches. First, there was psychotherapy, in which treatment aimed to help the mother understand the dynamics of her behaviour, and attempted to give the child insight into the way he was using dependency as a means of control. The giving of insight is often an important part of treatment, but it is usually insufficient in itself. Understanding does not necessarily lead to a change in behaviour unless specific steps are taken to ensure that it does. In fact in Levy's cases a psychotherapeutic approach was not particularly successful because there was a lack of motivation to change. Without some alteration in the family pattern there was no incentive for either the mother or child to move to a different form of interaction. In other cases psychotherapy designed to provide insight might be the treatment of choice, but with these families other measures were necessary.

Environmental or manipulative therapy was the second approach tried and this was more successful. This involved a direct attempt to manipulate those factors shown to be related to the development of overprotection. The father was encouraged to take a more active role in the family, especially with respect to the child. Efforts were made to find ways in which the parents might share mutually enjoyable activities, and steps were taken to dilute the intensity of mother–child interaction by widening the scope of the mother's interests and by encouraging the child to undertake activities independent of his mother.

The third treatment method was educational therapy which focused on giving the mother skills in dealing with the situations which caused most difficulty. Thus she was shown how to deal with the child's demands, how to ignore his attention-seeking behaviour and how to get him to be more self-reliant and independent. This too seemed to be an effective mode of therapeutic intervention.

Levy's study concerned a relatively small group of families with one particular pattern of interaction. The importance of the investigation lies less in its findings about this pattern (although these are important in their own right) than in its demonstration of how to analyse any pattern of parental behaviour in order to discover its origins and to develop an appropriate method of treatment.

Patterns of dominance and of communication

Although some forms of family therapy have as their main aim the alteration of family patterns of dominance, there is little evidence that variations in parental dominance are very important in the causation of child psychiatric disorders.[76] Studies of the normal population have given rise to varied findings, but most have shown that the commonest pattern is for a balance of power in the home with husbands taking some decisions on their own, wives doing likewise and some decisions taken jointly.[33] Families in which the husband is generally dominant are somewhat commoner than wife-dominant families, but both are very much in the minority. At least in the cultural climate of the last few years wife-dominant families tend to be those associated with the least satisfactory marriages. The findings concerning families of children with emotional or behavioural problems are similarly varied. No consistent pattern has been found, although, perhaps, extremes of husband dominance or wife dominance may be more common. So far as can be judged from the available studies, variations in parental dominance as such are of little importance in leading to disorders in the children. However, the disagreements and tension, or the overprotection, which arise when one or other parent is dissatisfied with the dominance pattern are likely to be of more importance (see below). Also there may be difficulties when the dominance pattern leads to problems in family communication.

The psychiatric interest in patterns of family communications is of relatively recent origin but, even more than dominance, it has played a central role in the development of conjoint family therapy – that is, a form of treatment in which the whole family meet together with the therapist to discuss family concerns and problems. It is a difficult aspect of family interaction to study because it has to be observed directly. Not surprisingly people's reports about communication are not to be relied upon. Usually the method of investigation has involved asking the family to discuss together some problem which they are given, and to arrive at some mutually acceptable solution. There have been too few studies of this kind for our knowledge to be more than tentative. However, the results seem to show that such discussion situations give rise to more parental conflict and disagreement in families with either neurotic or delinquent children than they do in families with normal children.[76] Even more characteristic is that the families of problem children less often reach an agreed solution. There does not seem to be anything very distinctive about the sequence or patterns of communication, but what is different is the *efficiency* of communication. In families with disturbed children the limited available evidence seems to suggest that communication is more inefficient, both in the sense that it is associated with fruitless disputes and in the sense that it fails to achieve its object, namely an agreed solution.[54, 116] Of course these are artificial situations which have been studied, but the suggestion is that the poor communication in those circumstances is a valid sample of a failure in communication which pervades the family's usual mode of interaction and, in particular, their attempts to resolve family problems. Hence the development of conjoint family therapy which aims specifically to improve family communications.

An example of a family where this seemed to be the main issue was the Jameson family. Norman was an adolescent boy referred ostensibly because of a single episode of truancy and because of parental concern regarding his indifferent school work and recent failure in an examination. There was a longer history of frequent clashes between the father and Norman, mainly over homework, but of sufficient severity to greatly sour their relationship. Norman was jealous of his more successful younger sister and father seemed resentful of Norman's closer relationship with mother. Norman had some difficulty with friendships, tending to be over-eager in a way which led to rebuffs. In early childhood there had been several periods when mother and Norman had been separated from father for as long as three or four months as a result of father's work. Also Norman had spent a rather unhappy five months with his paternal grandmother when he was aged four years. Father was a self-made man with a professional job. Mother was an Italian university graduate. Mother's father shared the home and had recently been causing trouble by spreading stories in the town about supposed marital difficulties. Norman had become increasingly unhappy and resentful and wondered if his father really cared for him. Both parents were reasonably stable people of sound personality who shared a good marital relationship, but there were increasingly heated arguments over Norman and over father's method of dealing with him. Norman constantly provoked father and father could no longer recognize Norman's successes (which were several).

This family were all concerned about their difficulties and were anxious to improve matters. In spite of this they had got into a pattern in which there was much argument and mutual recrimination but little real communication. Each family member found it difficult to see the others' point of view, and in spite of a lot of positive feelings they tended to rub each other up the wrong way. The situation was discussed with the family and it was agreed that they would meet as a family group with the therapist: They did this over the course of some six months during which time they were encouraged to talk about the issues which split the family. It became apparent that irritation was sometimes expressed regarding Norman when the real, but hitherto unrecognized, anger was towards the disruptive grandfather. It became possible to discuss this anger more openly. Norman's early separations had impeded the development of his relationship with his father and this too was discussed. The discussions became more frank but also more relaxed. The daily clashes over homework were greatly reduced, Norman was more appreciated by his father and worked harder. Once the pattern of better communications became established, the family were able to deal with most of their difficulties outside the therapeutic sessions. The problems did not disappear and

Norman remained a slightly difficult adolescent, but the family had found more efficient and more acceptable ways of coping with these now rather everyday difficulties.

Separation and loss

It was once claimed that prolonged separation experiences were the foremost cause of delinquency, and even short separations were regarded with such alarm that in 1951 the WHO advised that the use of day nurseries inevitably caused permanent psychological damage. We now know that these views were exaggerated and unnecessarily pessimistic.[152, 156] Nevertheless it has been shown that certain sorts of separation experiences constitute important causes of short-term distress, and that in some circumstances they may play a part in the development of more prolonged psychological disorders. So the key question is: what is special about the separations which cause distress and disorder; what differentiates them from those which do not cause harm and which may indeed even be happy and positive experiences?

Acute distress reactions

The characteristic patterns of distress shown by some young children when they are admitted to hospital or to a residential nursery have been well described by the Robertsons and Bowlby in terms of three phases.[138] The first phase, in those children who show the acute distress reaction, is described in terms of 'protest' – the infant cries and screams for his mother, shows panic, clings when she visits and howls angrily when she leaves. After a few days this is replaced by the phase of 'despair' in which the infant is more withdrawn and appears miserable and unhappy. Eating and sleeping problems are common at this time and often there is much thumb-sucking and rocking, especially if the child is confined to bed. There may then be a final third phase, 'detachment', in which the child seems to lose interest in his parents and appears no longer concerned whether or not they are there. When the child returns to his parents he may ignore them at first or turn away and seem to reject them. Then, for several weeks or even months, he is 'difficult', bad-tempered and clinging. He follows his mother everywhere around the house, holding on to her skirts and appearing very reluctant to leave her even for a moment. At the same time he often seems angry and demanding and may hit out at his parents. In this situation the mother and father may become cross and fed-up with the child's tiresome behaviour and push him away or reprimand him. This usually results in a further increase in the child's clinging and demanding.

It would be wrong to regard the acute distress reaction as rigid or stereotyped, as it is not. Not all reactions take quite this form, but the three phases described do give a realistic picture of how the reaction often develops. A more important fact is that by no means all children admitted to hospital or to a residential nursery develop this reaction.[156] Whether or not they do is in part dependent on them and in part on their experiences while in the hospital or nursery. So far as the children are concerned, the ones most likely to develop an acute distress reaction are those between seven months and four years of age, who have had little experience of visiting other people's houses, who have had a recent traumatic separation, who have had difficulties in making friends, who show poor emotional adjustment or who come from an unhappy home. There is also some suggestion that boys may be more likely than girls to become upset in hospital.

Regarding the experiences during separation, the factors that *reduce* the risk of acute distress are the presence of a family member or friend, frequent visiting, *familiar* staff who spend time with the child and show affection to him, ample provision of toys and play activities, adequate preparation of the child for admission, the keeping of favourite toys and objects during the separation, the continuation as far as possible of familiar home routines and the reduction of unpleasant hospital procedures. With young children it is particularly important that they have the opportunity of showing attachments even when away from home, and this means that there must be a few staff members who have a special interest in the child and who are regularly available at the key times of meals, getting up and going to bed. When these conditions are met, separations may not lead to the distress reaction at all. For example, the Robertsons fostered several young children while the mothers entered hospital for a confinement.[139] Mrs Robertson had only met the infants once just before the separation, but she went to some lengths to ensure that familiar routines were followed whenever possible, she was constantly available to the children (some of whom developed attachments to her even during the brief period of ten days or so they spent with her), and she kept the memory of mother alive by talking to the child about his home and his family. In this happy situation, although the children showed some emotional response to the change, none showed the acute distress reaction exhibited by the children admitted to a residential nursery in similar circumstances for a similar period at a comparable age.

Young children under the age of about seven years tend to think in *egocentric* and *animistic* terms, believing that they are the cause of events around them. This may result in their seeing illness or operations as a punishment for their misdeeds, perhaps particularly in children aged four to seven years. These kinds of worries may constitute the major stress associated with hospital admission. Studies have shown that the opportunity for children of this age to discuss their feelings and anxieties during their hospital stay reduces the likelihood of their showing emotional disturbance after return home.[199] During the period in hospital this psychotherapeutic experience may increase worries for the time being, but the findings show that the resolution of the anxieties through discussion improves the children's adjustment after leaving hospital.

The cause of the hospital admission will also affect the likelihood of a distress reaction. Severe burns, operations and anaesthetics are particularly likely to lead to emotional disturbance, because of the associated pain and the child's fears of surgery and unconsciousness, but also because of the parental distress. Joan Woodward[200] showed that children's emotional disturbance following severe burns could be considerably reduced by instituting daily visiting and by getting a psychiatric social worker to talk with the mothers. Some of the children's problems stemmed from the mother's guilt about allowing the burn to occur and from their inability to cope with the children's aggression and anxiety following the burn. The hospital experience is a stress for parents as well as for children and both may benefit from an opportunity to discuss and deal with their anxiety and anger.

In a study of infant monkeys' responses to separation, Hinde[78, 79] showed that much of the infants' emotional disturbance following reunion with the mother stemmed from tensions in the mother–infant relationship. The same probably applies to humans. Children are often very difficult after a hospital admission and, unless parents understand why this is and how the children are feeling, their irritation with the child's demanding behaviour may make matters worse. An example of this kind is given below.

We are now in a position to draw conclusions about what makes some separations stressful for young children. The separation itself is a stress, important in some children with insecure relationships or unused to separations, but not usually the major factor. In this connection it should be said that, although separation is often talked about in terms of the child's separation from his mother, it is separation from people to whom he is attached which is important. The mother is one of these but by no means the only one. Separation reactions are usually most marked when they involve separation from the whole family and also involve removal to a strange environment. The loss of the opportunity for the child to show attachment behaviour to a familiar person is probably the critical factor in many separations. The reaction of the parents to the child's clinging and demanding behaviour on return home is probably an important influence in the continuation of the distress reaction. The physical traumata associated with hospital care aggravate distress in may cases. Both the child's fantasies concerning his illness or operation and the parental guilt and anxiety about what has happened also often serve to intensify the emotional disturbance.

The therapist's role with respect to acute distress reactions is mainly concerned with efforts to improve conditions for the children in hospital, residential nurseries and other institutions;

with encouraging parents to foster adaptability and emotional security in their children by carefully graded, short, happy separation experiences (e.g. staying with friends or with granny for a few hours and then later overnight); and with psychotherapeutic discussions with children and their parents to reduce distress during such admissions. However, occasionally children are referred for disorders following separation in which the true nature of the problem has not been recognized. The case of James is one in point.

James was a handicapped boy of four years with a severe developmental disorder which meant that he had very little speech and showed marked difficulties in developing social relationships. In the past there had been a variety of behavioural problems including temper tantrums, which the parents had learned to deal with by withdrawing attention during the tantrum and giving attention and affection immediately the tantrum ceased. This approach had proved effective, the tempers greatly diminished and James was becoming increasingly affectionate and responsive. He then spent a fortnight in a holiday home for handicapped children and on his return his behaviour was quite changed. He did not seem to know his parents; he was withdrawn, miserable and apathetic; he was clinging and demanding and there was a return of aggressive behaviour. The parents were intelligent and concerned people, but rather undemonstrative individuals who did not find it easy to appreciate young children's feelings. They responded to the new behaviour problem as before by withdrawing their attention when James was difficult. Unfortunately this only served to increase the difficulties and as there was no opportunity to give affection again after the tantrums the withdrawal had no beneficial effect. At this stage the parents became increasingly concerned and began to worry that there might be some organic illness which was causing this deterioration and I was asked to see him for the first time. At interview James stayed close to his parents and kept looking at them. He was the picture of misery and seemed very anxious in case they were going to leave him. His lack of speech meant that he could not express what he was feeling but the story and the picture he presented seemed characteristic of the acute distress reactions associated with an unpleasant separation experience. His social difficulties and language incapacity had made it more difficult for him to cope with the new demands of a holiday home (which was a good one where children were usually happy). James's parents had quite misinterpreted the meaning of his behaviour, and their response of withdrawal was such as to aggravate the situation. There was no sign of organic deterioration. The significance of what happened was discussed with the parents who were advised to give James extra attention and affection. Within a week James was again his old self, apart from being rather more clinging than before.

Long-term disorders following separation experiences

The acute distress reactions following an unpleasant separation experience usually last some weeks or a few months. The next issue is how often acute separations lead on to more prolonged psychiatric disorders. Studies have usually shown that children who have been *repeatedly* admitted to hospital during early childhood have an increased risk of later emotional or behavioural disorders. However, the risk associated with a *single* hospital admission is quite small, even when the admission has been a very prolonged one. Bowlby and his colleagues[17] studied children who had been in a TB sanatorium for several months below the age of four years. When followed up some years later these children showed only slightly more behavioural disturbances than a control group of children who had not been in hospital.

Whether the increased risk of multiple hospital admissions is due to the cumulative effect of these repeated experiences or whether children who go into hospital many times come from more disturbed families or are different in other ways is not known. However, there are studies showing how the psychological implications differ according to the nature of the child's separation experience. For example, Douglas found that the risk for later bed-wetting was trivial if the child was separated from his mother but looked after by someone he knew in a familiar environment. The risk was slightly greater if either the care-taker or the environment was unfamiliar, but it was when *both* were strange to the child that the risk went up markedly.[96] Rutter[152] showed that when the child was separated from both his parents because of family discord or parental disorder the risk of later antisocial problems was much increased. In contrast, children separated for the same period of time (one month or more) because of hospital admission or a prolonged, usually convalescent, holiday showed *no* increased risk of psychiatric disorder. Again it appeared that it was not separation as such which did the damage but rather the unpleasant circumstances which surrounded some separations. It is this which explains the high psychiatric risk for children who have been admitted 'into care' (i.e. placed in a children's home or with a foster family) for short periods. Studies by several workers have shown that children placed in short-term care tend both to come from and return to disturbed families. It is the long-term family disturbance which causes most of the psychological harm rather than the brief separation itself.

Other acute stresses

In adults it has been shown that acute stresses, other than those involving separation, may serve to bring about psychiatric disorders and especially depression. The matter has been very little investigated in children, but from the limited evidence available it seems that stresses may have a similar effect in childhood. Douglas[96] found that a high number of stress events in the first four years were associated with an increased likelihood of later bed-wetting. Some of the events which were included involved separations, but others such as the birth of a younger sib and a move of home did not. The latter group were not looked at separately. Heisel *et al.*[73] also found that a high number of stresses were more common in children with psychiatric disorders and with certain physical disorders than in children in general. Unfortunately he too made no differentiation according to the type of event.

The birth of a younger brother or sister is one of the commonest stresses experienced by children and it is fairly usual for there to be a period of mild difficulties. This may show itself as jealousy of the new baby, as temporary regression (in which the child reverts back to the bottle or recommences bed-wetting) or as aggression to the mother. These reactions are much commoner when the child is below the age of three years when the sib is born and are distinctly uncommon if the child is over six years at the time of the sib's birth. It seems reasonable to suppose that adverse reactions should be less if the child can be involved in the care of the new baby and if steps are taken (perhaps by father's greater involvement in family activities) to ensure that the new arrival does not mean any reduction in parental attention and time spent with the older child. However, systematic information on these points is lacking.

Bereavement

Rutter[150] showed that there was a connection between bereavement and psychiatric disorder in children. Although only a small minority of children attending psychiatric clinics have lost a parent by death, the proportion is significantly greater than that in the general population. While the association with child psychiatric disorder is not as strong as when the child has lost a parent by divorce or separation (see page 165), there is a significant, if small, increase in the risk of psychiatric disturbance. This risk appears to be greatest when the parent dies during the child's third or fourth year of life, and there is some suggestion that the risk is increased if the death involves the parent of the same sex as the child. This may be because the same-sexed parent has a special importance in the processes of identification or because he is needed as a model for appropriate sex-role behaviour in later childhood and adolescence. In this connection it is relevant that most of the disorders in Rutter's study did not arise until well after the parent's death.

In young children personal grief is generally not as marked and not as prolonged as it is in adults. To a considerable extent the mechanisms by which bereavement is associated with later psychiatric disorder involve factors other than the child's grief. These include the effects of the parental illness which preceded death, the grief of the surviving parent, the family disruption following the death (such as the child going into care or to stay with relatives), the social and economic difficulties consequent upon the loss of the family wage-earner and the problems which may develop later in connection with parental remarriage.

However, particularly in older children there may be a grief reaction of a kind similar to that seen in adults, and in such cases the bereavement need not necessarily involve loss of a parent. This is illustrated by Nathan.

Nathan was a young adolescent who was referred by his family doctor to determine if his severe head injury over a year ago had led to his present unhappiness, poor school performance and preoccupation with violence. He had been involved in a bad road accident in which his closest friend was killed. Nathan had a fractured skull with some damage to the brain, was expected to die at first and was in an intensive care unit for a while. However, he made a good recovery and returned home after a month, going back to school four months later. Previously he had been a cheerful popular boy near the top of his class, but now he was morose, quiet and withdrawn, complained of headaches, and showed irritable behaviour with tantrums. At night he sat outside his bedroom or walked around, and at times he talked of suicide. He was sensitive to criticism and became preoccupied with violence as shown in drawings and pictures. At school he mainly went around with a boy who was something of a trouble-maker and he lost interest in schoolwork. He kept thinking of his dead friend and said that his friend talked to him at night. The family was harmonious and his parents were obviously fond of Nathan, but they very rarely talked about the accident. By the time he came to the clinic Nathan was already improving, but the same problems persisted in lesser degree. There was no abnormality on neurological examination and psychological testing showed him to have good concentration and memory and to be of above average intelligence.

Nathan had suffered some mild brain damage but this had not left any serious after-effects. It probably made him more vulnerable to emotional disturbance, but it had not caused it directly. The form of depression, the preoccupation with the dead friend and the occasional feelings that he could hear him talking are all very typical of grief reactions. His family had not recognized the importance of the bereavement, and avoiding talk about the accident probably made it more difficult for Nathan to cope with his grief. The trouble-making friend he took up with at school (and whose friendship played a part in the fall-off in Nathan's schoolwork) was a third member of the trio made up of Nathan and the boy who died. Nathan naturally turned to him in despair, although before the accident they had not been very close. The opportunity to discuss what had happened helped Nathan to recover from his bereavement and some coaching enabled him to regain his confidence and catch up again with his schoolwork.

Working mothers

Although it has sometimes been claimed that the children of working mothers are particularly likely to become delinquent or develop some psychiatric disorder, there is abundant evidence that this is not so.[152, 205] Indeed in some circumstances children with working mothers may even be better off, as this may mean that the mothers have an increased range of interests, are more content and so have more to give to the family. There are no ill-effects from a child having several mother-figures, provided that stable relationships and good care are provided by each. This is an important proviso, but one which applies equally to mothers who are not working. It should be noted that a situation in which the mother-figures keep changing so that the child does not have an opportunity of forming a persisting relationship with any of them is not satisfactory.

Broken homes and family discord

There is an extensive literature linking 'broken homes' with delinquency, and it is certainly true that children from a broken home have an increased risk of antisocial problems.[156] Interestingly, this association does not seem to apply to neurosis and emotional disorders, at least not in older children. However, if this association is to be used to help children with antisocial disorders, we must know what it means. Why is there this association and what psychological mechanism mediates the effect? Is it the break-up as such or is it the circumstances leading to or following the break which do the harm?

The clue lies in the observation, made in three separate investigations, that the risk of delinquency is much increased if the parents divorce or separate, but that the risk is only slightly raised if a parent dies.[152] This suggests that it may be the family discord and disharmony, rather than the break-up of the family as such, which leads to antisocial behaviour. To test that hypothesis it was necessary to show directly that parental discord is associated with antisocial disorder in the children even when the home is unbroken. There is good evidence from several studies that this is indeed the case. In fact it appears that delinquency may actually be commoner in unhappy unbroken homes than it is in harmonious but broken ones. In short, it may be concluded that it is the ongoing disturbance in family relationships which does the damage rather than the family break-up.

In order to obtain a proper understanding of the mechanisms involved, however, it is necessary to go into the matter more thoroughly. The first question is: what sort of family discord leads to delinquency and antisocial problems? Emphasis was initially placed on the child who was rejected by his parents. Rejection may be shown by a tendency to talk of the child in derogatory ways, to blame him for things and to extend criticism of his misdeeds to all kinds of trivia, so that he becomes a sort of family scapegoat. There may be actual physical neglect or brutality, but also there may be compensatory over-protection and solicitude. Often rejection takes place against a background of tension, quarrelling and discord, but it can also occur in stable families in which the parents have a harmonious relationship. The feelings of rejection are often mixed with those of love and affection and it is important to try to understand how the negative feelings arose.

Elizabeth was referred at three because of sleep disturbance, breath-holding attacks, screaming, tantrums and demanding behaviour. The attacks had begun at age six months and the excessive crying, irritability and tempers developed at about one year. Elizabeth was unusually attached to her father and was much more affectionate with him than with her mother. Father blamed mother for Elizabeth's dependency on him and there was a good deal of friction between the parents on how to handle Elizabeth. Father was frequently away from home and mother resented this. The paternal grandmother had opposed her son's marriage and she remained hostile to mother and critical of her handling of Elizabeth. Mother had never felt close to Elizabeth and said quite frankly that there were times when she hated her. The first year of her marriage was very stressful and she became very depressed. This continued into the pregnancy, she lacked confidence on how she would deal with the baby when it arrived and looked to her own mother for help with this. Maternal grandmother died suddenly during the pregnancy, mother felt drained of emotion and was unable to grieve. After Elizabeth was born, mother turned to the paternal grandmother for help. She agreed to come and assist mother but then did not, going off to look after a young nephew. Mother was very distressed and the first year of Elizabeth's life was a very difficult one. A second child was born two years later. By then mother was less depressed, the baby was easy and responsive and a good mother–child relationship developed. The second child was affectionate and attached to mother and mother found her rewarding.

Elizabeth's mother did not openly reject her but she expressed a lot of negative feelings and, if the situation did not improve, it was likely that frank rejection and scape-goating would develop. The mother was an anxious, insecure person but also warm and responsive. The negative response to Elizabeth could clearly be linked with mother's depression at the time of her birth and the double blow of her own mother's death and rejection by her mother-in-law. Elizabeth was her first child and she did not know how to cope, father was often away and the mother-in-law constantly interfered. Elizabeth became a family focus of discontent and mother got little pleasure from the situation. Things were much easier with respect to the birth of the next child, mother was more experienced in looking after babies and the infant had a warm, responsive temperament. In these better circumstances a quite different mother–child relationship developed.

Social casework constituted the mainstay of treatment. As is usually the case, this involved a variety of techniques, explanation, interpretations, ventilation of feelings, specific advice, modelling and the use of a relationship as a means of learning. First, the caseworker discussed with mother our diagnostic formulation (as above). Previously, mother had thought of Elizabeth's breath-holding attacks in terms of some physical illness. It was explained that we thought Elizabeth's problems were emotional in origin and that in large part they arose as a result of difficulties in her relationship with mother. The caseworker emphasized mother's good relationship with her second child and said that the difficulties with Elizabeth were explicable in terms of special problems associated with Elizabeth's birth. In order to help mother cope with, and overcome, the hostile feelings which she found so upsetting, it was necessary for mother to gain some insight into how the problems arose. This was done by encouraging mother to talk about her own earlier life as well as Elizabeth's upbringing. Mother spoke of her unhappy childhood, her expectation that having a child would somehow right it and her disappointment when this did not happen. She talked of how Elizabeth's birth was unhappily associated in her mind with her own mother's death, her inability to mourn at the time, her rejection by her mother-in-law and her depression after Elizabeth was born. The therapist aided the development of insight by linking these feelings and events with current problems by means of interpretations and suggestions. In doing this, mother was also helped to see that her easy, positive relationship with her second child showed that she had the necessary mothering 'instincts' and that the difficulties with Elizabeth were reversible.

Mother was angry with her mother-in-law's interference and with father's inconsistency and lack of support, but at home she had only been able to respond by unhappy withdrawal or by quarrelling. The caseworker encouraged mother to ventilate these feelings during the treatment sessions. In this way mother was helped to come to terms with the situation and to decide what she could change and what she would have to accept. In addition she learned that it was possible to express anger without losing control.

These gains in understanding would have been of only limited benefit if mother had not also been helped to deal with the specific day-to-day problems that arose. This involved three elements – the avoidance of situations which upset Elizabeth, the solution of immediate behavioural problems and the development of a more positive parent–child interaction. The first, for example, involved the need for mother to avoid fighting with her mother-in-law over Elizabeth in Elizabeth's presence. Mother and father were given direct advice to avoid conflict in front of the child and to discuss the difficulties with mother-in-law away from Elizabeth. Father's cooperation was sought and, in the context of understanding Elizabeth's needs, he was advised to be more consistent in his approach, so that the child could count on him and not have to make unlimited demands (previously father had swung between overinvolvement with and neglect of Elizabeth). There was a specific discussion of how the parents might handle Elizabeth's sleeping difficulties. They were advised how, when Elizabeth came to their bed in the night, they should return her to her own bed and settle her there. Medicines were used as an interim measure in order to help Elizabeth get into a regular sleeping routine.

As well as seeing mother on her own or with father, the caseworker had some sessions with mother and Elizabeth together, in order to focus on how they responded to each other. Mother tended to be insecure, uncertain and vacillating with Elizabeth and the model provided by the therapist's play with Elizabeth was useful to mother in helping her to learn better ways of responding. The caseworker showed through her own interactions with the child that it was possible to be sympathetic and understanding but at the same time firm and realistic. Through her relationship with the caseworker, mother also gained confidence in her parenting skills. By identifying with someone who responded differently from her own mother and mother-in-law, both of whom provided such unsatisfactory relationships, mother gained experience in personal interaction which she was able to generalize to her relationships at home. These experiences were linked with particular suggestions as to how mother might find enjoyable ways of playing and doing things with Elizabeth. As mother learned to be more affectionate, Elizabeth relaxed and became more responsive and rewarding for mother to be with.

As a result of these endeavours, mother's relationship with Elizabeth improved greatly, she began to enjoy being with her daughter in spite of the feelings of resentment and anger which recurred from time to time, and both the tantrums and sleeping difficulties diminished. However, there were difficulties in gaining father's full cooperation and problems with grandmother's continuing interference remained. The future depends very much on how far it will prove possible to improve the marital situation.

In the case of Elizabeth the main problem was the mother's negative feelings towards her child, although this had arisen against a background of marital discord. In other cases the parent–child relationship may be quite good in spite of quarrels and hostility between the parents, and it is the marital discord which constitutes the major issue. Does this also put the child at psychiatric risk? Studies show that it does. The worst situation for the child is when there is both marital discord and rejection of the child, but either are likely to be associated with behavioural disturbances in the children. In families where there is gross marital disharmony it may be very difficult, and often impossible, to help the parents return to a happy, peaceful relationship. Accordingly it is necessary in a bad marital situation to determine which factors help protect the child.

There have been only a few investigations which have tried to disentangle the threads in these circumstances, but the available evidence provides a number of important leads.[152] First, children may be harmed by either open hostility in the home or by a lack of warmth and positive affection. However, it seems that on the whole it is overt quarrelling and discord which are the more serious. Therefore there is something to be gained by the parents trying to avoid their differences leading to arguments, fights and an atmosphere in the home, even if their relationship remains cool and strained. Second, the effect on the child is worse if he becomes embroiled in the parental disputes. If the marriage becomes very difficult or if the parents separate or divorce, it is very important to help both parents realize that, whatever their differences, they remain father and mother to the child. Disputes over custody and access are likely to harm the child, and denigration of the parent will do the same. It is sometimes hard for parents to realize that the child will probably go on loving *both* of them even though the marriage has broken down irretrievably.

Third, the child is more likely to be damaged if the discord is prolonged over many years. Whereas this is almost self-evident, it means that the sooner marital disputes can be resolved the better it will be for the child. Fourth, the ill-effects are not necessarily irreversible. Rutter and his colleagues[152] found that, if there was a change for the better in the family relationship, the outlook for the child's psychological development correspondingly improved. However, it remains uncertain how readily, how completely and how often the adverse effects of disturbed relationships in early childhood may be reversed. Fifth, the child is at a specially high risk if in addition to the marital discord one or both parents have a personality disorder of such severity as to cause a chronic handicap. This means, in effect, that where the parents have shown disordered behaviour or relationships throughout their adult life, as well as not making a successful marriage, the outlook for the child is particularly poor. In these circumstances careful thought needs to be given to the question of whether the child might not be better being placed away from his family. Finally, as already noted, a good relationship with one parent can make up to a considerable extent for a bad relationship with the other or for gross marital discord. Whether or not this also means that a *good* relationship with someone outside the home (another relative, a teacher, or a friend) may also exert some protective effect is uncertain, but it certainly seems worthwhile striving to make sure that the child has at least one sound, lasting relationship he can rely on.

Clearly it would be helpful if we understood just how family discord leads to disorder in the children. Unfortunately we do not. However, there are three main mechanisms which are probably the most important. First, children need to have stable, warm, intimate family relationships upon which to build their own social behaviour and relationships outside the home. Discord and quarrelling interfere with the development of such family relationships, and in so far as they do the child is likely to be harmed. The evidence in support of this hypothesized mechanism concerns the findings, already discussed, suggesting the protective effect of good relationships in a hostile environment. Second, quarrelling parents provide a deviant model of interpersonal behaviour and in so far as the child follows this model his own behaviour may become disturbed. This hypothesis is discussed further when considering mentally ill and criminal parents. The findings are inconclusive, but it seems that deviant modelling exerts some influence. Third, it might be supposed that where there is severe marital discord the child is likely to find it more difficult to learn how he is expected to behave. That is, that parents who are engaged in marital disputes are more likely than other parents to provide inconsistent discipline and child-rearing. Again there is some evidence in support of this view, but the critical comparisons which could determine the relative importance of each of these mechanisms have yet to be undertaken. Finally, when parents are in dispute, the child may have conflicting loyalties which give rise to strain and anxiety.

One-parent families

Children who are brought up in homes with one parent are more likely than are other children to have behavioural problems or to be delinquent. However, it is much less certain how far the children's problems stem from the lack of a father (or mother) and how far from the many adverse factors that happen to be associated with the situation of having only one parent. These adverse factors concern both the circumstances which lead to there being only one parent and also the circumstances which follow such a situation. Thus the three main reasons for a child being reared in a one-parent home are illegitimacy, parental divorce or separation and parental death. The National Child Development study[41] showed that illegitimate children, at age seven years, were twice as likely to be maladjusted, compared with legitimate children. They were also considerably more likely than the legitimate to have problems with reading. But, interestingly, the illegitimate children living with two parents were, if anything, *more* likely than those with one parent to show problems. It seems clear that, while illegitimacy put the child at risk, the additional factor of being reared in a one-parent family made little difference. With homes

broken by divorce or separation it is the discord and disharmony preceding the break which constitute the main stress
factor. It remains uncertain how far parental remarriage helps
or hinders the child's psychological development. Much the
same applies to parental death.

The circumstances following the loss of one parent are also
very important. It has been found that single-parent households
have a lower income than do two-parent homes.[81] Furthermore
single parents tend to be less well educated and their homes are
more likely to be overcrowded and to lack basic household
amenities. This social privation may well be at least as important for the child's development as the lack of a parent.

Of course there are specific issues associated with having only
one parent. First, there is the effect on the remaining parent who
will lack the emotional, social and material support usually provided by the spouse. When things go wrong, the single parent
will have to look outside the immediate family for advice and
help. Society too puts special pressures and stresses on the unmarried mother and on the separated parent. Second, the child
is himself subject to the social discriminations associated with
the lack of a parent. Third, the child lacks the opportunity of
seeing how two adults live together in a close and harmonious
relationship – a lack which may make marital relationships
more difficult for him later. Fourth, if the same-sexed parent
is missing from the home, the child will lack an important
model of sex-appropriate behaviour and the opportunity
parents provide for same-sexed identification.

For all these reasons it has usually been supposed that boys
brought up in a home without a father will tend to be more
effeminate and will lack masculine identity. The converse has
been thought to apply to girls reared without a mother. In fact,
although the evidence is shaky and unsatisfactory, it seems that
this does not usually occur.[75] Most boys reared only by mothers
are as masculine as any other boys. Of course that does not
mean that fathers are unimportant. To the contrary, there is
good evidence that they have a substantial influence on their
children's development. Obviously, too, there are many advantages to being brought up by two parents. However, the findings

do suggest that the parents are not the only available source of masculine or feminine identity and that the absence of a father from the home does not necessarily impair a boy's masculine identity.

In summary, although there are ill-effects stemming from being brought up in a one-parent family, the effects are probably less uniform and less severe than is widely assumed. In general the number of parents in the home is probably less crucial to the child's development than the relationships and behaviour provided by whoever is present. Furthermore family life is determined not only by the particular characteristics of the individual family members but also by the social circumstances and environment within which the family live.

Lack of bonding

At the beginning of this chapter we noted the importance of the child developing emotional bonds. We need now to consider the circumstances in which there may be a failure of bonding and the consequence when this occurs. In spite of a strong psychiatric interest in this question over many years there is little good evidence on the subject. However, the findings seem to suggest that bond formation is least likely to occur in a non-stimulating environment, where there is only low intensity of personal interactions, where care is provided at routine times rather than in response to the infant's demands and where there are multiple care-takers, none of whom have regular interaction with the child over a period of many months or longer.[156] This can occur in an ordinary family setting but it is probably most likely to occur in an old-style institution or in circumstances where the child has gone from pillar to post in early childhood with multiple separations and periods of substitute care without continuity. The very limited findings available suggest that these circumstances may lead in early and middle childhood to disinhibited, attention-seeking behaviour with indiscriminate friendliness, so that strangers and parents are treated alike in a non-discriminatory fashion. Later on this may lead to a personality characterized by lack of guilt, an inability to keep rules and a failure to form lasting relationships.

This train of events certainly occurs and the damaged personality that is left is one of the most seriously handicapping of psychiatric disorders. However, many questions remain. How early must the child have the opportunity to develop bonds if these later consequences are not to develop?

The normal child first develops bonds between seven and eighteen months. However, bond formation can first take place up to three years of age. Probably it can occur after that too, but it becomes increasingly more difficult for bonds to be developed for the first time later in childhood. A related question is: how reversible is this chain of events? We do not know, but the answer *seems* to be that by the time the child has reached school age complete reversibility becomes increasingly difficult. Nevertheless reversibility will necessarily depend on both the severity of the early damage and on the quality of the environment later. Another question is: given a seriously depriving environment will there always be a lack of bonding? The answer to that is, no. Children are surprisingly resilient creatures and there are always some children who emerge unscathed from even the worst forms of upbringing. The result will always depend on factors in the child as much as in the environment. Finally, are affectionless personalities always due to lack of bonding in infancy? Again the answer is, no. This type of personality disorder certainly arises in other ways as well, although we do not adequately understand its genesis.

The issues that have to be faced in psychiatric practice with respect to a lack of bonding are best illustrated by two cases:

Carol was a girl of twenty-six months referred because her prospective adoptive parents expressed concern that, although she had been with them five months, she was still cold and unresponsive. Carol's biological mother was a single woman who had herself been brought up in an institution. For the first fifteen months Carol was looked after by dozens of strangers while mother went from one living-in job to another. Mother then became pregnant and Carol was placed in care for five weeks, during which time she was very unsettled. She returned to her mother for nine weeks, but then mother disappeared after a party and Carol was placed with another set of foster parents where she remained for three months until going to her present parents at age twenty-one months.

She did not seem upset at leaving her foster parents and she quickly settled in her new home. However, she did not discriminate between people, and would go off with any adult. Carol was solemn, unsmiling, uncuddly and miserable when first placed with her prospective adoptive parents, but she gradually became more cheerful and lively and was increasingly responsive. During the month before she came to the clinic she had become a more friendly affectionate child who differentiated between her new parents and other adults, who cuddled and ran to mother and showed pleasurable excitement when father returned home in the evening. At the clinic she was a little tearful and, although she played imaginatively with the doctor, she was guarded and solemn. Psychological testing showed her to be of above average intelligence.

Carol's start in life could hardly have been more unfortunate and there was little doubt that the combination of indifferent parenting from her biological mother and . an inordinate number of mother-substitutes had prevented her from developing the usual bonds and attachments. The adoptive mother had expected a warm and affectionate response when she came from this disturbed background to a happy and cosy household. However, this was too much to hope for all at once and inevitably she was disappointed. Nevertheless the child's progress, especially in the last month, clearly demonstrated that bonds were now forming and that, provided she remained in a stable, warm family environment, there was no serious cause for concern. The reasons for these developments were discussed fully with the parents, who were reassured that all was well. A follow-up report later indicated that Carol was continuing to make good progress and hopefully should have no important consequences of her unhappy early experiences. Carol's development illustrates both the ill-effects of lack of bonding and also the potential for recovery given an early enough change to a good environment. Her good intelligence also reflects the fact that an environment which constitutes emotional privation is not necessarily lacking in what is needed for intellectual growth.

Peter was referred at the age of nine years with a long history of severely disturbed behaviour and the query as to whether he should be placed away from home. At age four years he tore up the bed-clothes when in hospital for a minor operation, but otherwise there was no problem with his behaviour in the preschool years. However, difficulties began soon after he started school. He was over-active, impulsive, disobedient, and generally disruptive in the classroom, although he was cheerful and friendly. He made friends, although he tended to fight with them and in spite of his dis-obedience he seemed attached to his parents. This behaviour varied markedly with the situation, and with some people he was very responsive and well behaved. He was first seen at another clinic at the age of seven years because of severely destructive behaviour at home. Peter had wet the bed since his hernia operation, he ate paper and recently he had been in trouble with the police for stealing. This started shortly after mother became pregnant for the sixth time. At a year old he spent three months in hospital with a severe burn, during which time he was visited only infrequently. At age four years he spent three weeks in a foster home while a brother was born. He had twice changed schools because of his disturbed be-haviour. Father was a rather anxious man who had had a very unhappy childhood, and who never got on with his very harsh and unkind stepfather. As a result he could not bear to discipline his own children in case they suffered from cruelty as he had. Mother had chronic ill-health and came from a poor home. The maternal grandfather was very strict, but mother's childhood was basically happy. Family discipline was chaotic and the parents frequently argued over how to deal with Peter. Father was very indulgent and mother oscillated between very firm discipline, restricting Peter to the house, and leaving him alone. Both parents were warm-hearted and fond of their children. Two of Peter's brothers had also stolen and another brother wet the bed. The housing conditions were very poor and there had been several moves of home. At interview Peter was a chirpy, rather scruffy little boy, somewhat disinhibited but not overactive. His intelligence was below average and he was quite backward in his reading.

Peter had had three separations in early childhood which might have given rise to difficulties in bonding. The separations had clearly been stressful and his bed-wetting started during one of them. He was a rather overfriendly, even if disobedient, child who had some difficulties in personal relationships. Never-theless he seemed to have formed bonds and was attached to his parents. A lack of bonding did not appear to be the main trouble. Rather, the problems stemmed from the stresses of a combination of unpleasant experiences in the past and totally disorganized discipline from his parents. In the circumstances it was inappropriate to remove him from home. Rather, an attempt was made to help the parents work out better ways of coping with Peter's disruptive behaviour and a psychologist visited the school to advise on how to deal with the behavioural difficulties he showed there.

It is often very difficult to sort out exactly what mechanisms have been operative in the link between a 'bad' family background and disturbed behaviour. However, the research evidence shows that there are a number of quite different psychological mechanisms which may be operative. These have different effects and require different solutions. One of the psychiatric tasks is to assemble the clinical evidence with each child referred, to derive hypotheses about possible mechanisms and, so far as possible, to test these hypotheses in terms of response to treatment.

Parental deviance
Parental neurosis and personality disorder

Several studies have shown that parents with a chronic depressive or neurotic condition or with a personality disorder are more likely than other parents to have children with emotional or behavioural problems.[150] In general, neurotic parents tend to have children with emotional disorders and parents with personality disorders to have youngsters with conduct disturbances involving antisocial or aggressive behaviour. Again the question has to be asked: what mechanisms mediate the association? Several processes seem to be at work. It should be emphasized that in many families with neurotic parents the children are perfectly normal so that any explanation must account for the observation that only some children are affected.

First, genetic factors may sometimes play a part. It is known that there is an important hereditary element in both neuroses and personality disorders, so that the parents may pass on a biologically increased vulnerability. On the other hand most children with emotional disorders do not become neurotic adults and it is rather uncertain how far the childhood and adult disorders are genetically similar. So far as antisocial disorders in childhood are concerned, the genetic component is fairly small and it seems unlikely that heredity constitutes the main link with adult personality disorder, although doubtless it is important in some cases.

Second, there are the direct effects of the parental mental disorder on family life. Parents who are depressed are frequently very irritable and often this impinges greatly on the children. Alternatively some forms of depression make parents withdrawn and unresponsive. Parental anxiety and fears may lead to the children being restricted in their activities because the parents are worried about what might happen to them. Parents with a severe obsessional illness sometimes want to involve other family members in their rituals and this can be very distressing for the children. Delusions and hallucinations, associated with more severe mental illness in parents, may lead to bizarre and disruptive behaviour. Also, when parents are suffering severely from some neurotic or other type of mental disorder, they may become so handicapped that household tasks and child care are neglected.

Third, there are possible influences through imitation and identification. A parent with particular fears and phobias very readily transmits these fears to the children. When the father or mother responds to stress through hypochondriacal complaints, the children may learn to do likewise. It has been shown that, when a husband is neurotic, over the course of several years the wife tends also to become neurotic. A similar process may operate with the children.

Fourth, when parents have a mental disorder, there is an increased likelihood of marital disharmony, family discord and break-up of the marriage. These family disturbances are known to be associated with the development of psychiatric disorder in children. It may often be that the mental disorder in the parents is followed by psychiatric problems in the children only because parental illness tends to be associated with family disharmony.

On the whole it appears that the mechanisms which lead to disorder in the children of mentally ill parents are not very different from those operating in the children of parents without mental illness. The form of treatment that is needed will depend on individual circumstances and the ways in which family life is disturbed. Several examples have already been given of children whose parents had a psychiatric disorder. Caroline is an example of a child where the link with the parental disorder was more direct.

Caroline was referred by the psychiatrist treating her mother. She was a five-year-old girl who had been frightened and anxious for the last two years since her mother became ill. Caroline had become dry, but then started wetting her bed again at three. She was very faddy over food at home, mainly living off potatoes and biscuits, but ate much better away from home. She cried and screamed in her sleep and mother often had to comfort her. There were many fears: of old people, of TV programmes, of the clock, of insects and of noises. Most of these were much more marked at home. She was often tearful and became upset if her mother left her. The family lived in very poor and overcrowded circumstances and the parents attributed all the troubles to the housing difficulties. There was an adult brother and sister, both of whom were very fond of Caroline. The large age gap between them and Caroline was determined by the housing difficulties, as the parents only later decided to have another child before mother was too old. Mother became increasingly depressed while Caroline was a toddler, and developed a variety of phobias, including a marked fear of cats. She was exasperated by the difficulties with Caroline and got irritable with her, but was also overprotective and solicitous. Caroline was not directly involved in any of her mother's phobias, but mother's fearfulness was very evident in her dealing with the child. Although Caroline shared some of mother's fears she also enjoyed baiting mother about those she did not share.

Mother's depressive/phobic disorder had probably led to Caroline's fearfulness both through the child learning mother's fears directly and through the effect of mother's symptoms on the way she dealt with the child. She tended to fuss over Caroline and restrict her, with the result that the girl had not learned to cope with things on her own, mother's anxiety was contagious when Caroline was upset and her swinging from anxious solicitude to irritated exasperation only served to increase

Caroline's fears. Conversely the mother's worries over Caroline and Caroline's provocative behaviour tended to aggravate the mother's problems. The fact that mother was now in her forties and had not had to look after an infant for well over a dozen years also probably made it more difficult for her to cope. Mother had been on antidepressant drugs for the last year with some benefit, but she remained quite handicapped. When the link between the disorders in mother and child was realized, Caroline was referred. Mother was seen regularly by a psychiatric social worker and the mother–child interaction was discussed. Mother was helped to find ways of coping with Caroline's fears and she was encouraged to let the child become more independent. She continued to take the antidepressants for some time but over the course of the next year she gradually improved. Caroline stopped being fearful and settled well at school, which also helped her to be less dependent on her mother.

Parental criminality

Investigations of delinquents have consistently shown a high rate of deviant or criminal behaviour in the parents, especially in the fathers.[194] Studies in this country have shown that the same association applies to aggressive and antisocial disorders in youngsters who have not come before the Courts. The main explanation probably lies in the fact that criminal parents have a much increased rate of family discord and disruption, and it is the unhappy marital relationships and interparental conflict which lead to disorder in the children. As we have already discussed, homes where the parents are frequently quarrelling and fighting or are cold, hostile and isolated from one another provide a setting which is very conducive to the development of conduct disorders, particularly in boys.

However, there are also other mechanisms. Psychologists have shown how, in an experimental situation, imitation of an aggressive model is an important factor in the development of aggressive behaviour in children. The same probably applies in real life outside the research laboratory. Children may learn to act in a socially deviant manner by copying their parents. Also, in some criminal families, the children may learn from their parents social attitudes in which stealing or other delinquent activities are regarded as acceptable behaviour, provided they occur outside the home. In addition some criminal parents have markedly inconsistent and arbitrary methods of discipline, another factor shown to be conducive to conduct disorders in children.

Lack of stimulation

Meaningful stimulation and an adequate range of experiences have been found to be essential ingredients for optimal intellectual development and the normal growth of language. This means an adequate provision of toys and play-activities, but most of all it means that the parents should talk and do things with the child in a way which is understandable and enjoyable for him. In the past, poor quality institutions have provided the environment where lack of stimulation has been most evident. However, as Barbara Tizard's recent studies[189] have shown, residential nurseries for children can be stimulating places which give the kind of experiences needed for normal intellectual development. Furthermore other investigations have demonstrated that there can be a serious lack of stimulation in ordinary families. It should not be assumed that this only occurs when there is a lack of feeling for the children. On the contrary, to a considerable extent social and cultural norms determine what parents do with their children. For example, it has been found that, on average, West Indian parents play less and talk less with their children than do native English parents, in spite of normal warmth and affection for them.

In addition there are personal reasons why parents may give less than the optimal play and conversation needed for their child's development. For example, parents who are seriously depressed frequently interact less with their children. Also to some people parenting skills do not come naturally and they may inadvertently be neglectful. Josephine was a child where this seemed to have happened.

Josephine was referred at the age of three and a half because her

speech development was delayed. She had a few single words only
at two years and then a few months later stopped using even those.
At age three years speech began to develop and during the next six
months her vocabulary increased, so that by the time she came to
the clinic she was beginning to use phrases and short sentences.
Otherwise her development had been normal except that she had
become rather demanding after her sister was born a few months
before referral. She was a happy child and quite affectionate (although she had been less so when younger). Her play and games
were quite appropriate for her age, but she had not learned to share
toys with other children. Father had married late and was an
affectionate but undemonstrative man. Mother was younger and
came from a rather rigid, unhappy home in Scotland where the
maternal grandmother was said never to show affection. Mother was
a capable woman who had supported her husband financially for
the first few years of the marriage. She did not enjoy romping on the
floor with her child, as she felt self-conscious doing this. She had
periods of depression, and when depressed found it more difficult to
relate to people. She returned to work soon after Josephine was
born, but was able to work at home. Apart from when she was fed
and bathed, Josephine was left in a room on her own and was not
played with or talked with by mother. However, there was an ample
provision of toys. Mother would not let father discipline Josephine
in case he did it the wrong way. Nevertheless he played with her
with enjoyment when he returned home from work each evening.
Mother was very dedicated to the child in spite of the lack of interaction. Shortly before Josephine was three, mother became increasingly concerned that she had neglected her. She gave up work and
spent a lot of time with Josephine, and also with her sister when she
was born.

Josephine's hearing was tested and found to be normal and there
were no abnormalities on medical examination. Psychological testing showed her to be of normal intelligence.

It seemed clear that the major factor in Josephine's speech
delay was the marked isolation and lack of conversation during
most of her first three years. Both parents were obviously fond
of her and showed their affection, she was physically well
looked after and there were plenty of toys and games in the
house. As a consequence the speech delay stood out in contrast
to her normal social and intellectual development. The reason
for mother's inadequate interaction with Josephine lay partly in

an intellectual failure to understand that play and conversation were important for babies, partly in mother's rather rigid and self-conscious personality and partly in her own bad experience of mothering which equipped her poorly for parenthood. By the time she came to the clinic, mother had recognized the child's need and there was now no shortage of mother–child interaction. Nevertheless she needed support to avoid this becoming too intense and stressful, and guidance was required on the ways she might do things with Josephine. The situation rapidly improved and mother got much more enjoyment from the child, although mothering never came easily to her. Two years later the child showed no abnormalities and was doing well at an ordinary school.

Family composition

Ordinal position

There is a slight but consistent tendency for the eldest child to have a greater likelihood of developing an emotional disorder.[162] The reasons for this are not fully understood, but two factors are probably the most important. First, the parents are anxious and inexperienced, so that their handling of the child is likely to be both less confident and less skilled. Second, the eldest child has the problem of adjusting to the arrival of brothers or sisters, a stress not experienced by the youngest child in the family. However, the eldest also has some advantages in that he tends to have a higher level of scholastic and work achievement than later-born children.

Family size

Children from a large family, that is, one with at least four or five children, are at a disadvantage in several ways. On average they have a lower verbal intelligence score and a poorer level of reading attainment and in addition they have an increased risk of delinquency or conduct disorder. These findings are not accountable for in terms of social class differences and the effect is evident by the early school years.[47, 48, 158]

In terms of the poorer verbal intelligence and reading, the explanation probably lies in the patterns of communication and verbal stimulation in large families. Although the matter has not been adequately explored, two factors seem important. First, in large families there tends to be more talking all at once, so that the linguistic environment for the young child may be rather confusing and lacking in meaning. Second, the parents will necessarily have less time to spend with each child. As a result verbal interchange will more often be with the other children, who possibly provide less adequate stimulation in that their vocabulary, speech and ideas are more limited.

With regard to the association between large family size and delinquency, part of the explanation is a follow-up from the reading failure, as children who are poor readers are more likely to develop conduct disorders (see chapter 8). However, it may also be that large families have less well organized discipline and more frequent discord and disharmony.

Inter-generational cycles

It will have been apparent in several of the case histories that the reasons for poor parenting often went back to the parents' own childhoods. Sometimes it was a matter of the parents lacking an experience of normal family life and so having no model of how to bring up their own children. This probably applied to Carol's biological mother (see page 175) who had been raised in a rather poor, old-style institution. Sometimes it was because one parent had had a rather cold relationship with his own parents and so had failed to develop easy and spontaneous, affectionate relationships. This was true of Josephine's mother (see page 182) who felt warmth and loved her child but found difficulty in expressing these feelings and didn't know how to talk to a young child. In other cases it was a question of parents reacting against unhappy experiences in their own childhood. Overprotection and overindulgence sometimes arise in this way when the parents have themselves experienced cruel discipline. This was so with Peter's father (see page 176).

There is limited research evidence to confirm the clinical impression that childhood experiences can influence parenting skills in later life. For example, Illsley and Thompson[83] showed that women whose parents had divorced or separated during their childhood were particularly likely to have illegitimate children or to conceive before marriage. Frommer and O'Shea[60] found that women who had experienced traumatic separations from their parents before the age of eleven years were more likely to leave their baby to feed himself from a propped-up bottle, to be irritable and unwell during the year after the baby was born, to have a second pregnancy very soon after the first and to have sex problems in their marriage. Other investigations have indicated that individuals who grow up in homes broken by divorce or separation are more likely themselves to show marital instability when adult.[70, 99] Several studies have shown that parents who batter their children have frequently come from unhappy homes themselves and have often experienced cruelty at the hands of their parents.[174] Sometimes child-battering recurs throughout several generations of the same family.[122] It might be thought that this merely reflects an inherited personality defect, but experimental studies with monkeys have shown that animals isolated and deprived of social contact during infancy later go on to become neglectful, incompetent and sometimes cruel parents.[156] Although, doubtless, genetic factors play a part in these inter-generational cycles of bad parenting, it seems highly likely that poor childhood experiences in themselves predispose individuals to become poor parents.

Unfortunately we know all too little about how these inter-generational effects arise and, if we are to prevent some of these cycles of misfortune being further perpetuated, there must be research to identify the various processes which are at work. In the meantime we have to help the parents of our child-patients today. Sometimes it is necessary to discuss with the parents how their own upbringing has affected their parenting. In other cases it is more useful to focus on the here and now, helping the parents to deal better with the immediate issues that face them. Either way, however, it is helpful for the clinician to understand the inter-generational processes, and it is for this reason that, when children come to the psychiatric clinic, their parents will usually be asked about their own childhood and early home life.

5 Communities, Schools and Peer Groups

In the last chapter I discussed how family variables and inter-actions within the home can contribute to the development of psychiatric disorders in children. In this chapter a broader per-spective will be taken in looking at influences in the community, the school and the peer group. Families are but one part of a wider social network and are subject to forces stemming from the neighbourhood in which they live and the people with whom they mix. These influences need to be assessed if there is to be a proper understanding of why families behave in the way that they do. Also, from the moment they enter the educational system, children are increasingly open to a host of pressures, inducements, compensations and stresses arising from factors outside the house, but especially from the school and from their group of friends.

Area differences

It is well known that within big cities there are areas with un-usually high delinquency rates. In this country this was first shown by Sir Cyril Burt half a century ago, and numerous investigators have found the same phenomenon in the United States and elsewhere. Interestingly these high-delinquency areas remain remarkably stable over time, as Wallis and Maliphant showed when they repeated Burt's London survey forty years later.[191] More recently Gath and his colleagues[62] found that area differences in the rate of referral to child-guidance clinics followed much the same pattern as those for juvenile de-linquency. On the whole the areas with high delinquency rates are 'slummy' parts of cities – poor, overcrowded areas of low social status; but high-delinquency areas have also been found in new housing estates. In general, too, delinquency is more frequent in large cities than in industrial towns, and commoner in both of these than in non-industrial towns or country areas. Backwardness in reading has also been associated with low-social-class areas.

The facts regarding the existence of these area differences in delinquency and psychiatric disorder are well recognized, but the reasons for the differences remain poorly understood. It was in an attempt to elucidate these that Rutter, Yule and Berger and their colleagues recently made a comparative study of psychiatric and educational disorders among ten-year-old children living on the Isle of Wight and in one of London's inner boroughs.[158] As expected, they found that both sorts of problems were twice as common in the metropolis as on the Island – an area of countryside and small towns. By a more detailed study of a large number of individual families they went on to determine what factors were associated with child psychiatric disorder. These were quite similar in the two areas and fell into four main groups: (a) family discord and discipline, (b) parental mental disorder and criminality, (c) social disadvantage and poor living conditions and (d) various school characteristics. These findings were very much in keeping with previous investigations. However, what was even more interesting was that these same factors differentiated the two areas, that is to say, London had *more* of the various characteristics associated with disorder. It was concluded that the high prevalence of psychiatric disorder and reading difficulties in London ten year olds was due in part to the fact that a relatively high proportion of London families are discordant and disrupted, that families are often large and living in overcrowded homes which they do not own and that the schools are more often characterized by a high turnover in staff and pupils.

These findings provide important clues as to aspects of family life, social circumstances and school conditions which require attention if the rate of psychiatric and educational problems in children is to be reduced. Nevertheless the results do not show why it is that these family, social and school circumstances should be worse in London. The results showed that it was not a question of problem families moving into London.

The same pattern was evident with children born and bred in London of parents born and bred in London. It seemed to be something about life in an inner-London borough which predisposed to deviance, discord and disorder. But just what that something is we do not know, although some clues are available.

In animals it is well known that overcrowding leads to increased fighting and other signs of disturbance, and it has been suggested that overcrowding is an important source of stress in humans too. In this connection it is necessary to specify what is meant by overcrowding. Does this mean the density of population, that is, the number of people living on each acre of ground? Recent work suggests that that is not a very important factor. For example, a study in Chicago by Galle and others[61] showed that there was no relationship between population density and various indices of social pathology, including juvenile delinquency. Alternatively, does overcrowding mean restriction in personal living-space in the house – the number of persons per room? The Chicago study showed that that was an important factor and investigators in this country have shown the same. Why overcrowding in the home is associated with higher rates of delinquency, psychiatric disorder and reading difficulties is uncertain. It may be that in such an environment parents are more likely to become tense and irritable, or that such negative emotions are more likely to impinge on the children if they all have to live in the same room. It will be more difficult for children to study, so that school work may suffer. Also it will be less easy for them to play at home with other children, so that they are more likely to seek activities outside. If meeting places and play facilities in the neighbourhoods are limited, this may push them into street-corner and building-site activities which are conducive to delinquency. In addition parental discipline and control will probably pose more problems in an overcrowded house or flat.

The evidence on the benefits of rehousing is inconclusive. The high delinquency rates in many new housing-estates certainly demonstrate that better housing provides no immediate return so far as reduction in delinquency is concerned. It may be that it takes a long time to change well-established patterns of behaviour, or it could be that the gain in housing was at the cost of community support. Often the price of rehousing is removal to a neighbourhood in which the old social contacts and supports are lost or at least diluted. Or again the improvement in living standards may be offset by other disadvantageous aspects of the neighbourhood, such as the lack of social amenities, the isolation imposed by the high-rise dwellings or the high noise-level in so many modern blocks of flats. So far there are no convincing answers to these questions, but for too long we have largely ignored the consequences for families of their living conditions. We need to find out what are the optimal conditions and to ensure that these are made available.

In this connection it is not enough to be concerned with housing space. The type of housing is also important.[118] Is it better to build tower blocks or individual houses or some other mode of housing? Tower blocks have rightly come in for a good deal of criticism on the grounds of mothers' dissatisfaction and of the difficulty of allowing preschool children to play outside. Whether they lead to a higher rate of psychiatric disorder, however, seems more uncertain. Again research is needed to find out.

Quite apart from housing, it is also necessary to think in terms of the organization of the neighbourhood. Another aspect of overcrowding in animals is competition for scarce resources. In humans the equivalent may be in the provision of play space, sports facilities, social clubs, coffee bars and the like. Often one aspect of 'slummy' areas is the relative lack of these resources.

In the sociological literature there has been much discussion of the importance of the 'community' or 'neighbourhood' in which people live.[132] This is a confusing concept, as it refers to both a geographical area and a set of social relationships which may or may not coincide. Our knowledge of the factors that lead people to make most of their social contacts locally and to become involved in neighbourhood activities and organizations is very limited. Also the psychiatric benefits of community involvement have been little investigated. However, it seems that people identify with quite a small area (a radius of about half a mile) and that community involvement is greatest when people work in the same area as that in which they live, when there is social heterogeneity and when people have lived in the area for at least several years. It may also be that clear demarcation of areas increases social involvement. Of course people differ in their needs and in their preferred patterns of social life, and this implies that a variety of community organizations are needed.

A further aspect of the areas in which people live concerns their social status. This is not a matter of absolute standards with respect to housing or any other feature. Rather it is a question of the relative standing of the area *vis-à-vis* other areas. In part this is a function of how far neighbourhoods are socially homogeneous, with some very prosperous and others very deprived, and in part it is a question of how people view the area. Areas of low social standing are usually areas in which there are high rates of delinquency, psychiatric disorder and educational failure. The reasons for this are complex. To some extent it is simply a matter of 'problem' families moving to low-status areas as the only areas in which they can find housing. To some extent it is a question of 'contagion' – of people copying the behaviour and coming to accept the standards and attitudes of their neighbourhood. And to some extent it may be a consequence of the dejection and demoralization which follows the labelling of families as failures because they come from a 'failure area'. The second mechanism, 'contagion', probably applies to immigrant groups. Areas with a high proportion of recent immigrants are often areas with high delinquency rates, but interestingly most of the delinquency is not carried out by the immigrants themselves, who may even have a crime rate below average. For example, this is what Lambert[98] found in Birmingham. However, in the next generation there is a tendency for the delinquency rates in the immigrant families to increase and go up to the high levels in the host population. The labelling effect may occur with families in 'half-way' housing or other forms of institution for the homeless. Although not well documented, it seems that the poor reputation of these forms of housing may make it increasingly difficult for the parents to get work because employers are wary of employing anyone from such an address.

It will have been all too evident from the discussion this far that, although area differences in rates of psychiatric and educational disturbance are large and well demonstrated, our knowledge on which neighbourhood influences are important in this connection is quite meagre. In ordinary clinical psychiatric practice it is difficult to take much account of their wider forces when treating individual children and their families. It is sometimes important to provide medical support for applications concerning rehousing, use may well be made of community agencies, families may be put in touch with social organizations in their neighbourhood and, in treatment, attention may have to be paid to family relationships with neighbours. However, that has often been the limit of psychiatric involvement with the community. This is now changing as clinics have increasingly come to serve a particular local area and as clinic personnel have become aware of the psychiatric implications of neighbourhood structure and community resources. If clinics are to have a preventative, as well as therapeutic, function it will be necessary for them to become more involved in decisions about what is done for the community which they serve. It is not that psychiatrists have any well-tested solutions, for they have not, but rather that all should be aware of the possible psychiatric implications of decisions on town planning and on community services.

'Sub-cultural delinquency'

A variety of theories have been put forward to explain the association between the area in which people live and the rate of delinquency. Most recent writers have seen the link in terms of some type of cultural stress or conflict. As indicated above, there seems to be something in this, although the nature of the stresses or the conflict has yet to be adequately defined. Alternatively some theorists have suggested that the answer lies in the effects of socially-biased labelling or stigma. The very limited research so far undertaken into this question suggests that labelling does have some effect – that is, people may come to behave in a deviant way more often simply because they are labelled deviant – but that this effect is fairly small in most instances.[195] Another type of theory suggests that much delinquency in youngsters from socially deprived neighbour-hoods constitutes a *normal* sub-cultural pattern. For example, Mays[111] suggested this with respect to his studies in Liverpool. The suggestion is that, whereas delinquency in children from more prosperous areas may arise as a response to family patho-logy or personal maladjustment, in children from deprived areas this is less often the case. Rather their stealing or playing truant represents a pattern of behaviour which is normal in the social groups in which they live, although it is against the *mores* of society as a whole.

There are several ways in which this hypothesis might be tested. First, it implies that, compared with other delinquents, those from a deprived background should show a lower rate of personal maladjustment or emotional disturbance. Studies by Conger and Miller,[37] Robins[140] and Stott[184] have all proved negative on this point, although it should be added that there are problems with respect to their definitions of maladjustment. Second, whereas delinquency is ordinarily associated with un-popularity and poor relationships with other children, this should not apply to delinquents from deprived areas. Roff and his colleagues[143] have provided evidence on this point. They showed that in all socio-economic groups more intelligent chil-dren were more popular in third grade (about age eight years). When followed up to ninth and tenth grade, in the upper and the middle socio-economic groups the unpopular boys were those most likely to have become delinquent. In the lowest social group the delinquents were most likely to be those pre-viously rated as either most popular *or* most unpopular. In short, some of the children from low-social-status groups followed the same pattern as in other sections of the community, but some followed a different pattern which was consistent with the view of a 'normal' sub-cultural delinquency.

A third approach is to determine whether, within socially disadvantaged high-delinquency areas, delinquency is associ-ated with the same indices of family discord, disruption and disorganization that are important in higher-social-status groups. The findings from several different studies suggest that much the same family variables are associated with delinquency and conduct disorder in all areas and all social groups, although some variations are found.

It appears that in all social groups much of persistent delinquency is associated with personal maladjustment and family problems. This applies to socially disadvantaged areas as well as others. However, there are some types of crime – e.g. filching things off the back of lorries in dock areas – which are so widespread as to be regarded as normal. Furthermore, whereas in all social groups a proportion of delinquents appear psychiatrically normal and well adjusted to their own cultural group, this proportion may be rather high among youngsters from socially deprived backgrounds. For obvious reasons very few of these children ever come to psychiatrists.

Social class

Much has been made of supposed social-class differences in rates of child psychiatric disorder. However, surveys of the total population show that, in contrast to the situation in adult life, the prevalence of disorder does not vary at all consistently with social class, as measured by the father's occupation.[166] There is a tendency for delinquency, and conduct disorders especially, to be somewhat common when the father has a labouring or semi-skilled manual job than when he has a skilled manual or a non-manual job. However, the tendency applies mainly to the extreme bottom end of the social scale, the association is usually of only moderate strength and it is found only in some populations and not in others. It seems that it is not the father's job as such which is important in the genesis of child psychiatric disorder. Rather it is factors such as family discord and inconsistent discipline or, alternatively, variables such as personal overcrowding which predispose towards disorder. It is when low social class is associated with these factors that there is a secondary association with child psychiatric disorder.

On the other hand low social class is associated with a lower IQ and with poorer educational attainment. This is partially explicable in genetic terms and partially in terms of different, and to some extent limited, experiences and linguistic opportunities. As reading backwardness and, to a lesser extent, low IQ are both known to be quite strongly associated with a higher rate of psychiatric disorders, and especially conduct problems (see chapters 7 and 8), this provides another mechanism by which low social class might come to be associated with an increased prevalence of behavioural problems.

A further factor is that low social status is also associated with more complications in pregnancy and a somewhat higher infantile mortality. This is probably a consequence of poorer maternal health, poorer living conditions and poorer provision and utilization of medical services. Prenatal complications only rarely lead to psychiatric disorder but when there is brain damage and impaired intelligence these undoubtedly constitute a psychiatric risk.

Migration

Moving house to a new neighbourhood often involves the breaking of old social ties and the development of new friendships. In addition, if the community is a very different one, it may mean the learning of a new set of social habits and new ways of doing things. Kantor,[91] in a study of children living in an American city, found that multiple moves of home constituted no psychiatric hazard if the moves were in the same neighbourhood. Even if the moves involved adjustment to a quite new area, most children adapted easily. However, if marked social changes were involved, some children found this stressful. Whether the stresses are greater when a very large number of moves are involved as may be the case with fathers who have to move jobs or place of work frequently (as do members of the Armed Forces) is uncertain. It may also be that the difficulties are greater when the moves involve changes in the style of teaching at school.

All these factors are magnified greatly in the case of children who move from one country to another, or whose family origin is different from the social group in which they are reared. In England this phenomenon is most apparent in the children of parents who came from Asia and the West Indies during the wave of immigration in the 1950s. Much political heat has been engendered by concerns about the supposedly 'alien' culture within our midst, but there have been surprisingly few studies which have attempted to determine the extent to which the way of life is really different in these families of migrants, or have sought to assess whether the rate of psychiatric problems is any different in the children from that in the indigenous (non-immigrant) population. However, data are available from a systematic study in London, comparing the families of West Indian immigrants with those of indigenous English families.[168]

In terms of educational background the West Indian parents were broadly similar to the indigenous parents, but in spite of this a higher proportion of West Indians held unskilled or semiskilled manual jobs. In view of the PEP (Political and Economic Planning) study findings there can be no doubt that racial discrimination exists and that it restricts job opportunities. Discrimination is a hazard which faces children from early in their schooling, but it becomes more overt during adolescence and it is most marked in its effects when the youngster comes to leave school and searches for a job and later a home. As might be expected from their lower occupational status, the West Indian families were in many respects living in less satisfactory housing conditions. Overcrowding was twice as frequent, and a higher proportion of families did not possess or had to share the basic amenities of hot running water, a bathroom, lavatory and kitchen. Particularly when they first came to this country many of the West Indian parents had to live in the most dreadful privately rented accommodation, often at exorbitant rents. Nevertheless, in one respect, a major change had taken place following migration. Nearly half the West Indian families owned their own house compared with less than one in five of the indigenous families. This meant that in spite of discrimination in housing and other adverse circumstances the West Indian families had done a great deal to improve their situation. However, a price was paid in terms of wives working long hours (much more so than in the indigenous families) and the property was often old, poor quality and bought under disadvantageous financial arrangements.

A further difference between the West Indian and nonimmigrant families concerned family size. Three fifths of the West Indian mothers had at least five children, a rate over double that in the indigenous group. As this was frequently associated with overcrowding, and in view of the known association between large family size and low reading attainment, this large number of children may have serious educational consequences.

Many more children in West Indian families had been looked after by non-relatives – other studies have shown the often poor quality of these arrangements – and more had been taken into care of the local authority. The West Indian parents were deeply concerned for their children and usually had good relationships with them. But Pollak[129] found that they provided fewer toys and interacted less with their children in the preschool period, probably a reflection of the lesser emphasis in West Indian families on the importance of play in children's development.

The quality of family relationships in the West Indian families was found to be just as good as in the indigenous families, and there were no differences in the rates of parental mental disorder or criminality. Also, contrary to popular belief, in most respects the family pattern in the two groups was closely similar. In both, the 'nuclear family' consisting of stable marriages was the norm, and the fathers were quite involved in the family.

In one respect the pattern of discipline did differ. West Indian children were expected to help more at home and they were generally more self-reliant. On the other hand they were rather more restricted in their social activities. West Indian parents sometimes complain that discipline in schools is lax and inefficient. Conversely teachers sometimes feel that West Indian parents are unduly harsh. This arises through a cultural difference in attitudes to discipline, but children may sometimes find the disparity between what is expected at home and what is expected at school confusing and troublesome.

The London study also showed that the educational attainments of West Indian children were well below those of indigenous children. But attainment differed markedly according to the child's place of birth. Children born in this country had a reading age ten months above their counterparts born in the West Indies, in spite of the fact that the educational-occupational level of the parents in the two groups was similar. The reality of this difference was confirmed by the finding that the level of attainment was related to the duration of time the children had spent in this country. There are many possible reasons for this observed difference in attainment according to place of birth. Malnutrition in early life is much commoner in the West Indies than it is in the UK and this may affect intellectual development. The disruption of moving from one cultural setting to another and differences in the children's early life experiences may also have played a part. Nevertheless it seemed that the experience of schooling in this country may have been one of the main factors accounting for the better reading attainments of children born in England.

The psychiatric findings were rather different. Taken as a whole the rate of psychiatric disorder in the children of West Indian migrants was much the same as that in non-immigrant families. The groups did not differ with respect to behavioural difficulties at home, but the West Indian children did show a somewhat higher rate of conduct problems at school (fighting, disruptive behaviour, stealing, etc.). There was also one other difference. Whereas in English girls with psychiatric problems the disorder is usually emotional in type (anxiety, fears, depression, etc.), in West Indian girls conduct disorders predominated.

There are a variety of reasons why West Indian children might show more behavioural difficulties at school. These include their often lower educational attainment, the disparity between home and school patterns of discipline, the effects of racial prejudice and the consequences of attending poorer schools (as they tended to). It should be added that in some respects the conduct disorders in West Indian children seemed not to have quite the same significance as those in indigenous children. The relative lack of emotional problems and of difficulties with other children suggests (but does not prove) that the sources of the conduct disorders in West Indian children were less pervasive and less deeply entrenched than those in indigenous children.

Interestingly the rate of conduct disorders did not differ according to the children's place of birth. It seemed that, although the maladaptive experiences associated with an upbringing in the UK differed in pattern from those associated with life in the West Indies, the level of 'bad' experiences was much the same. However, it should be borne in mind that these findings refer to children who migrated from the West Indies early during their school years. Clinical experience suggests that the much smaller number of youngsters coming to the UK during adolescence to join their parents may experience many more problems.

For example, Matthew was referred to the clinic at age thirteen years with the complaint that he was disobedient at home, appeared sullen and resentful and had stolen small sums of money from his mother's purse. He had spent all his childhood in the West Indies until age twelve years, when his mother sent for him. Up to that time he had been looked after by his grandmother in a small village where he was very happy. Matthew had little memory of his mother, whom he had not seen since he was a toddler, and he had not wanted to come to England. He joined a well-organized home with very firm discipline and he was expected to adapt immediately to this new situation. His mother was a very able, ambitious woman who worked hard and had very high standards. The house was kept spotless and Matthew found in his room a set of regulations which were to apply to him as they had to the lodger who preceded him. Matthew had never known his father, and mother's husband, whom she had married since leaving the West Indies, was a complete stranger to him.

The husband worked very long hours and, although he got on quite well with Matthew, they saw very little of each other. Matthew became increasingly miserable after his arrival in this country and was resentful and rebellious concerning the regulations at home which he regarded as unreasonable. His defiance was sharply punished and he became more conforming on the surface, but soon began pinching things from his mother's purse. Starting a new school was initially quite stressful, but he was an intelligent, athletic boy who was well liked, and his closest ties came to be formed with his teachers and with other boys at school. Matthew's mother was a forceful, dominant personality; she could be quite warm but she completely failed to appreciate Matthew's difficulties and was very angry about his 'dishonesty'.

In this case the move to England was the major factor in the development of emotional and behavioural problems. Matthew had a resilient personality and his adaptation to school in England was remarkably good. His intelligence and his skill at games undoubtedly helped in that respect. The move to a different culture, and even more important the breaking of his social ties in adolescence, was the first stress, and the clash with his mother was the final precipitant. He presented no general delinquency problem and the stealing was a fairly direct expression of his resentment of his mother. Mother was helped to understand that Matthew needed both time and support if he was to adapt and come to accept his new family. Matthew was seen to discuss his feelings about the move to England and to a new home. His main outlet lay in the school and a teacher/counsellor gave him a lot of support there. Over the course of the next year he made a good adjustment and there were no further episodes of stealing. He never developed a warm relationship with his mother but they got on much better. At school he made very good progress and soon had a circle of friends with whom he got on well.

Matthew came to this country at both a difficult time in his life and in difficult circumstances, so that migration proved much more of a stress to him than it does to most immigrant children. Many show some signs of disturbance shortly after migration, but they usually quickly settle. The evidence from the London study suggests that, although West Indian children have rather more than their share of difficulties at school, they do not have an appreciably increased rate of psychiatric disorder. To a considerable extent the factors that cause disorder in them are closely similar to those in any other child. However, it is important for the psychiatrist to be aware of the possible effects of racial discrimination and of the different cultural patterns both with regard to child rearing and to the utilization of services. A further issue, although not one apparent at age ten years, is the disparity between the strict religious standards in some of the West Indian homes and the quite different values which the adolescent finds both at school and among his black friends. In this situation there is the potential for an exaggeration of the normal clash between parental and adolescent attitudes and standards.

So far this discussion has largely focused on children from West Indian families, because that is the group about which most is known. Nevertheless it is important to appreciate that there are several other larger immigrant groups (such as those from Eire, Cyprus, India and Pakistan) whose situation differs in several crucial respects. Their cultures are not the same and to a varying extent differences in skin colour, language and religion influence the children's adjustment and attainments.

Schools

Michael Power and his colleagues[131] were the first people to provide good evidence for the very marked variation between schools in rates of delinquency, although this had been suspected for some time. They studied an inner-London borough and found that there was a *twelve-fold* difference in the average annual delinquency rate among secondary schools serving the area (selective schools and special schools having been excluded). When the neighbourhood where the children lived had been taken into account, very large differences between schools remained. These differences were unrelated to formal characteristics of the school, such as old or new, single sex or co-education, large or small, voluntary or local authority. Closely similar findings for an outer-London borough were reported by Gath, Cooper and Gattoni,[62] who went on to show that the same variability between schools applied to child-guidance referral rates. Neither study was able to identify what were the features of 'good' and 'bad' schools in this connection.

Rutter and his co-workers[158] found that this marked variability between schools applied also in the field of primary education. They showed variability in both reading difficulties and also behavioural deviance as assessed by teacher questionnaire. As all the ten-year-old children in the borough had been studied in the same way, the findings could not have been due to varying police practices or referral rates – which just conceivably might have accounted for the Power and Gath findings, although their evidence suggested that this was unlikely. Rutter had only limited data on school characteristics, but these were enough to show that the variability between schools in terms of children's progress *was* related to differences in the schools. Nevertheless behavioural difficulties and low attainments in reading were much commoner in schools with high rates of teacher and pupil turnover. Schools which lacked stability in staffing and which had a high proportion of children coming and going were those with the most problems. The teacher–child ratio made little difference, but problems were also greater in schools with a large proportion of children eligible for free school meals (i.e. poor children) or of immigrant children. These last two findings, it should be noted, applied to children who were not themselves either poor or immigrant. It seemed that it was something about the school itself and the composition of its children which was associated with the marked differences between schools in rates of low educational attainment and behavioural deviance.

None of these studies was able to prove that the schools actually influenced the children's behaviour and attainments, although that was the inference. In order to test whether the differences were truly due to school influences rather than selective intake, it would be necessary to examine *changes* in children's behaviour after they came to the school. Using this method, West and Farrington[195] showed that there were selective biases in intake. Our own findings show the same but also indicate that, in addition, schools can influence children's behaviour (as well as their attainments) for better or worse.

Much earlier studies had produced findings which suggested that schools could influence attitudes and, what is more, that the attitude changes were remarkably persistent. Newcomb[117] investigated the attitudes of students attending an American college and showed that during their time at the college the students became progressively less conservative in their attitudes in spite of coming from conservative families. This change to a more liberal viewpoint did not occur among students at other colleges. The findings were explicable in terms of the fact that liberal views were associated with popularity and prestige among students and also with involvement in college affairs. The college had a liberal ethos which had developed over the years and which seemed to influence each new lot of students in a predictable way. Twenty years later a follow-up study showed that the ex-students had tended to select like-minded, non-conservative people to marry and that for the most part their liberal views persisted.

If schools are likely to influence children for better or worse, it is important that everyone should know how to ensure that it will be for the better. Unfortunately there are very few hard facts on this issue, although there are some useful leads to follow. Let us consider what some of these are. Hargreaves[72] in a most interesting participant–observer study of social relations in a secondary school noted some of the effects of rigid streaming. There was very little mixing between streams – children mostly chose friends from within their own stream – and there was considerable antagonism between the upper and lower streams. This antagonism broke down to some extent when there were joint activities, such as rugby football. In the upper streams there were quite good teacher–pupil relationships and the youngsters were generally committed to both the school and the educational process. Less-experienced staff took the lower streams, the teachers had negative expectations of boys in the lower streams and there were fewer educational rewards there. Essentially the lowest streams formed an antischool subculture in which there was a high delinquency rate. Children in these streams were exposed to middle-class and academic values but were constantly frustrated by their being denied any status in that system.

That was just one study, but its findings are in keeping with other people's experience. If it is used to draw lessons, it would seem that a demarcation between highly-valued and less-valued children (by streaming or by any other means) is likely to lead to resentment in the latter group. Ways need to be found of ensuring that less-able youngsters as well as the more intelligent ones get plenty of rewards from the school system. There are various ways in which this might be achieved: such as by providing rewards for gains in achievement rather than for an absolute level and by giving comparably great rewards for achievements in non-academic subjects (art, woodwork, etc.), in sport and in hobbies or other non-classroom activities linked with the school. The object would be to ensure that all children are able to get rewards and encouragement for what they do at school. A second and complementary approach is to ensure that the non-academic children achieve a degree of commitment to the school by their being involved in important aspects of its work and by giving them responsibility in the school system. Studies with adults show that being given responsibility in a social structure (such as in a factory) leads people to shift in their attitudes towards a further adoption of the values of that system.[92] Even playing a role serves to influence attitudes. It is probable that the same phenomenon applies in childhood. A third measure is to ensure that negative labels are avoided and that a premium is placed on encouragement rather than discouragement. This means that grading children (by posting up marks or by streaming) should be avoided. It may encourage those at the top, but there is bound to be a bottom half in any list or group of streams and the children there will be discouraged. It is better to pick out the things that they are good at and give praise for those. Children, like adults, tend to live up (or down) to what is expected of them. Labelling a child as a failure might make it more likely that he will be so.

Another aspect of schooling concerns the clash between the values and *mores* in school and the youth culture outside it. Sugarman[185] in a study of four London secondary schools found that high commitment to teenage culture tended to involve a repudiation of the values and norms of the school. He suggested that this clash might be reduced if the school included more of the teenage social system by both increasing the range of extra-curricular activities *and* giving the adolescents responsibility in organizing these activities.

For many children a similar clash exists between the culture of the school and the culture of the home. Where the family does not regard education as important or where there is a 'them' and 'us' dichotomy with teachers seen as unsympathetic authority figures concerned with an alien set of values, the child is faced with a conflict between the attitudes he experiences in the two settings. Douglas[47] and others have shown how children's scholastic progress is much better when the parents express interest and involvement in their children's schooling. Bronfenbrenner's careful, critical review[22] of the results of the American preschool education programme concluded that the single most important factor leading to the children's *continuing* academic progress was the extent to which parents could be actively involved in the educational programme. The suggestion is that something is to be gained by breaking down the wall between family and school. This might be done by getting parents to actively participate in school affairs, by having them talk about their jobs, by taking children to visit their place of work, by taking a leading role in extra-curricular activities and generally by being recognized as important partners in the educational process.

The style of teaching may also have an impact both on personal relationships in the school and on the efficiency of learning. For example, White and Lippitt[196] compared authoritarian, democratic and *laissez-faire* approaches in getting ten- and eleven-year-old children to make masks at school. The authoritarian approach meant giving orders and not involving the children in decision-making; this group made the most masks but were rather aggressive to the leader. The democratic approach meant that they were led and guided, but the children were involved in decision-making; they made nearly as many masks as the first group, worked slightly better when the leader was out of the room and got on best with the leader. The *laissez-faire* group was given neither orders nor guided discussion and did worst on all criteria. This study and others have demonstrated that children need leadership and do not benefit from complete freedom and lack of structure. Efficient learning is most often obtained in the immediate situation by a firm, structured, authoritarian approach, and for some sorts of teaching of older children this may have benefits. On the other hand friendly relations are more readily obtained with a democratic approach and with this regime children are inclined to persist better when left to continue on their own. Both these advantages make it the preferred approach in most situations.

The organization of groups and determination of goals also have important effects on interpersonal relationships. In the famous Robbers' Cave Experiment, Sherif and his associates[178] found that, when adolescents were organized in competing groups working towards a goal obtainable only by one side (e.g. becoming a winner in competitive games), strong and productive in-group loyalties were produced, but there was also hostile intergroup interaction. When the groups were both working towards a common goal (e.g. developing a safe water supply), there was friendly and cooperative group interaction. As the youngsters did not know each other before the experiment, the presumption is that it was the definition of groups and goals which led to these effects. If these findings can be applied to schools, the lesson would seem to be that there are benefits in getting children to work together in groups, but that competition between groups may sometimes have undesirable side-effects.

A further issue is the model of behaviour provided by the teachers both in their interaction with children and with each other. If the staff are harsh, intolerant and bad-tempered, they are likely to encourage similar behaviour in the children. Extensive use of violence in discipline, as by corporal punishment, may set an example of dealing with problems by aggression. This may partly explain why Clegg and Megson[36] found in a survey of West Riding schools that behaviour was best and delinquency least in schools where corporal punishment was used sparingly or not at all. They also reported on the changes introduced into a severely disruptive school by a Head in the process of transforming it into a harmonious, well-respected school. One of the serious problems was the general slackness of staff, who were poor time-keepers and showed little interest in the school. They set a model of idleness and non-involvement for the children, and one of the Head's tasks was to increase the standards, motivation and involvement of his teachers. This also emphasizes that, if a school is to run smoothly, it is important that the staff feel they are doing a good job, get satisfaction from their work, have harmonious relationships among themselves and become really involved in the school as an institution. Studies in a different type of institution have suggested that interstaff conflict tends to have bad effects on others and the same probably applies with teachers and children.

Of course, if there is to be an ethos which has a good influence in the school, it is important that there be adequate stability of staffing. If teachers are constantly coming and going, as applies in some schools, it is difficult to have any kind of consistent social structure.

In addition to these broader social influences in the school, the details of how teachers interact with children in the classroom are also very important. Through the work of psychologists much progress in this connection has been made in recent years.[11] The principles are those of behaviour modification which stress that situations should be structured so as to maximize the occurrence of desired behaviours; that approval, praise and other rewards encourage the continuation of activities; that a lack of response to an activity or ignoring it tends to lead to a diminution of that activity and that, if approval is to be effective, it must be given immediately. Thus Becker,[7] Hall[71] and others showed that disruptive behaviours in the classroom diminished if the teacher ignored them *and* if he gave approval and attention in increased amounts when the children were behaving well. The effect was to increase the rewards of good behaviour and to ensure that disruptive, attention-seeking behaviour no longer achieved its object of gaining attention. In this situation it appeared that attention from the teacher (even if punitive) constituted the most important reward for the children. Of course it may also be necessary to give reprimands for certain behaviours. O'Leary and his colleagues[121] showed that soft reprimands were more effective than loud ones, presumably because loud reprimands disrupted the work of other children and drew attention to the disruptive child. Kounin[97] also found that firm quiet reprimands were more effective than angry punitive responses. Discipline was better with teachers who could cope with more than one issue at a time, who were in touch with the group situation in the class, who were active teachers and who could maintain interest and involvement in the task.

These specific techniques will not always be effective in quite the same way. Thus, in another study, ignoring disruptive behaviour merely led to pandemonium. This may happen if it is largely attention from other children, rather than from the teacher, which acts as a reward. In this situation it will be necessary to do something to alter other children's responses to disruption. For example, in one study Patterson and his colleagues,[127] when treating a very overactive, disruptive child, so organized the classroom that rewards for the *other* children were made contingent on the good behaviour of that one very disturbed child. This had the effect of making the other children encourage that child to behave better, and so he did. It is also necessary to ensure that the children have the desired 'good' behaviour in their repertoire. It is no good expecting them to stop misbehaving if they do not know anything better to do. It may be necessary to first teach them the necessary social skills or give them the appropriate remedial help with subjects they are finding difficult. This will have to be individualized in approach and in the first instance the remedial teaching is often best done in a one-to-one situation.

This is necessary because, once a child is severely behind in his schoolwork, one of the initial tasks will be to regain his cooperation and involvement, to increase his motivation and give him the will to succeed. To do this, some knowledge of the individual child is required and it is necessary to tailor teaching to his needs. Studies have shown that 'progress' and remedial classes are of very limited benefit at best and may sometimes actually make things worse by, in effect, providing the label of failure.

These various studies do not show at all conclusively what the requirements of a good school are, but they do give some indication of the areas of school life which may require attention.

In the last few years psychiatrists, psychologists (both clinical and educational) and psychiatric social workers have increasingly worked with teachers in order to help them deal with emotional and behavioural difficulties in the children they teach. In this situation it is important to appreciate that the clinician is not treating the child himself as he might in the hospital or clinic. What he is trying to do is help the teachers do their own job better: by trying to give them an understanding of the sociological and psychological factors which may be operative in the school environment or in an individual's behaviour, or by providing them with help in specific techniques of dealing with various types of problem behaviour.

In my own clinic this is done in several different ways. With one secondary school an interdisciplinary team regularly meets with the staff to discuss issues related to problems in the school or in the children. The teacher is very much alone in coping with a classroom of children and, particularly if the group is a difficult one, he can readily feel isolated and lose confidence. The opportunity to discuss with other people the difficulties he faces and the way he copes with them may lead to an increase in assurance, quite apart from any specific suggestions the clinician may have to offer with respect to the children's or teacher's problems. Psychologists from the clinic have also developed special links with certain primary schools in the area to help teachers learn what to look for in observing children and to give them understanding of the ways in which ordinary methods of teacher–child interaction may be improved, so as to encourage cooperative and discourage disruptive behaviour in the classroom. On other occasions clinic staff may meet with teachers to discuss the referral of children before they are seen at the clinic. After the child is seen at the clinic, the psychologist has a key role in communication with the school. Teachers may know a great deal about the child which can be helpful in planning treatment. Also, with parental consent and within the limits of confidentiality, the psychologist may help the teacher understand better the nature of the child's problems. The results of psychological testing may assist the teacher in planning how best to help the child with scholastic difficulties. Finally, in some cases working with teachers constitutes the main focus of treatment. The case of Brigitta described in chapter 6 page 225 is one example of this, while that of Charles is another.

Charles was referred at age ten years because he was severely behind in reading and spelling and because his behaviour was troublesome. He did not settle to things and moved restlessly from room to room. At school he behaved in a silly, attention-seeking fashion and this was taken advantage of by other children who readily led him into mischief. He had no class friends and did not play with other children at home. His interests were very few and most of his spare time was spent watching television. Charles irritated his parents by pestering them to do things, by not engaging in proper conversation and by always fiddling with something. He was generally happy but tended to sulk in a babyish way and sometimes brooded in the evening. Affectionate and rather sensitive, he was easily upset over things like his rabbits' death and even more so by his uncle's death. His early development was unremarkable, but his school reports had been bad from the very beginning. Psychological testing showed him to be of low average intelligence and he was almost a non-reader, his achievements being well below those expected of a boy of his age and intelligence. At interview he was restless and monosyllabic although he smiled warmly. His concentration was very poor. Father had been treated for depression in the past and had periods when he thought of injuring Charles. He was a rather bumbling, ineffectual man. Mother worked part-time and was indulgent and inconsistent with the boy. There was one older sister and a younger brother, and the family lived together in an old house due for demolition. The maternal grandmother lived nearby and constantly interfered in Charles's upbringing. At first, treatment was focused on dealing with the family difficulties and on the parents' way of responding to Charles's disturbed behaviour at home. This proved rather unproductive because, although well meaning, the parents were of quite limited ability and found it difficult both to understand what was needed and to alter their behaviour in any way. When Charles was seen individually, he expressed some of his misery and frustration, but little progress was made because of his difficulties in communication. It became apparent that his behaviour was worse at school than at home and a school visit was paid by the clinic psychologist. It was decided, with the teachers, to observe what happened in the classroom and then to develop a plan of action. Charles was seen to be an overactive, ungainly and socially incompetent boy who kept moving around the classroom and provoking other children by pinching or hitting them. He was very anxious to please the teacher and sought his attention both by mischievous, 'silly' behaviour and by volunteering to do things. His offers of help were invariably turned down because he was thought unreliable. Charles was unpopular with the other children, who laughed at him and never chose him until last for team games. His disruptive behaviour resulted in a lot of attention from other children as well as from the teacher, while his appropriate behaviour less often drew notice although some praise was given. It was decided to get all the teachers to look out for when Charles was behaving well or getting on well with other children and to give systematic praise and encouragement at these times. His disruptive behaviours were to be completely ignored. Charles was given individual help with reading, as his illiteracy was interfering with all school learning. In order to improve his interaction with other children, it was agreed that Charles should be given as much responsibility and leadership as he could cope with and that other children should be given attention and praise when they responded positively towards Charles. This programme had to be started only in the middle of his last term at primary school, but even after five weeks there had been a dramatic fall in the amount of disruptive behaviour, his attention and motivation in class were better and his relationships with other children were beginning to improve.

This programme resulted in very dramatic short-term gains which might well have been built on if he had remained at the same school. Unfortunately the family moved away from London and his new (secondary) school found him so well behaved in the first weeks that they said no further help was needed. A month or so later all the old difficulties returned and in the next term assistance was sought by the school. They were reluctant to adopt the previous programme in its entirety and in any case there were practical difficulties in view of the many teachers and many classes of children who would be involved. Similar principles were used but in an attenuated form. Progress was again made, but it was much slower. Two years later Charles was holding his own socially and presented no marked behavioural problems. However, he had made almost no progress in reading in spite of increased confidence.

Peer group

A child's relationships with other children are most important, both because persistent disturbed relationships are a sensitive indicator of something going wrong in psychological development and because the peer group plays an increasingly important role in influencing behaviour and attitudes as the child grows older.[30] Although there are temperamental differences in the extent to which children are socially outgoing, most young children actively seek friendship and in so doing tend to imitate other children's group behaviour as a means of joining the group. When a young schoolchild is introduced to a new group of children, he tends to watch for a while to learn what is expected, and then makes overtures by copying the remarks, actions and gestures of the most active group members. Acceptance by the peer group and popularity within it are related to various personal characteristics such as intelligence, pleasing appearance, cheerfulness and friendliness, and also to prowess in the activities which constitute the focus of that particular peer group. For this reason, athletic prowess and strength aid popularity in boys. This means that, if children can be helped to gain skills in the things that matter most in the group with whom they want to mix (whether those skills be in football, playing the guitar, dancing, telling funny stories or whatever), this may make their social acceptance easier. However, there are also specifically social skills which are important in any group. Youngsters need to be able to make other children feel accepted and involved, to recognize their needs and how they are feeling, and generally to act in ways which promote friendly interaction within the group. In short it is not just personal qualities but also interpersonal skills which are important. Particularly among older children popularity tends to go to those who contribute to others. Leadership is often a function of an ability to plan and initiate interesting group activities and to make the most of a group situation. Leaders tend to be sensitive to group feelings but also to anticipate group needs which have not yet been articulated, so that, in initiating new styles of behaviour, leaders are a little ahead of the group but not much.

Children who are socially isolated or rejected by other children are considerably more likely than other children to have psychiatric problems. Sociometric studies (that is studies in which children name those with whom they would most like and least like to play, sit, work etc.) show that youngsters with emotional or behavioural disorders are less likely to be chosen by other children as desirable companions and more likely to be named as an undesirable playmate. This is a two-way process in that the characteristics of the psychiatric disorder may make popularity less likely, but then the ensuing isolation may aggravate the disorder, and a vicious circle is set up. Unpopularity and social rejection also predict psychiatric and behavioural problems many years later. As already noted, Roff found that children who were social isolates or rejects in the third grade in American schools had a much increased likelihood of being delinquent six years later.[143] Furthermore longer-term follow-up studies have also shown links with psychiatric disorders in adult life.

As well as being influenced by personal factors, friendships are to some extent shaped by structural variables, by the opportunity for interaction and by adult behaviour. For example, among preadolescent campers friendships were more likely to develop among children who shared the same cabin and also, within cabins, among those with adjacent bunks[30]. Much the same applies within the school with respect to classroom and desk distribution, and, outside school, friendships are more likely to be found with children living in the same neighbourhood. As we have seen already when discussing schools, peer acceptance is encouraged if the child is a member of a group sharing a common purpose and having to work together to reach a goal. Experimental studies have also shown that praise from teachers can influence popularity. For example, Flanders and Havumaki[56] showed that when teachers restricted praise in a group discussion to students sitting in odd-numbered seats, these praised students later received more positive sociometric choices. All these findings mean that, to some extent, parents and teachers can influence the development of friendships by the choice of where to live and which school the child will go to, by structural and social organization within the school and by the way they behave towards different children.

This is of some practical importance in view of the influence of the peer group on children's behaviour and attitudes. This is easily seen in the way children conform to fads and fashion in dress, hair styles, pop music, styles of speech and the like. It can also be shown experimentally. Thus it has been shown that, when asked to judge the length of a set of black lines, in a group situation children tend to follow the majority of other children.[10] The strength of this influence is demonstrated when the other children are stooges who have been taught to make deliberately wrong estimates of length. In this situation, children who made accurate estimates when tested individually, later made inaccurate ones in a group setting. Young children are more likely to conform, girls are more suggestible than boys, low-status children follow group norms more than high-status children and temperamental differences also influence conformity.

To what extent children are led into deviant behaviour through their association with other children remains quite uncertain. The sociologist, Sutherland, first expressed the view that delinquency was a behaviour learned through interaction with other people and thus that the likelihood of persons becoming delinquent was directly related to the frequency and consistency of his contacts with delinquent individuals.[42] Clearly there is something in this view which has been widely taken up by others, but research has not yet shown how important differential association is in the genesis of delinquent behaviour or any other forms of deviance or behavioural disturbance.

The importance of these matters to the psychiatrist lies in the value of learning about a child's peer relationships as one indicator of social and psychological development, of appreciating the difficulties of the socially isolated child, of examining the possible influence of peer-group values in shaping the child's behaviour and in the need to determine when it may be therapeutic to influence peer-group interaction and when children need specific help in gaining social skills. Michael Argyle[2] has been a foremost advocate of the importance of social skills, and he and others have gone on to carry out studies which suggest the value of social training for some individuals with psychiatric problems. The case of Charles, discussed above, involved a focus on peer-group interaction, and with Graham special training in social skills was undertaken.

Graham was a young man of twenty who first attended the clinic many years ago with infantile autism. As a young child he had been delayed in his speech and failed to develop the normal bonds and attachments, and had showed a variety of bizarre and ritualistic behaviours. Gradually all these problems diminished and Graham made slow but steady progress. He became fluent in speech, lost many of his weird ways of behaving and came to want friendship and social contacts. He was of above average intelligence, went to school and eventually gained several 'O' levels in national examinations. However, in late adolescence he was still considerably handicapped by his social ineptitude. He wanted to make friends, but he put people off by immediately bombarding them with personal questions, not listening to what they said and then replying with a series of facts on his obsessions of the moment (such as bus timetables). He was fidgety and restless, had an odd manner and tended to go off at a tangent in conversations because he suddenly thought of some interesting fact (but unrelated to the topic being discussed) or because he was distracted by some interesting aspect of the environment. He recognized his social problem but did not understand what to do to improve matters in spite of the fact that his difficulties had been discussed at length on many occasions. One of the psychologists with special experience in social training undertook treatment with Graham. He was interviewed first to assess the specific social faults he showed and then a videotape recording was made of his talking to a young female psychologist whom he had not previously met. Graham was told to act as if he were meeting her at a party. This brought out all his oddities of social behaviour. He was then shown the videotape film and asked which aspects of his behaviour he thought needed changing. He did not immediately pick out the crucial elements but, with help, he was able to see the social deficits. Using role-playing techniques and making use of videotapes, Graham was taught to look at people's eyes, to listen to what they said before he replied, to speak in a less personal manner and to develop conversations in a less stereotyped manner. In this, emphasis was placed on Graham's observing and understanding what happened in social interactions, and the necessary pieces of social behaviour were taught one by one. This programme led to considerable improvements in his style of interacting with people although he remained rather awkward and would revert to his previous form of behaviour on occasions. He became much more acceptable socially and this proved an important factor in his gaining and holding a regular job.

The value of such techniques of social training in the treatment of psychiatric disorders in children, adolescents and adults has yet to be systematically evaluated. However, it seems probable that developments in this field will prove to be of considerable value for some types of problem.

6 Emotional Disorders

In previous chapters there has been an emphasis on factors in the child and in his environment which may have played a part in causing psychiatric disorders, and on the need to gain an understanding of the nature of the child's problems and how they arose. These are important issues, but it is not always possible to determine how and why a particular disorder developed and, moreover, in some cases it may not be necessary to know the causes in order to plan treatment. It should also be added that, in our present state of knowledge, there are many children for whom we have no really effective means of providing help. In this chapter, and the next, some of the commoner psychiatric problems will be considered with particular focus on what forms of treatment are available and how a particular treatment is selected.

As already noted, many normal children have mild and transient emotional disturbances which are just a part of growing up and are no cause for concern. In addition there are some aspects of normal development which, on the surface, look like psychiatric symptoms but which are not. For example, separation anxiety is normal in the toddler, and fears of the dark and of animals are common in the preschool period. Young children frequently have periods of being irritable and bad tempered and also they often show behaviours which appear obsessional and ritualistic. For example, children in their games may have to avoid stepping on the cracks of the pavement, touch every second tree or pick up a stick before the next person walks by. These have the same element of performing an act to avoid a disaster that is characteristic of an obsessional compulsion. However, they are not identical in that, unlike the psychiatric symptoms, the rituals are not felt as imposed or compulsory and the child does not resist the act. This behaviour develops as part of a childish game and not as a maladaptive means of dealing with excessive anxiety.

Emotional disorders differ from these behaviours in terms both of abnormality (assessed in the term described in chapter 1) and social impairment. These disorders have many features in common with the neuroses of adult life, but the two groups of conditions are also dissimilar in several respects.

Whereas adult neuroses are much commoner in women than in men, emotional disorders in childhood occur with about the same frequency in the two sexes, being only marginally more frequent in girls. It is only during adolescence that the sex ratio begins to shift towards the adult pattern. There are also a number of interesting age-specificities with respect to emotional disorders, the meaning of which is not yet fully understood. For example, animal phobias (fears of dogs, cats, etc.) almost always begin in childhood, and usually early childhood. In sharp contrast agoraphobia (a fear of going into open spaces) rarely begins before adult life. Social phobias (e.g. fears of meeting people) are less consistent in their age of onset but generally develop about the time of puberty. Although misery and unhappiness are quite common symptoms in childhood, depressive disorders in the form they are seen in adult life are fairly infrequent until the child reaches puberty. Suicide is extremely rare before puberty and suicidal attempts too are less common than in adult life.

Although a few children with emotional disorders grow up to become neurotic adults, most do not. The prognosis for emotional disorders is generally good and, on the whole, it is probably better than that for adult neuroses. However, in the minority where the disorder does persist into adult life the adult problem is almost always of a neurosis or depressive condition.

Genetic factors are of some importance in leading to vulnerability to emotional disorders, but they are probably particularly influential in the most severe and persistent emotional disorders. Precipitating factors, in terms of environmental stresses, are relatively frequent. There is no one characteristic type of family circumstances or of parent–child interaction which leads to emotional disorder. However, parental constraint and overprotection seem to be important factors in some cases and, as discussed in Chapter 4, other family influences may also be relevant. Severe emotional disorders may be associated with a falling off in schoolwork but, unlike conduct disorders, there is no particular association with specific reading retardation.

Fears, phobias and anxiety states

Fears or phobias can occur at any stage but are especially common in early childhood and again around the time of puberty. The fear may be specific to one particular type of object or situation, or it may be quite generalized and unfocused.[9] Children, like adults, are much influenced by the fears of those about them and phobias may be 'learned' from other family members. The extreme contagion of fear may be seen most dramatically in its acute form by the panic which spreads rapidly through crowds in times of disaster. It is quite difficult to remain calm and at ease when other people all around are panic-stricken or even just very anxious. As well as this general spread of anxiety in social situations, children also learn to be confident or afraid in specific situations according to how their parents behave. When mother or father are very afraid of thunderstorms, cows or water, the child is more likely to develop similar fears. In other cases the fears may stem from personal experiences, as when a child becomes afraid of dogs after being bitten by one. Less dramatically the fear may arise because of the child's incompetence in some situation. A child may be very anxious meeting people, because he lacks social skills. For related reasons, when a child becomes generally depressed or anxious, this increases the likelihood of specific fears developing.

Fears may also arise because the child is uncertain and unsettled in his personal relationships. If the child lacks confidence in his mother's love or in his mother's ability to be there when she is needed, he may begin to develop anxieties and fears about what has happened to her. In this way children may come to be afraid to leave parents in case they are ill or have an accident. Especially when this fear appears silly or is greeted with mockery or lack of sympathy, the fear may become *displaced* on to some other object. Thus, the fear may be focused on the school when in fact the child is really afraid of losing his parents.

Particularly in the case of specific isolated phobias, behavioural methods of treatment focused on the symptoms are usually the most effective. Some examples are given below and others are provided in chapter 9. However, it is also necessary to take account of any currently active factors in the child or in his environment which are leading to the fear. Unless these too are altered, there is the likelihood that the fear will simply recur.

An example of an occasion in which a behavioural approach was sufficient on its own is provided by Martin who was referred at age six with a severe and incapacitating dog phobia. He was then so terrified of dogs that his mother was unable to take him out shopping with her or go on walks or visits to the seaside, and on several occasions Martin had run out on to the road, heedless of traffic, in order to avoid an encounter with a dog on the pavement. If dogs came near he screamed, cried and ran away. The fear of dogs first started when Martin was a year old when he was repeatedly frightened by two very large and noisy hounds in the adjoining garden. The dogs never attacked Martin, but they would put their paws on top of the fence and snarl and bark at him. Martin would either stand still, screaming and terrified, or would rush into the house in tears. The parents protested to the neighbours in vain. This went on until Martin was three and a half. Martin did not mind seeing pictures of dogs, but he would become anxious and bite his nails if there was a dog in the film he was watching. His parents tried to get him used to dogs by introducing him to puppies, but these attempts came to an end when as a result of Martin's clumsy overtures one snapped at him, making him frightened. Martin was a generally happy boy who showed no other problems. He was slightly timorous in new situations and a year before he had refused to eat school lunches for a few weeks. However, that difficulty was soon overcome and generally he appeared a rather jaunty, outgoing and friendly little boy. He had had no separations from his family and both parents were sensible people, fond of Martin, and without any fears of their own. There were some slight marital difficulties, but both parents had a good relationship with the boy.

In Martin's case the phobia certainly warranted treatment, in that it was quite incapacitating. However, it was an isolated problem and the causal factors seemed to lie in the past with Martin's unpleasant early experiences with dogs rather than any other factors in his current situation. It was decided to treat the problem by means of *desensitization*. This involves first drawing up a hierarchy with the most feared situation at one end and the least feared at the other. In Martin's case, pictures of dogs or other animals produced no anxiety, small furry animals in real life (such as a docile guinea pig) produced only a little anxiety, whereas any live dog produced a lot of anxiety which reached a peak if the animal was large, moving fast and approaching. Treatment, after getting to know the child and gaining his confidence, consists of getting the child used to the situations which arouse very little anxiety and then gradually introducing very small changes in the situation, so that the child can slowly move up the hierarchy without at any stage having more than slight anxiety. It is often helpful to combine this with some activity which counteracts anxiety. This may be relaxation (which the child is taught to do) or it may be something like chewing a sweet or chocolate. In essence the procedure is no more than a sophisticated version of the well-tested family 'treatment' of dog phobias by getting children used to puppies before they are introduced to dogs. However, it relies on very careful grading of situations, so that there can be a steady progression up the hierarchy without the child ever becoming afraid. With Martin the treatment was carried out by gradually introducing him to live animals of increasing size and similarity to dogs. Guinea pigs, rats, rabbits, monkeys, sheep and goats were used (taking advantage of the animals available in a nearby research unit), in each case using chocolates or stroking the animal to reduce anxiety. At the fifth weekly session he was first introduced to a small, docile, obedient dog and encouraged to approach it gradually. In later sessions small, frisky dogs and finally larger dogs were employed. At first the dogs were on a leash held by the therapist, then off the leash and then on a leash held by Martin. The treatment methods were discussed in detail with the parents (as well as with Martin), so that they could similarly grade his contacts with animals and ensure that he did not encounter any frisky animals before he was ready for them. By the end of treatment, after ten weekly sessions, Martin was spontaneously approaching and patting small dogs at home. A follow-up interview six months later showed that Martin's improvement had been maintained. He was now happy with dogs and there was no difficulty in going out for walks. The only times he appeared at all afraid were when suddenly and unexpectedly confronted with an unleashed dog (such as when one came up to him from behind). Because Martin was so terrified in the presence of dogs, the treatment was undertaken at the clinic, in this case by a psychologist. However, in other, milder cases the same procedure may be followed by the parents on advice from the clinic but without the need for the child himself to attend.

In other cases the phobia may be less circumscribed or there may be current causative factors which also require treatment. Ann was a ten year old referred to the clinic because she had refused to go to school since the start of the new term three months ago. She also complained of fears of the dark and was preoccupied with thoughts of death. The trouble started at the end of the previous term when Ann was reprimanded for talking to her very close friend. The teacher decided to separate the girls and Ann had to sit next to a boy she did not like. The following day Ann was fearful and anxious but went to school when her friend arrived to collect her. She then developed tonsilitis and was off school for the last three days of term. When school re-opened at the beginning of the next term, Ann was very upset, cried, hid behind the furniture and refused to go. She complained of dizziness and tummy pains and was kept off school. The next morning the same happened, but mother took Ann to school. On arrival she ran home. This happened for four more days and then mother got Ann to stay at school. A few hours later she was sent home by the teacher because she complained of pains. The family doctor advised that she be kept off school and for the remainder of term she was at home, well and happy, playing contentedly with a younger child who lived next door. She played out in the streets with her friend without anxiety, but as soon as

school was mentioned she burst into tears and complained of dizziness and tummy pains. While off school she began later to have
difficulty sleeping and she worried that her tummy-aches meant that
she would have to go into hospital and might die.

Until age five years Ann had been an unusually clinging child, but
she settled early at school and there were no difficulties in separation. A year later mother became depressed and father left home
for a while. Ann coped well with this situation as she did also with
the stresses two years later when her father was very seriously ill
with a bowel infection. Ann's development was normal and she got
on well at school. However, she worried a good deal over maths
lessons and got very worked up over her homework. Although she
was a friendly, cheerful child, she was very dependent on her one
very close friend. At school the two girls were inseparable.

Mother was a rather tense, anxious woman who became low-
spirited just before her periods and who had had three episodes of
depression since Ann was born, the last being a year previously and
resulting in psychiatric treatment. She had a good, but rather close,
relationship with Ann. Father was a stubborn, tough, confident man
who was rather resentful of authority. He was very fond of Ann.
The marriage was now a happy one and there were plenty of joint
family activities. At interview Ann was rather tense and anxious but
talked freely. She expressed worries about arithmetic, saying that
she was below the standard of other children and could not cope
with the lessons.

The precipitating factor in Ann's school refusal was the
forced separation in class from her friend, and her worries
about arithmetic constituted a subsidiary contributory factor
(although testing showed that in fact she was not behind in her
attainments). There were features in the family background
(mother's depression, father's serious illness and the earlier
marital disharmony) which probably played a part in sensitizing
Ann to emotional difficulties, but they did not seem to be major
influences in the current situation. Ann showed some dependence on her mother and some separation anxiety, but these
were not marked features and she was able to separate in order
to play with her friends. The timing of the refusal and the
anxiety about school suggested that school factors were more
important. Her tummy-ache revived fears associated with her
father's illness, but these fears followed rather than preceded

the school refusal and so were thought to be secondary. She first attended the clinic at the start of a school holiday, so that just over two weeks were available before she had to return to school. During that time, contact was made with her class teacher who agreed that Ann might sit next to her friend again. The psychologist gave Ann intensive remedial teaching in mathematics which resulted in a marked upsurge in confidence and a demonstrable increase in her skills. She learned how to do money multiplications and simple fractions, realized that she could do all that was required and, after four sessions with the psychologist whom she obviously liked, she was actually enjoying doing sums. Ann was given sleeping pills for a few nights to re-establish her sleep patterns and the social worker saw mother both to help her cope with her anxieties over Ann and to work out the best ways of dealing with Ann when she became afraid and upset on school mornings. Two weeks later she returned to school, being taken by mother and being greeted by her class teacher (whom she had had for the last two years and whom she liked). She came home for lunch to begin with and was taken back to school by her mother each afternoon. Ann again sat next to her friend and rapidly settled at school without difficulties. On school mornings over the next two months she occasionally had abdominal pains, but these were given little attention and never stopped her going to school. She attended the clinic three more times and was happy and animated. A follow-up a year later showed that there had been no further difficulties.

With both Martin and Ann the problems were quite circumscribed and response to treatment was marked, rapid and lasting. Of course this will not always be the case, even with isolated disorders. Elective mutism is a case in point, as illustrated by Brigitta's problems (see page 225). This is a much rarer disorder than either dog phobias or school refusal, but it is of interest because it is usually focused so specifically on the school situation and because it exemplifies another approach to treatment.

Elective mutism simply means that the child is able to speak but does so only in certain situations.[59] Most typically the child speaks normally at home and with his friends but does not speak at all at school. In mild degree this is quite common as a transient phenomenon with shy children when they first start school. In this new and anxiety-provoking situation they may not speak at all in class or will do so only in monosyllables or whispers. Gradually, as they get used to school and make friends, they relax and start speaking more without anything very special needing to be done. However, in a very few children this is a much more severe and lasting disorder, and youngsters may be referred to the clinic not ever having spoken at school over a period of several years. The children vary in personality, but most possess temperamental features which are abnormal in some respect. Some children are apathetic, morose, unprepossessing and withdrawn. Others are timid, anxious and fearful. Usually, but not always, there is an abnormally strong tie between the child and his mother, who is frequently anxious, dominating and overprotective. Elective mutism is an emotional disorder, but in some children there is also an underlying speech or language handicap which is important through giving rise to teasing and mockery. This played some part in Brigitta's mutism.

Brigitta was a nine year old referred because she had never talked at school after her first two months there, when she was teased about her foreign accent and slight difficulties in pronunciation. Individual psychotherapy at another clinic started in her second year at school and this continued for two years without influencing the situation. Then the parents invited her class teacher home on several occasions, hoping that this might help. It did to the extent that Brigitta would now talk to her teacher in the lunch break provided that they were alone. At home and outside school Brigitta talked normally and fluently. She was lively and popular with other children and never lacked companions. With her parents she was affectionate and easy to get along with. Most of the time she was cheerful and happy but her mood tended to have short swings both up and down. Both parents had been married before, the marriages ending in divorce. Mother had been treated for depression after the breakdown of her first marriage and the paternal grandmother had also had a 'nervous breakdown' in the past. In the first few years after Brigitta was born father was away a good deal and this was a difficult time for everyone. Family relationships seemed happy.

There was no evidence of separation anxiety and Brigitta was mute at school irrespective of her parents' presence or absence. She showed a high anxiety in the classroom but was not otherwise a particularly anxious child. Because of her mutism she got a lot of special privileges at school and also a lot of attention from teachers. She gestured when she needed to make her needs known and her mutism in no way interfered with her friendships. She was of good average intelligence and her scholastic attainments were up to standard.

The problem was one of elective mutism associated with a high level of specific anxiety in the classroom situation. It may have been precipitated by the teasing regarding her speech when she first started school, but it was unclear why this had led to such a marked withdrawal of speech. However it began, it seemed that the mutism was now being maintained by the advantages it brought her in terms of privileges and a means of avoiding stress, and by the fact that, surprisingly, it caused no disadvantages. Nothing was to be gained by searching around for the initial causes and it appeared preferable to focus specifically on the factors in the current situation which were serving to perpetuate the mutism. Accordingly it was decided to use a behavioural approach in which things should be organized to give maximum encouragement for speaking at school, in parallel with a withdrawal of the advantages which had accrued from the mutism. Because of the high anxiety, it would be necessary to ensure a very relaxing and supportive situation when she was first asked to speak. There were a series of meetings with the child, with the parents and with the school teacher to work out how to do this. The first aim was to get Brigitta sufficiently relaxed in the classroom to speak on her own with the teacher in the lunch break and then by encouragement and praise gradually to get her to speak more in other situations. A graduated approach was used, in which first one and then several children were introduced into the lunch-time conversations. In class she was only expected to say 'yes' to the morning register at first and then step by step she was encouraged to say more. Because Brigitta found whispering less stressful, she was allowed to begin speaking in whispers and only later was she asked to speak at normal volume.

In order to facilitate this process it was decided to institute a points system in which her class teacher would allocate a sliding scale of points, ranging from a small number for just saying 'yes' to the register to a much larger number for reading aloud in class. These points would then be exchanged by the parents for money, sweets, toys and the like. By the end of the first term on this regimen Brigitta was talking in class quite well. She would answer questions and would sometimes initiate requests or conversations. As she improved, the scale was gradually amended, so that she had to talk more in order to earn her points. She stayed to school lunches for the first time, was able to read aloud in class and planned for the first time to have a birthday party. She remained self-conscious about her speech, but she was able to cope with her anxiety.

In this case the treatment programme deliberately ignored the causes of the disorder, which lay in the distant past, and instead focused on altering the contingencies in the current situation which influenced the use of speech. It was important that Brigitta wanted to speak and that she was freely brought into the planning of the programme. The main onus in treatment fell on Brigitta's class teacher who proved very adept at judging how hard to press Brigitta and when to let her be. This is a good example of how, when a problem occurs in one situation away from the clinic, it is important to take the treatment to the situation. Schools are not involved in cooperation with clinics often enough and teachers have a lot to give children with emotional and behavioural problems if they can be guided as to how to help.

Depression

In adolescents and adults depressive disorders are usually shown by misery and unhappiness together with loss of appetite, sleeplessness, social withdrawal, irritability, loss of interest and of concentration and frequently a preoccupation with physical complaints. In children before the age of puberty the same clinical picture may be seen but often the manifestations are less clear cut. Because of this, psychiatrists are still somewhat divided on the question of how often depression occurs in young children and how it is shown if it does not take the form characteristic of depression in adults. The relevant facts which might provide answers are rather thin upon the ground. Followup studies suggest that pre-pubertal children with emotional disorders do not often develop into adults with depression, which could argue that depression is less common in childhood. As already noted, suicide is exceedingly rare before puberty. This too might indicate that depression is less common, but also it might simply mean that children who are depressed have less resolve or less know-how to end their life. Some studies have suggested that many emotional disorders in childhood respond to antidepressants, but few studies of this kind have been undertaken and there are problems in their interpretation. If the limited evidence available is brought together,[157] it may be concluded that manic-depressive psychosis (a severe form of depression in adults which may swing into periods of abnormal excitement and elevation of mood) is decidedly uncommon before puberty. More ordinary varieties of depressive disorder certainly occur in children, but they are probably less common before puberty than they are during adolescence or adult life. When they occur, depressive disorders in young children tend to differ from those in adult life in being more tied to specific situations, in being more transient, and in having less often the features of loss of weight and a general slowing of physical activities. Symptoms of misery and unhappiness, however, are very common in childhood as part of other kinds of disorders – of both an emotional and a conduct type.

As in adults, genetic factors play a significant role in aetiology, but environmental factors are also very important. The breaking of a close bond or relationship seems to be a particularly important precipitant of depression.[156] This may act at the time by leading to an immediate depression, but also it may act later when anniversaries or the like serve to revive the memories of the loss. For example, this was apparent with one socially withdrawn adolescent boy who had to be admitted to hospital with a quite severe depressive disorder following his father's sudden death. He recovered within about two months, but the next year in the week preceding the anniversary of his father's death he again became increasingly depressed and agitated and treatment was again urgently required. On the second anniversary of his father's death he was slightly depressed for a few weeks but soon recovered.

Not all children with depression require antidepressant medication and, when drugs are given, some form of psychotherapy is usually needed in addition, to deal with the environmental stresses causing the depression. This was so, for example, with Barbara.

Barbara, a teenager, was seen at the clinic after being sent home from boarding school because she had become extremely emotionally upset. About nine months earlier she had broken off with a long-standing friend, with much resulting distress. Shortly after this she started sleeping poorly, lost her appetite and began to feel worried and depressed. She felt she had some physical illness and was only partially reassured when medical examinations and tests showed no abnormality. She thought she was losing the power in her legs and had to keep checking that she could move them. By the end of term she was improved, although not back to her usual self. The next term passed fairly uneventfully, although she remained periodically worried and low spirited, particularly when she thought about her friend. During the spring holidays the feelings of depression built up again. At Easter she started to feel very guilty and got thoughts that something terrible would happen if she did not do certain things. She started praying and felt that she must make amends for past peccadilloes. Also she began to worry about eating meat on Fridays. She started compulsively checking that she had done things and at times had to keep touching leaves or wood to prevent disaster occurring. She recognized that this was silly but felt under pressure to do it. She felt that she was a bad person and blamed herself for all sorts of actions. At the same time she was aware that this was foolish and unnecessary, but the moods still occurred. Sometimes Barbara felt that she could not carry on any longer and she thought of taking sleeping tablets. During this time she continued to put on a fairly convincing social front. She wanted to confide her feelings to her family, but this was difficult at the time because of family visitors. She worried about returning to school and thought she would never have friends again (although in fact she had plenty of friends). The first week or so of term passed, but then the thoughts and compulsions increased once more as she became more depressed. Things came to a head with two very disturbed nights in which she was obsessed with thoughts of heaven and hell, and was preoccupied with the thought that, if she could not sort out her thoughts, God might never forgive her. When interviewed at the clinic Barbara was anxious, tense and full of indecision, self-doubt and self-deprecation. Nevertheless she talked easily and frankly and was evidently a girl of superior intelligence.

Barbara had had no previous episodes of emotional difficulties apart from a short period at age eight years when she became very worried. She was a highly conscientious girl, always thoughtful, helpful and well liked but also rather possessive and insecure in her close friendships, in spite of a generally ebullient and outgoing nature. The family was a generally happy one, but there had been a lot of worries about Barbara's older sister who had been physically and mentally handicapped since infancy. Mother worried a great deal over the sister and at the time of Barbara's emotional difficulties she had been under some strain. Mother invested a lot of herself in Barbara and when Barbara became depressed mother became somewhat overinvolved and her own feelings of anxiety, guilt and tension about her depressed daughter were very evident. Some years ago mother herself had had a depressive disorder necessitating treatment.

Barbara had a depressive disorder with some secondary obsessional features as shown in the ruminations about God and in the compulsions to touch things. Her accompanying loss of weight and difficulty in sleeping were characteristic of depression, especially in adolescence and adult life. The hypochondriacal fears about having some physical illness and the feelings of guilt and self-blame were also typical of depressive disorders. Barbara's turning to prayer and the guilt over eating meat on Fridays were part of the religious preoccupations that sometimes accompany depression. In her case this was probably intensified by the fact that the family were active Catholics, although Barbara herself had not previously been very religious. Depression tends to run in families to some extent and it may be that genetic factors were important in making Barbara vulnerable to depression. However, the immediate precipitants lay in the environment. As already noted, several studies have shown that depression is particularly likely to occur after the breaking of some close relationship. This is most obvious in terms of grief reactions following bereavement, but it may also be seen with respect to people who lose friends or relations by moving house to another part of the country. In Barbara's case the break-up of the long-standing friendship with another girl undoubtedly played a part in the onset of the depression. This was particularly stressful because of Barbara's tendency to develop possessive, all-encompassing friendships. In addition mother's own tensions were high at the time and these markedly increased when she first found out about Barbara's difficulties during the Easter vacation. The intense interaction with a very anxious mother probably had some effect in prolonging the depression once it had started. The onset of puberty and the normal strains of adolescence are thought to increase the risk of emotional disorders, and these too played a part in the genesis of Barbara's disorder.

One of the features of depressive disorders is that a point is reached when they tend to become self-perpetuating, even though the cause is an environmental stress. This stage had been reached with Barbara and it was necessary to prescribe antidepressant medication. When first seen she was in no state to be at school, so she was advised to remain at home. However, although antidepressants could be expected to relieve the symptoms, they would not affect the girl's problems about friendship or about the overintense interaction with her anxious mother. Accordingly Barbara was seen for weekly psychotherapy by one therapist and her parents were seen by another. During the next four weeks Barbara gradually improved and soon she was able to return to school. Mother was very much aware of the importance of what was happening in the family in terms of her involvement with Barbara and her high expectations of the girl (increased because of her other handicapped daughter). She was able to modify her behaviour to some extent and tensions relaxed at home, although the moods of mother and of Barbara still tended to fluctuate and interact. Barbara got a new close friend at school, which helped, but this was a less possessive relationship and part of a wider circle of friends. Appointments with Barbara and mother became less frequent after the first two months and antidepressants were stopped five months after Barbara was first seen. A year later she remained well. There were some minor tensions and uncertainties both at school and at home, but Barbara was coping well with these and there were no signs of depression.

Other emotional disorders

Emotional disorders may take a variety of other forms. These include obsessive-compulsive states, 'hysterical' conversion reactions and hypochondriasis. Obsessive-compulsive states are those in which compulsive actions or thoughts, usually recognized by the patient as unreasonable and resisted by him, constitute the most prominent symptoms.[89] In mild degree these were present with Barbara who kept ruminating in an obsessive manner about God, heaven and hell, thoughts which kept coming into her mind and would not go away. Barbara's ruminations were part of a depressive disorder and, perhaps because of this, her thoughts centred around major issues involving life and death. However, the ruminations often concern much more mundane topics, such as with an eight-year-old boy who was handicapped by recurrent thoughts about an old rusty pram that he had seen in the street on his way to school. Throughout the day, whatever he was doing, he kept returning to thoughts about the pram – what was it doing there? whose pram had it been? how long had it been there? etc. – in an endlessly revolving stream. Frequently these obsessive thoughts are linked to compulsive action as with Barbara who had to keep touching leaves, wood and other objects to prevent disasters. In a more severe form this was evident with Toby – the boy discussed in chapter 1 who had to wash his hands thirty times a day for fear of germs and uncleanliness.

With adults the compulsions are usually limited to the individual himself, but with children the acts often involve the rest of the family. For example, with Robin the compulsions consisted of his asking a fixed series of stereotyped questions to which his father had to give a set of predetermined replies. If he refused, Robin would go into a rising crescendo of panic and anger, so that the father would eventually capitulate but feel resentful and angry in doing so. In the case of Terence his life and that of his family centred around the problem of ensuring that no 'dirt' from school ever passed into his bedroom. There had to be a complete change of clothes on returning from school before he would enter the room and if he, or anyone else, touched any school books they would have to wash immediately before doing anything else. However the obsessions arise, one effect is that they come to be a means of controlling the rest of the family. When that happens, the very 'reward' of the control brought by the obsessions tends to prolong the disorder and treatment may have to focus on altering the family response to the child's behaviour.

The exact origins of obsessional symptomatology are uncertain. Psychoanalytic theory has it that all neuroses are due to excessive anxiety and that the symptoms are manifestations of that anxiety, the anxiety having been transformed, as it were, by one or other of the various psychological defence mechanisms (repression, projection, displacement, reaction formation, etc.). Clearly there is something in this view. The mechanisms do exist, and symptoms often are a consequence of anxiety. The problem arises from the very universality of the explanation. It has been said that 'anxiety is the most pervasive but the least perspicuous of concepts'. By explaining everything, in effect it comes to explain nothing. The same applies to the psychological defence mechanisms. They are important in that it is necessary to recognize them if there is to be a proper understanding of people's feelings and of interpersonal interactions. Thus, when a child says he is afraid of school, this may constitute a fear of something else which has been *displaced*. Or, when a child is angry with his parents, he may kick the dog or the furniture. He is not allowed to be aggressive to his parents so the aggression is displaced. Exactly comparable phenomena may be seen in animals where they are usually called 're-directed' activities. Worries may be *denied*, as by the girl who says 'I'm not afraid,' when she is quaking with apprehension. Alternatively the feelings may be *repressed* so that they do not reach conscious awareness. Someone who feels hate for his child may be so upset by this thought that he will repress it. The thought is still there in the mind and may come out in dreams or in other ways, but it is not consciously recognized for what it is. Sometimes a person may compensate for these unpleasant feelings by behaving in the opposite way – *reaction formation.* In chapter 4 we saw how maternal hostility might sometimes appear in the form of compensatory oversolicitude, an example of this mechanism. *Rationalization* is the finding of reasons which allow one to do something which really occurs for some other reason. *Withdrawal* is simply not entering the situation which causes pain or distress. *Regression* is behaving in a way more appropriate to an earlier stage of development, as when a young child reverts to the bottle or to thumb-sucking at times of stress. *Projection* is another common mechanism, which refers to what happens when the undesirable thought or action is attributed to someone else. Thus a child who feels angry with his father may project these feelings on to the father in thinking that his father is being hostile and punitive towards him.

Of course, before it is claimed that one of these mechanisms is operative, it is necessary to obtain evidence that this is the case. It may be that the child really is afraid of school or is angry with the dog, that the mother's solicitude is due to love not hostility and that the father truly is punitive. Other behaviour will usually provide the clue as to the true state of affairs.

However, all of us use defence mechanisms, so that their existence is *not* an indication of any kind of disorder. Also, although some mechanisms may be more adaptive than others, the type of defence mechanisms employed is of very little diagnostic or prognostic importance. All these considerations mean that attention must be paid to possible defence mechanisms if there is to be a proper understanding of what is happening, but not much significance should be attached to which mechanism is being employed.

To return to obsessional states, it appears that the compulsions are sometimes a means of coping with excessive anxiety, a means which rapidly turns into a vicious circle, in that anxiety is attached to a concern to slavishly complete each compulsive action properly. Also, the obsessive thoughts may be a response to feelings or wishes which have been repressed as unacceptable. In some cases the obsession arises through repressed aggressive or sexual thoughts.

As with other emotional disorders, the treatment needs to be focused both on the underlying problems (when they exist) and on removal of the symptoms. Individual psychotherapy may be needed to help the child come to terms with his anxieties and to find more adaptive solutions to his problems. Attention will also need to be paid to whatever family difficulties there are. Children with obsessive disorders often come from rather perfectionist families with rather rigid and restricting patterns of upbringing, but there is no consistent pattern of family interaction. When the obsessions are secondary to a more widespread anxiety state or depression (as with Barbara), it is usually best to deal with the main emotional disorder and as that improves so usually will the obsessive symptoms. However, it may sometimes be necessary to find ways of directly influencing the symptoms, and here a wide range of behavioural techniques are available (see chapter 9).

'Hysterical' conversion reactions are disorders in which physical symptoms (other than those involving the autonomic nervous system) arise on a psychological basis.[32] The word 'conversion' implies that anxieties have been converted into physical symptoms and traditionally there is supposed to be an emotional indifference. In fact, although there is often an inappropriate indifference to the physical symptoms, most children with 'hysterical' conversion reactions also show considerable anxiety, and often also misery. While it is usually true that the reaction is a response to anxiety, it is misleading to suppose that that disposes of the anxiety. The physical symptoms can take many forms including paralyses, limps, blindness, a loss of sensation and an inability to swallow. The onset is usually, but not always, fairly sudden and a slow progression of symptoms over many months is so unusual as always to make one suspect physical disease. In fact, studies of children diagnosed as having 'hysterical' conversion reactions show that as many as half may have organic diseases which have been missed, so that the diagnosis needs to be made with great caution. While conversion reactions often develop following some stress situation, this is also true of some physical disorders, so that it is an unreliable diagnostic pointer. Usually the conversion symptoms directly serve a psychological purpose, in that they act as means of avoiding some stress or of obtaining some reward, quite apart from acting as response to anxiety. While this is a useful diagnostic point, it has to be borne in mind that children may also use organic disease in the same way.

In some cases the conversion symptom is the only indication of psychiatric disorder, but often the symptom is merely part of a more widespread disorder. This was so, for example, with Malcolm.

Malcolm was referred to the clinic at twelve with paralysis and pain in one arm, which had occurred after he received an injection. He complained bitterly about his arm and a month later developed paralysis of a leg. Repeated hospital investigations showed no physical cause. Malcolm was irritable, aggressive, anxious and demanding and mother gave up her job to devote herself to caring for him full time while he remained in bed. Often he cried all night. He would not allow his arm or leg to be touched and both became very dirty with very long nails. He swore at and threatened first his mother, and later his therapist. Malcolm had been difficult in his behaviour from the time he started school. He was frequently away from school because of tummy-aches and mother was forever writing notes of excuse for him. He had various fears and, when mother was admitted to hospital with back pain (later thought to be 'hysterical'), he kept rushing out into the garden screaming. Malcolm had always been moody and determined and his parents usually gave in to him. He was very close to his mother and had been very 'spoiled' by both parents.

Father was a taciturn, morose man who had been orphaned when young and had had an unhappy childhood. Mother had suffered from a host of physical complaints since Malcolm's birth and had had seven surgical operations. A year before Malcolm's referral to the clinic she had had psychiatric treatment for a disorder characteristic of depression, 'hysterical' back pain and feelings that people were against her. The marriage was an unhappy one and there were frequent rows. There were four much older sisters who were adults and had left home. The housing conditions were very poor.

Psychotherapeutic treatment was started on an out-patient basis but it soon became clear that admission would be needed. When in hospital Malcolm talked to his therapist about the family rows and about his anxieties. His mother was seen by the social worker in order to deal with some of these problems, but she rarely turned up for the appointments offered. Within a month of admission the paralyses had gone, but Malcolm remained depressed and anxious. Later he became aggressive and destructive in the ward and for a while was a very disruptive influence. After nine months in hospital he was discharged to a special boarding school as his behaviour remained disturbed and the family difficulties had not been resolved. The next school holiday he was much improved but later in the year mother removed him from school against advice. There were no further episodes of conversion symptoms but he remained a difficult boy and the family relationships continued disturbed.

Malcolm's paralysis merely constituted an acute dramatic episode in a much longer history of emotional, and later conduct, disturbance. The disturbed family situation was undoubtedly important in the development of Malcolm's disorder, and the specifically conversion symptoms also had their roots in the home. From early childhood Malcolm had learned that he could avoid stressful situations by means of physical symptoms and all his life he had controlled his family through the use of one symptom or another. Mother, to whom he was very close, presented a model of 'hysterical' conversion symptoms in terms of her disorder a year earlier and also the multiple physical complaints which gave rise to repeated operations. The injection was the immediate precipitant of the paralysis but was otherwise not very important. Once having developed the paralysis, Malcolm very soon discovered that this was a very potent source of power in the home. In fact it was so much so that mother gave up her job to nurse him at home. The disorder had its origins in emotional disturbance, but it also brought about psychological gain, as is typical of 'hysterical' conversion reactions. Psychotherapy, plus the total change of situation implied in admission to hospital, rapidly relieved the conversion symptoms, but it was less successful in dealing with the other aspects of Malcolm's disorder.

In Malcolm's case the 'hysterical' conversion reaction constituted a psychiatric disorder in an individual child. These disorders are equally common in boys and in girls. However, there is another variety, called 'epidemic hysteria' which is very much commoner in girls.[8] Characteristically this occurs in a closed community of some kind such as a girls' boarding school. What happens is that one girl develops 'hysterical' fainting attacks or convulsions, then another does so and soon the 'hysteria' spreads through the community to involve many girls. The girls who first show the 'hysterical' conversion symptoms are often severely disturbed individuals, but this is less often the case with later-affected girls who may be quite ordinary, but perhaps rather dependent, youngsters. The spread of the disorder is to be sought in the social milieu as much as in the personality features of the individuals.

Hypochondriasis consists of physically unjustified or exaggerated complaints. Most of these consist of headaches, stomach-aches and back-aches. These pains often arise in the first instance as the somatic aspects of anxiety. (Of course most children have stomach-aches or headaches of this kind at some time or another and they would only be regarded as indicative of disorder if severe, persistent and associated with social impairment.) As part of anxiety there is usually muscular tension (which may cause pain) and also a variety of symptoms pertaining to the autonomic nervous system, including nausea, diarrhoea and frequency of passing urine. This very readily becomes part of a learned pattern of behaviour which serves as a means of either avoiding stress or gaining attention or both. Thus the child may learn that stomach-aches can be used to avoid school or that headaches bring attention, comfort and sympathy from mother. The mechanisms are thereby similar to those in conversion symptoms, but the disorder is much nearer to the reality situation and hence is usually more easily treated. Most children have little difficulty in talking about their emotional problems and in seeing the connection between these and the physical symptoms. Treatment consists of dealing with the stresses which gave rise to the disorder and in helping the child find better ways of dealing with stresses. It is also very important that the parents learn *not* to give undue attention to the child's physical complaints, so that they no longer serve to gain attention.

Frequently, there is a family pattern of hypochondriasis, so that one or other of the parents also tends to react to stress with physical complaints. Often too the parents have been unduly fussy and protective when the child has been ill. In many cases the child's hypochondriasis develops against a background of misery and unhappiness or of overt depression.

7 Aggression, Overactivity and Delinquency

Conduct disorders are conditions in which the main problem lies in socially disapproved behaviour. This behaviour may take many forms but would include troubles in getting along with other children as shown by fighting and bullying, other non-delinquent activities such as aggression, defiance, destructiveness and lying, and finally delinquent acts such as stealing, playing truant, arson and serious mischief involving damage to other people's property. There are important links between these various behaviours, so that children who are aggressive and bullying in their early school years are quite likely to become delinquent when they are older. In terms of causation, associated disabilities and prognosis, children with conduct disorders do have quite a lot in common with one another but, as we shall see, it is a far from homogeneous group of disorders.

The most immediately obvious feature is that conduct disorders are very much more frequent in boys than they are in girls. This is particularly so with delinquency, where male delinquents outnumber female delinquents in a ratio of up to ten to one.[194] However, a male preponderance is also evident with non-delinquent disorders of conduct.[166] The preponderance is less but the ratio is still about three to one.

Isolated delinquent acts are exceedingly common and are of relatively little significance. Even among delinquent youngsters brought to Court, half are never re-convicted. Many of these lads are essentially normal and do not have a conduct disorder in the sense used in this chapter. However, the prognosis for an established conduct disorder is poor, particularly when the onset goes back to early childhood. In a classic study of children referred to American child-guidance clinics in the 1920s, Lee

Robins[140] followed their progress over a thirty-year period into middle adult life. She found that children referred to the clinic for antisocial behaviour had a generally poor outlook. Not only were they more often arrested and imprisoned as adults than were the control group of non-clinic children, but they also had more marital difficulties, poorer occupational and economic histories, more impoverished social relationships, poorer Armed Service records and a higher rate of excessive use of alcohol and to some extent even poorer physical health. Only one in six of the antisocial children was completely free of psychiatric disorder in adult life and over a quarter showed a sociopathic (psychopathic) personality disorder. This very poor outcome was most likely when the antisocial behaviour in childhood was both frequent and varied, and when it was shown outside the family and the child's own circle of friends. Children who developed into adults with a sociopathic personality disorder were more likely as children to have been aggressive towards strangers, towards authority figures and towards organizations. The prognosis was better for children who only stole from their family and for children who just played truant.

The Robins study referred to children attending child-guidance clinics many years ago in the United States and it should not necessarily be assumed that the findings apply exactly to children attending psychiatric clinics in England today. Also, of course, the findings should not be extended to the many delinquents who never get referred to psychiatrists. Nevertheless other studies[141] have confirmed the general pattern of outcome described by Robins and have suggested that the findings are probably applicable to English children today with conduct disorders. The prognosis for children with conduct disorders confined to the family or with isolated delinquent acts is better, but the outlook for those with serious and widespread antisocial disorders is very bleak, and much worse than that for youngsters with emotional disorders.

Many factors are known to be of importance in aetiology. Temperamentally many of the children are unusual from the outset in being impulsive, unpredictable and unmalleable. Aggressiveness and assertiveness are common and sometimes there

242 Aggression, Overactivity and Delinquency

appears to be a lack of feeling for others. Recent studies also suggest that aggressive boys tend to be less responsive than other boys to praise and encouragement.[125,126] Typically the children with persistent disorders come from families where there is discord and quarrelling; where affection is lacking; where discipline is inconsistent, ineffective and either extremely severe or lax; where the family has broken up through divorce or separation; or where the children have had periods of being placed 'in care' at times of family crisis.[130, 152, 156]

Children with conduct disorder are more likely than other children to come from very large families with at least four or five children. The precise reasons why such children should be especially at risk are uncertain, but they include the much increased rate of reading difficulties in children from large families, the greater problems of supervision when there are many children and the somewhat greater likelihood of family discord when the family is large. In addition several surveys have shown that large families are much more likely than others to live in poor-quality, overcrowded housing and to have financial difficulties.

One of the most consistent associations with conduct disorder is serious educational backwardness.[166] About a third of anti-social boys have specific reading difficulties (see chapter 8), a rate many times that in the general population. Again the reasons for this association are ill understood, but probably several mechanisms are at work. First, the temperamental characteristics which lead to conduct disorder are closely similar to those which predispose to reading problems. Second, the adverse family situations which put the child at risk for conduct disorder are often associated with those linked with reading difficulties. For example, large size is linked with both. Third, it seems that in some children the very fact of educational failure leads to disillusion and resentment which may go on to rebellion, aggression and delinquent behaviour.

Most children with conduct disorders are of normal intelligence, but there is some tendency for an IQ a little below average to be associated with an increased likelihood of aggressive, antisocial or delinquent behaviour. The same applies to brain damage. That is to say it increases the risk of conduct disorder but the association applies to only a minority of children. A few years ago there was much publicity attached to the finding that a particular chromosome abnormality (XYY) was associated with aggressive behaviour. Subsequent investigations have confirmed that the association exists but is not very strong. The vast majority of children with conduct disorders do *not* have any chromosome anomaly and most XYY individuals are not abnormally aggressive.[120]

In earlier chapters we saw that schools and geographical areas vary greatly in their rates of delinquency and of conduct disorders. There seems to be something about the *ethos* in schools or about the styles of teaching or discipline which may predispose a child towards or protect him from delinquency, but just what these influences are and how strong is their effect are still poorly understood.

Varieties of conduct disorder

As noted in chapter 1 (page 35), the main subdivision usually made within the overall group of conduct disorders is that between socialized delinquency and unsocialized, aggressive behaviour. The idea, first developed by Hewitt and Jenkins,[77] is that the socialized delinquent is not emotionally disturbed and that he is relatively well adjusted within his own delinquent groups of friends and relatives. Such children are typically supposed to come from large families in bad neighbourhoods where there is inadequate discipline and supervision and where the available models provided by the immediate family and peer group are of deviant and antisocial behaviour. Frequently the father is away from home and the boy lacks an adequate masculine pattern for identification as well as the training and controls provided by fathers. There is habitual truancy from school and much of the stealing is done together with other boys.

In contrast the unsocialized, aggressive child gets on badly with other children and has poor relationships in his family. He is negativistic, aggressive, defiant and vengeful. Many of the parents are hostile to their children and there is a pattern of quarrelling, lack of affection and rejection.

In essence, the idea is that the socialized delinquent has no psychiatric disorder as such. It is simply that he has acquired standards which are at odds with society at large although in keeping with those of his family and immediate peer group. The unsocialized, aggressive child, however, does have a psychiatric disorder, as shown by his emotional disturbance and poor inter-personal relationship. Furthermore his difficulties have arisen as a result of family stress and discord. There is something in this idea, but it is an oversimplification. Peter Scott[173] has pointed out that the socialized group really includes two sub-categories; those who have failed to acquire any consistent set of standards and those who have a well-developed set of standards which happen to run counter to those of most other people.

The youngsters without consistent values are said to come from disorganized families in which gross inconsistencies of dis-cipline prevail and in which the parents are unable to demon-strate self-control or firm standards of behaviour. The resulting delinquency starts early, is varied in kind, not usually de-structive or aggressive and consists largely of evasions of things unpleasant and a mixed pattern of stealing. Both Scott and Jenkins[86] agree that psychiatric treatment has little to offer this group. Nevertheless the youngsters do require help because they suffer from their lack of direction and lack of internal controls. They need an opportunity to gain their own coherent set of values and to learn responsibility. In the following case history we see how Andrew presented a pattern of behaviour of this kind, although in his case it was complicated by bed-wetting and some aggressiveness when he was younger. The fact that the picture is atypical underlines the point that the categories are neither pure nor mutually exclusive. They provide some guidance to the main features and likely mechanisms but in no sense should be regarded as discrete categories.

Andrew was referred at age thirteen years with a long history of delinquent behaviour. Playing truant started when he was six and became more frequent as he got older. When he was nine Andrew was taken to Court for this offence. His behaviour at school was disturbed and difficult and he was placed at a day school for mal-adjusted children. A year later he was suspended from this school for breaking things and was placed at another special school. At eleven he was first taken to Court for theft—on that occasion stealing from an empty shop. Stealing with other boys from shops and yards continued from then on. He lied freely and had a rather belligerent anti-authority attitude. Andrew was a generally friendly and amusing lad who had plenty of friends, most of whom were also delinquent, and also several girlfriends. He was keen on sport and was an out-standing athlete. However, he was quick-tempered, selfish and aggressive to boys outside his circle of friends.

His early development was normal and he gained bladder control by eighteen months of age. Then at age five he started wetting again after a frightening attack in which he was mauled by an Alsatian. His father, who died in a road accident just before Andrew was born, had been an aggressive man who drank and gambled heavily and was usually out of work. His mother was a rather immature woman who had been orphaned in middle childhood and married immediately she left school. She remarried when Andrew was two. The step-father was a rather intolerant, selfish man. He had a small business of his own. Andrew had two older brothers both of whom had a long history of delinquent behaviour involving theft, breaking and entering and damage to public property. The oldest brother was also a heavy gambler and both had severe difficulties in reading. The three younger sisters posed less of a problem but they were all quick tempered and one had great difficulties in reading. Andrew was found to be of normal intelli-gence, but even at fourteen his reading and arithmetic were only at the standard normally expected of a seven year old.

The disorder in this case was one of socialized delinquency. There were no marked emotional problems and, although Andrew was rather aggressive, he got on quite well with his own group of delinquent friends. There was a strong family pattern of delinquent behaviour and the family was a rather dis-organized one without adequate discipline and with no clear set of standards. The delinquency arose through a combination of a lack of normal controls, a 'couldn't care less' approach in the family and models of deviant anti-authority behaviour. Andrew's own anti-authority attitude was increased by his total lack of success at school resulting from his severe reading disability. The enuresis probably primarily developed as a result of the acute stress of being attacked by a dog. Psychiatric treatment had little to offer with his sort of problem. What was needed was better social learning, remedial instruction in reading and the fostering of an identification with pro-social goals. This was better provided by the special school which Andrew attended. He was seen again at sixteen, at the time he left school. Stealing with other boys had continued and he had shown no interest in school work, attainments having risen only to the standard of an eight year old. Nevertheless bed-wetting had stopped two years ago, relationships with his family remained close, he had a number of friends and was a socially mature young man. This is the sort of problem to which we have no very adequate answers at the moment. Andrew saw no reason to change, his family were mostly unconcerned and the difficulty lay largely in the fact that he broke the law by stealing and playing truant frequently and that he did not wish to learn at school. There were other disturbances, as shown by his bed-wetting, the tempers and aggressiveness, but in many respects Andrew was fairly well adjusted within his own delinquent group.

Jenkins's category of 'socialized delinquency' would also include Scott's category of individuals who have learned inappropriate standards. He gives the example of an adolescent, convicted of shooting a policeman, who came from a family with an anti-authority ethos, who had seen his father assault his school teacher and who, both at home and in his peer group, had been encouraged to actively resist authority. His attack on the policeman was a natural outcome of the pattern of behaviour he had been taught since early childhood. In this situation more acceptable standards and values need to be learned and this process should include the family as well as the youngster. This is a tall order and the results of treatment show only limited successes.

In the case of Scott's boy who shot a policeman, few people would doubt that his standards were inappropriate. However, clearly there are dangers in assuming that standards different from our own are thereby wrong. The fifteen year old attending a poor-quality school with overcrowded classes who plays truant because he feels schooling has nothing to offer him is breaking the law. But it may be that the fault lies in the education he is receiving rather than in his values. The university student who experiments with marijuana is also liable to prosecution, but he may well be conforming to his own peer-group culture. Of course, there are dangers in using marijuana (although how much they exceed those associated with alcohol remains uncertain) but it would be unwise to assume that the use of this drug is equivalent to the possession of 'wrong' standards. Social conformity in itself is not necessarily desirable and it may even be undesirable in some circumstances. For example, most of us would regard conformity to a racist culture as a bad thing. It is easy to assume that these issues do not arise in our own society, but they do. Unfortunately, serious inequities and adverse discrimination still exist and sometimes rebellion may be a healthy, even if troublesome, response. In these circumstances it is the situation which needs changing rather than the individual. In short, care is needed before we assume that someone else's standards are wrong because they are different, and non-conformity can never be used as an indicator of psychiatric disorder.

Sometimes, children referred to psychiatrists show an uncomplicated picture of delinquent behaviour which is in keeping with sub-cultural norms, but among clinic children the more usual pattern is one where the child and family also show more generalized disturbance. Treatment is even more difficult in these circumstances. Maurice is a case in point.

Maurice was referred to the clinic at thirteen, although his behaviour had been disturbed from at least seven and he had been seen at another clinic when he was nine. He had no friends at school and would accuse other children of talking behind his back. There were frequent fights and Maurice attacked other children regardless of their size. His school essays were mainly about violence and horror and he was disobedient and defiant both at school and at home. Although he was of average intelligence, his school work was poor. When the boy was referred to the other clinic at nine, his father was extremely critical of everything that was suggested and would not cooperate in any form of treatment. During the next few years Maurice's tantrums and nagging got worse and worse and his parents, who at first refused to recognize that the boy had any problems, began to be concerned. Maurice was openly hostile to both of them and on occasions he hit his father. His school attendance was very poor. There was nothing unusual about Maurice's early development, but he had always been a rather cold and remote boy who did not make relationships at all easily. Father was intelligent and cheerful but had always been suspicious and hostile towards schools, clinics and all kinds of authority. He repeatedly used the threat of writing to his Member of Parliament as a way of dealing with all difficulties. Father had sent several letters both abusive and apologetic regarding Maurice's behaviour and in spite of many requests had always refused to see the headmaster about Maurice's problems at school. Mother was a thin, anxious, rather depressed woman, very subservient to her husband. The parents had no friends and virtually never went out together. At interview Maurice did not establish rapport at all easily, he was anxious and rarely smiled, and complained that teachers and children picked on him.

Father provided a strong model of anti-authority behaviour and for many years he had regarded his son's behaviour as entirely normal, although everyone else considered the boy severely disturbed. Undoubtedly this had had a strong influence on Maurice's behaviour. On the other hand it was also evident that he had been a rather odd boy from the outset and his personality was clearly abnormal at the time of his referral to the clinic. The reasons for the abnormal personality development were obscure. As the immediate problem seemed to reside in the abnormal family interactions, conjoint family interviews were started. Maurice dominated these with long monologues of complaint against his parents which resulted in his father losing his temper and his mother crying. It did not prove possible to alter this pattern and finally family sessions were discontinued and replaced by individual psychotherapy with the boy and casework with the parents. His behaviour at school deteriorated and he was finally excluded. A place at a boarding school was sought but none was available. He stole from local shops and boasted of this, claiming that it was justified because the shopkeepers overcharged. Nine months after his referral to the clinic he presented himself at the local Police Station, asking to be taken away from home because he was unhappy there. Eventually a place at a boarding school for maladjusted boys was obtained. Maurice settled well at first but soon complained of being bullied. Father was openly contemptuous of the school and frequently criticized it when speaking to his son. After a few months Maurice's behaviour at school got worse, he felt everyone was against him and, after an episode in which he ran amok in a local store causing considerable breakages, he was again excluded from school. At home his behaviour continued to be as difficult as it had been at school and there were frequent clashes between father and son. He was admitted to a psychiatric hospital and improved somewhat on tranquillizers. When last seen at age nineteen years he still felt people were against him and he was a belligerent, touchy, difficult individual in frequent altercations with other people. Maurice's disorders ended in a severely abnormal personality. The origins of this were never very clear and the early abnormalities in temperament suggested the possibility of genetic factors. Certainly father's personality was decidedly odd, although he functioned much better than his son in most ways and held a steady job. Father's anti-authority attitude provided a model of deviant behaviour, but neither that nor the anxious subservient mother were sufficient to account for Maurice's abnormalities in environmental terms. Although genetic factors are of less importance with respect to minor delinquencies, they are probably more important in the case of personality disorders.

Scott also uses a category of maladaptive, self-destructive behaviour to describe a persistent pattern of antisocial behaviour which resists training and psychotherapy and in which the youngster seems bent upon seeking punishment. Closer study usually shows that in fact the boy tries to avoid punishment, but his behaviour is so disturbed and maladaptive that detection and punishment almost invariably follow. This sort of behaviour is said to be most likely to occur when there is repeated frustration, excessive punishment, and an inability to escape from the situation. The family is often an unhappy one with discord and rejection but also punitiveness, inconsistency and a capricious inability to take a firm line on what is expected of the child. This category has something in common with Jenkins's 'unsocialized aggression'. Treatment methods for this type of conduct disorder are most unsatisfactory. It would seem reasonable to try to provide better family relationships, to reduce frustrations and to ensure a more consistent and reasonable pattern of discipline. In practice this is usually very difficult to achieve, partly because in many cases the family is not very concerned to change the situation or at least is not prepared to make the major adjustments necessary.

Brian was first referred at ten for increasingly aggressive behaviour, disobedience, defiance and some episodes of stealing both from home and school. For several years there had been frequent tantrums, restlessness and persistent disobedience. His relationship with his mother had been poor for a long time and the immediate episode that led to referral was Brian's throwing a bucket of cold water over her when she was lying in bed. She was furious and chased him all over the house beating him with a broom. Brian was not doing very well at school and, although he had a few friends, he tended to chop and change in his friendships, getting into frequent fights. On one occasion he deliberately wet the floor at school in defiance of the teacher. His father left his mother following long-standing marital discord when Brian was aged five. His mother had not remarried but there had been several liaisons, one of which involved cohabitation. Mother had had several depressive episodes and twice had had psychiatric treatment. When well she tended to be rather indulgent, although inconsistent, but she did not like Brian and tended to complain about him. When depressed she became more irritable and would frequently beat Brian in temper (which she occasionally also did at other times). At age three years Brian spent six months in a children's home when his mother was ill, and at age eight years he spent some weeks with his older sister for the same reason. He complained he was badly treated and moved to stay with his older brother until his mother returned. Brian's sister (who was in her mid-twenties) had been in frequent trouble when younger for stealing and playing truant and had spent several years in a Borstal. She used to throw crockery at her mother whom she disliked. After she left home she went from job to job and then made an unhappy marriage. The older brother had never been delinquent, but he was rather aggressive when a boy and was now often unemployed.

Brian had known only unhappy family relationships and he was the target of much of his mother's irritation and violence, especially when she was depressed. The pattern of discipline in the home was extremely inconsistent and Brian never knew what response his behaviour would evoke. Brian saw the psychiatrist, and his mother was seen by the social worker who tried to help her understand what was happening in the family and to alter her ways of dealing with Brian. Things improved at home and, although Brian remained a difficult, isolated, belligerent boy, there was no more stealing and no more episodes of marked aggression while he was attending the clinic. The family ceased attending after a few months.

Conduct disorders needing psychiatric treatment

All the cases referred to so far in this chapter have been ones in which psychiatric treatment has had relatively little to offer. However, this is not true of all conduct disorders and the need for psychiatric treatment is particularly indicated where the antisocial behaviour has developed as a response to some type of emotional disturbance or where the behaviour seems to have come about as a maladaptive means of coping with some personal problem or difficulty. In these cases the child has learned that some behaviour reduces anxiety or tension or relieves anger. A psychotherapeutic approach may then be employed. After the child's confidence has been gained, he may be helped to develop insight, in order to encourage him to find better ways of coping with stress. Alternatively, a behavioural approach may be employed to shape the child's behaviour away from the antisocial and towards a more acceptable and more adaptive solution. Mary and Sandra are examples of children with whom a psychotherapeutic approach was followed and Donald is one with whom behavioural methods were employed (see below).

Either way it is necessary to determine what purpose the behaviour is serving and what environmental circumstances are influencing the behaviour. A functional analysis as described in the first chapter needs to be undertaken to discover the particular characteristics of the disorder in each child. The possible alternatives are many. This may be illustrated by stealing. As already noted, stealing may be just acquisitive behaviour or it may reflect a lack of sense of property rights. However, it may also serve other purposes. For example, in Evelyn's case stealing was used to buy friendships. She was a rather pathetic girl who was not very popular with other children. When she had some sweets she found that giving them out served to attract other children, at least in the short term. She then began to steal sweets and other small items from local shops which she freely distributed at school in an attempt to gain popularity. Stealing cars to take 'joy-rides' is a popular pastime among certain groups of adolescents in big cities. The motivations are varied, but in some cases the main purpose seems to be an attempt to prove masculinity. The cars are not kept but are just abandoned after they have been raced around for a while.

In other cases stealing may constitute a highly specific act of protest, as it did with Mary.

Mary was seen at age twelve because she had been stealing from home. For the last year she had repeatedly stolen from her stepmother's purse, had taken her mother's collection of coins and had extracted money from a charity box kept by her parents. In addition she 'stole' sweets and fruit in the home which she was not allowed to eat without permission. There had been no stealing from outside the home, but she had stolen from father on one occasion and from her brother on one other. She appeared tense before the thefts took place but relieved and more relaxed afterwards. When confronted she was giggly. There were clashes with her parents but no other difficulties apart from occasional bed-wetting. She had wet from infancy but was now dry for months at a time. She was popular with other children and got on well with them. There were no problems at school and she was well liked by adults. Her moods went up and down but she was quick to recover after arguments.

Mary's early development was normal and she was an easy, responsive child. When she was seven years old her mother had an affair. For about a year after that there were quarrels between the parents over this and the mother left home to live with the other man whom she subsequently married. Mary stayed with her

mother's parents for several months, returned to her father and
then went to live with some family friends where she remained for
over two years. She was very happy there and father visited regularly. When father said he was going to remarry, Mary became
distressed and rather rebellious. She returned home after the marriage and it was a few months later that the stealing began. Father
was a shopkeeper, a reasonable man who was fond of Mary and
showed affection for her. He had had a lot of illness as a child and
was not a very assertive person. Stepmother had been a nurse and
this marriage, at the age of thirty-five years, was her first. She was a
tense, religious, rather rigid woman with very strict standards.
Mother was easily embarrassed by any talk of sex and she would
never mention or discuss her husband's first wife. She had very
much wanted to get on with Mary but was quite unprepared for
Mary's resentment of her and did not know how to cope with the
situation. She responded by imposing strict discipline and at the
time of referral all doors in the house were locked. While her standards were rather strict by any comparison, they stood out in stark
contrast to the free-and-easy style of living Mary had been used to
before her return to the family. Mother became quite depressed
over the difficulties with Mary and was put on antidepressants by
her family doctor. Father was torn between his loyalties to his
second wife and those to his daughter. Mary was a pleasant, chatty
adolescent who freely admitted her thefts. She wanted to remain
with her father and stepmother but said she had been lonely and
unhappy since her return.

Mary was getting on well outside the family and there could
be no doubt that the stealing (which was entirely restricted to
the home and was almost entirely from the stepmother) was her
way of expressing her resentment against her stepmother. The
stepmother had little understanding of children and completely
failed to appreciate that it would take time for Mary to adapt to
the new family situation and that she would have to earn
Mary's love and respect. Although Mary no longer had any
contact with her biological mother she was still fond of her and
resented her stepmother's dismissal of her as a 'bad woman'.
Further difficulties stemmed from the pattern of discipline imposed by stepmother which was quite different from that to
which Mary was accustomed. Mary was seen by the social
worker for weekly individual psychotherapy. At first Mary said

little, but gradually she relaxed and clearly enjoyed having an older woman whom she could trust and respect. She was encouraged to discuss her feelings about her father's new marriage and her return home. She was also helped to see that stepmother too was feeling insecure and uncertain and that it was necessary for Mary to meet her half-way. The psychiatrist saw father and stepmother together and helped them appreciate Mary's needs in the situation. Stepmother was able to relax discipline a little and was encouraged by Mary's greater responsiveness and friendliness to her. Gradually over the months the family situation improved, there was no more stealing and Mary and stepmother learned to get on with each other. A year later Mary was getting on well and there were no further problems, although stepmother was still somewhat depressed and uncertain in her role.

In Mary's case the antisocial behaviour was sharply focused. But sometimes antisocial behaviour may be an ill-coordinated hitting-out by a youngster in deep emotional distress. This was true, for example, of Michael.

Michael was thirteen years old when his mother died after a painful terminal illness. Michael became severely depressed and withdrew from all social contacts. In the evenings he used to pace around the house or go out for walks. He expressed great anger against the injustice of his mother dying at so early an age and spoke bitterly of God and of the Church. On one of his evening walks he knocked impulsively at the door of a house of a complete stranger. When a woman came to the door Michael hit out at her in unprovoked rage. He was brought to the clinic as an emergency.

Michael was suffering from a severe grief reaction following his bereavement. The aggression arose directly from this depression and did not need treatment in its own right. He had never been aggressive before and therapy was directed at relieving his depression and helping him work through his grief.

In other youngsters the socially disapproved behaviour may be a means of establishing a personal identity through rebellion. During adolescence boys and girls go through a period in which they still feel dependent on their parents but also need to assert their own individuality. In most cases this process occurs without interrupting good family relationships, although parent–child relationships alter in character, and without any behavioural disturbance. The task of developing a personal identity distinct from family standards is an important one for young people, but one generally accomplished without undue distress. However, the process may be much more troublesome when communication in the family is poor and the parents find it difficult to give support to the youngster. This was the situation with Sandra.

Sandra was referred at age fourteen because of rebellious behaviour, staying out late at night, mixing with undesirable people, promiscuity, occasional truancy, episodes of drunkenness and one occasion when she swallowed a large number of aspirins feeling that she did not care whether she lived or died. She was also falling behind in her school work. Sandra had got on very well at her primary school and there were no concerns about her development up to that time apart from two brief episodes of bed-wetting. She went to a selective secondary school, her friends all going elsewhere, and at the same time the family moved house, her older sister got married and a favourite uncle died. Her work at secondary school was never satisfactory and six months before referral her father contacted the school over this and she was kept behind after hours to do additional homework. Sandra was upset by this and became rebellious and irritable, neglecting her appearance. She joined up with a delinquent gang and became friendly with a man in his twenties who, shortly after, was sent to prison for fire-raising. She went out in promiscuous fashion with a variety of men, having sexual relations with some. Her parents, both in their mid-fifties, were rather conventional lower middle class and were very distressed by Sandra's behaviour. Both were very concerned to do the right thing, but in practice mother was overinvolved, overintrusive and always expected the worst. Concern over how to deal with Sandra led to marital quarrels and mother would sometimes sulk for days at a time. They took to checking on her movements, looked at her diary and intercepted her letters. But, fearing a confrontation, they also stopped setting any limits on Sandra's activities. The atmosphere at home became tense and difficult. Sandra herself was an attractive, mature girl, rather sulky and miserable but not overtly depressed. Psychological testing showed her to be of just average intelligence.

Several factors were thought to be important in Sandra's difficulties. The secondary school transfer had not worked out well, partly because Sandra was intellectually not up to the competition, partly because it involved the rupture of close personal friendships and partly because it coincided with various family crises. Having been successful up to that time, she now failed in everything she undertook and lost her self-esteem, a loss intensified by her parents making unfavourable comparisons with her older sister. Communications in the family were poor and Sandra felt that she could not confide in her parents. She wanted to assert her own identity but did not know how to do this or indeed what sort of identity she wanted. In the gang she got the admiration which she lacked at home and at school, and this fulfilled some of her needs, but she had made a point of not firmly identifying with this or any other group. Her parents provided a deviant model in that they were devious in checking up on Sandra and lied about how much they knew of her activities from her diary. They criticized what Sandra did but simultaneously failed to give her any support or controls by dropping all restrictions on her activities.

A psychotherapeutic approach was indicated to try and resolve these various problems. Sandra was seen weekly on her own and the parents were seen by the social worker. The parents were helped to gain a better understanding of how Sandra was feeling, and their role in the situation was discussed. It was suggested that, if Sandra was to resolve her problems, it was necessary for the atmosphere at home to be less strained and negative, and that they should be receptive to Sandra's wish to be able to talk with them. The effect on Sandra of their attempts to conceal (almost certainly unsuccessfully) their checking up on her was discussed, as was also the conflicting effect of criticizing all that Sandra did and yet not setting any limits. In this it was thought wise not to prohibit Sandra's contact with the delinquent gang, as the group was important to her, but rather to attempt to provide other outlets and sources of support. Mother especially was very anxious to begin with, and one of the chief needs in initial casework was to provide support for the parents in their difficulties as well as helping them find more adaptive ways of dealing with their anxieties.

In her first few interviews Sandra turned up with an assortment of friends, including on one occasion someone she had met in the street just five minutes before. She expressed her resentment about being pushed around in school and her feelings of being a failure there. Sandra particularly talked about her relationships with other people, of needing to tell people about her feelings, of wanting people to care and also about her anxiety when there were no controls. During the first few months she went around with a variety of 'hippie' or other anti-authority groups. She also experimented with drugs. The therapist encouraged her to talk about these activities and her feelings about them, but pointed out the meaning of her actions and indicated some of the dangers in what she was doing. During this time her experiments with drugs, sex and anti-authority groups remained unusually compartmentalized and Sandra was well aware of the defects of these activities as solutions to her problems. After some months she stopped seeing the delinquent gang, as she had been let down by them several times. She continued to have a number of 'undesirable' friends according to the parents' standards, but her friendships were now more stable and settled and she no longer picked up stray men. Relationships at home were getting better and Sandra was able to talk to her mother more than she had. She had developed considerable trust and reliance on her therapist and it now seemed appropriate to make contact with the school. Sandra's intellectual level was reported to them and they worked out a less academic programme for her and arranged for her to have some opportunities for responsibility. Her behaviour at school improved markedly and Sandra became generally more cheerful and positive in her approach to things. The improvement in her friendships and relationships continued and she got a steady boyfriend who had a regular job. Things remained better at home, although some tensions between mother and Sandra persisted. School reported that Sandra was much better there and treatment was stopped after one year, both Sandra and her parents stating that they felt the problems had been resolved.

With both Mary and Sandra the main emphasis in treatment was on helping the girls find better ways of dealing with their difficulties. Individual psychotherapy was employed for this purpose, as it was necessary for them to understand both the nature of the stresses they were experiencing and the meaning of their own emotional reactions, if they were to find more acceptable solutions. With the parents much the same applied.

During treatment a variety of specific suggestions were made as to what the parents might do to improve the situation in the family, but in order to get them to change their behaviour it was important to help them gain insight and understanding of what was happening. Social casework methods were used for this purpose.

Insight is not enough in itself – treatment must always be planned so that understanding leads to a change in behaviour. Nevertheless it is usually helpful for people to gain an understanding of the psychodynamics of the situation and of the mechanisms by which the disorder developed, in order for them to appreciate both why patterns of behaviour need to change and the kind of change required. However, in some cases the major focus of treatment must be in specifically aiding the parents to cope with the child's behavioural disturbance. This was the case with Donald.

Donald was referred at age nine for severe temper tantrums which had progressively become worse since he was a toddler. By the time of referral they were daily occurrences and had reached the stage where he was screaming, throwing objects, kicking and stabbing at his mother with a kitchen knife. His parents had tried many ways of dealing with the tantrums but had come to the point where they were frightened and just gave in to almost all of his demands. Donald made life unbearable for his three older brothers, breaking and stealing their possessions. He tormented the dog, kicking it and feeding it things to make it ill. He did not often play with other children when they visited his home, but he mixed well with them at school and his behaviour posed no problems there, except that his concentration was poor and he took little interest in work. Nevertheless he had missed a lot of school through refusing to go, and having rages when his parents tried to insist. He ate and slept poorly and was below weight for his age. He had a facial tic and a habit of biting his fingers as well as his nails. He had been seen at various other clinics in the past and family therapy and antidepressants had both been tried without success. On one occasion he was admitted to a children's ward in a general hospital. His behaviour there was normal at first, but then there were tantrums culminating in an episode in which he broke things and tore up bed-clothing. The parents had not had Donald until quite late in life and at the time of his referral had reached the end of their tether with him. Mother had lost nearly two stone in weight and had become very anxious and tense. She had been fond of Donald and tended to be indulgent with him, but now affection was swamped by feelings of desperation, anger and frustration. Donald had been a difficult baby from the very beginning, being less responsive than their other children, unpredictable in his behaviour and seeming 'odd' and different in some indefinable way. The parents had come to expect trouble all the time with everything he did and felt they could never leave him unsupervised. Father was a self-contained man who had had a rather unhappy, depressed childhood. He did not find it easy to express his feelings and had been somewhat depressed over the last two years. His work pattern meant that he had not been able to provide much support for his wife in dealing with Donald's outbursts. The marriage was basically happy, but mother felt the lack of support. Both parents felt that they had been blamed for Donald's behaviour and were very sensitive about this. Donald was a thin, awkward, clumsy boy of unusual build and odd appearance. He was rather shy and subdued but made a fair social relationship. Psychological testing showed him to be of average intelligence, but he could hardly read at all.

Donald came to the clinic with a severe and persistent conduct disorder which was associated with marked reading difficulties and some emotional problems. The most striking feature of the disorder was that, in spite of its severity, it was almost confined to the family situation. The origins of the disorder seemed to lie in his unusual temperament which made him an exceptionally difficult child for his parents to deal with. His odd appearance and his clumsiness raised the possibility of some congenital physical disorder, but none could be detected. His tantrums had rapidly led to a pattern where his parents lost control and the tempers served to dominate the whole household. However they began, it was clear that the parents must be helped to find better ways of dealing with them. Both parents were under severe strain and had largely unexpressed feelings of guilt, resentment and anger both against Donald and against the clinic personnel who had unsuccessfully tried to help. If treatment were going to be effective and acceptable, it would have to provide the opportunity to deal with these feelings as well as

giving the parents techniques for dealing with Donald's tantrums. When Donald first came to the clinic, things were at crisis
point at home and it was evident that he would have to be admitted to hospital to begin with, if only to relieve the parents.
Equally, however, as the main problems lay in the family, in-
patient treatment would be useless, unless the parents were
closely involved in all that went on and unless the parent–child
interaction was altered.

Donald was admitted to hospital and quickly settled there.
He was rather inept socially but got on quite well with other
children. There were occasional mild tempers, but they were
ignored by the staff and they never developed into a proper
tantrum. Donald was seen by the psychiatrist for individual
psychotherapy and the therapist tried to gain a better understanding of how Donald felt about his family and what triggered
off the tantrums. This proved difficult, as Donald was un-
forthcoming although quite friendly. He received individual
remedial help with his reading, the task of learning to read
being broken down into a series of small steps with a graded
series of rewards (in the form of tokens) for his successes. Both
parents were seen by a psychologist and psychiatric social
worker working together. At first, in order to understand better
how the tantrums arose, they talked over the problems presented by Donald and the ways the parents responded. Then the
therapists observed the parents with Donald behind a one-way
screen, and afterwards discussed with the parents what had happened. This gave a clearer picture of the train of events leading
to a tantrum. Donald made provocative and unreasonable requests, the parents said no but later became exasperated and
gave in. Also, at first, the parents found it difficult to play or do
things with Donald, so that the importuning and tempers were
serving as a means of getting parental attention. The parents
were helped to do more with Donald, to praise him for even the
little things he did well, to set appropriate limits as to what he
should be allowed to do and to be firm and consistent in sticking
to these limits. Negative behaviour was to be ignored or firmly
reprimanded. The parents initially saw Donald on the ward,
next took him out for short walks, then had him home over-

night and for weekends and finally Donald went home for pro-longed periods of a week or so. The parents came to enjoy being with Donald and learned how to cope with his outbursts which were now infrequent and less severe. During this process there were occasional setbacks, but the parents were encouraged to see how these might be dealt with and the setbacks were actu-ally useful in testing means of dealing with more severe out-bursts. At the same time as the parents were taught ways of responding to Donald's tantrums, they discussed some of their own angry feelings about Donald's difficulties and expressed guilt over their own role in his problems. In time the whole family situation became more relaxed. Donald continued to pose some problems at home, but the situation became a man-ageable one for the parents. As a result of the special remedial help he received, Donald improved in his reading skills, but, more important still, he showed a real interest in school work for the first time and worked with concentration and enjoy-ment.

Donald's treatment focused mainly on giving the parents quite specific behavioural techniques for dealing with the tan-trums, and for encouraging positive social behaviour. Their successes in this connection resulted in a considerable lowering of the tension at home and in a marked improvement in parent–child relationships. In this it was also important that they were able to come to terms with their own guilt and dis-tress at what was happening and Donald's improvement in reading gave him a confidence which aided his adjustment.

It could fairly be said that Donald's difficulties arose directly out of a disturbed relationship with his parents, and indeed his disorder was mainly confined to the home situation. It was understandable therefore that conjoint family therapy had been employed at another clinic. This did not work because it as-sumed that the disturbed relationships were primary and causal, because it served to increase parental guilt without providing any means of resolution and because the parents were still left without any means of coping with frightening and dangerous behaviour. That the disturbed parent–child relationships were an important factor in Donald's difficulties and that the parents' very ineffective and maladaptive way of responding to his tantrums greatly aggravated his disorder were not in doubt. However, it was important to note that none of their other three children showed any difficulties in development, and also that Donald was an odd, difficult, unresponsive infant. The methods of child-rearing which worked so well with the other three children failed completely with Donald. As a result Donald showed increasingly disturbed behaviour and as his behaviour got worse, so the parental difficulties increased and so the parent–child relationships deteriorated. A vicious circle had been created and, in order to break it, it was necessary to give the parents an effective means of coping with Donald's severely aggressive outbursts. Given this, their relationship with Donald started to improve. The basic cause lay in Donald's abnormal temperament, but this had not led directly to his problems. Its importance lay in its adverse effect on parent–child interaction and hence that is where treatment had to be directed.

Hyperkinetic syndrome

Many children with emotional disorders or with conduct disorders are restless and overactive, as indeed are children with all sorts of psychiatric problems. The overactivity is just one of many symptoms. However, there is a much less common condition in which extreme overactivity constitutes the main feature.[31] This is usually known as the hyperkinetic syndrome. In children with this disorder the overactivity is usually very marked, so that the parents report that the child is never still, he keeps getting up from the table at mealtimes, he won't remain seated on a bus or at the cinema and generally he seems to be always rushing about. The key features which differentiate the overactivity from the restlessness seen in so many children are its severity, its pervasiveness, its early onset and its association with a serious disorder of attention and concentration. Thus, not only do the parents complain of overactivity, but also the teachers report that the child cannot remain seated and is always moving about the classroom. The overactivity is always evident by the time the child goes to school and usually it is manifest by three or four years. The child tends to have a very short attention span so that he spends only a few moments on each activity before going on to something else. Often, too, he is very distractable, so that his attention is easily diverted by sounds and sights about him. Although called the hyperkinetic syndrome, the basic defect probably lies in the attention defect which usually persists as the child grows older. In many cases the overactivity does not continue and frequently during adolescence it is replaced by underactivity, inertia and a lack of drive. Usually the disorder is accompanied by developmental delays of one kind or another; most of the children have serious educational difficulties and many are of below average intelligence or have mild mental retardation. In some cases the overactivity seems to be an extreme variant of temperament, but in others it appears to have arisen as a result of some kind of early brain injury. Although the main problem lies in the child's motor behaviour and concentration, not surprisingly the overactivity is also frequently associated with serious difficulties in getting along with other children and with aggressive or disruptive behaviour. Whereas there is usually an underlying abnormality in the child's constitution, the development of these secondary conduct disorders is heavily influenced by environmental factors. Children with the hyperkinetic syndrome are very difficult youngsters to deal with and frequently drive both parents and teachers to despair. The outlook is not good and the majority of children with this disorder still have serious social problems in adolescence. The main emphasis in treatment usually lies in giving the parents means of behavioural control, in providing educational help and sometimes in the use of drugs. A combination of these techniques may often be most effective.

Bruce was referred at age four years because of severe overactivity and difficult behaviour. His early development had been rather slow and his speech was particularly delayed. At four he still wet the bed. He had an epileptic fit at eighteen months and over the next two years there were about two dozen further fits. Most of these were major convulsive attacks, but one was a psychomotor fit which began with a stomach-ache and in which the main manifestations were a glazed look, drooling at the mouth and saying silly things. From the time he was a toddler he was very active, being on the go all the day, rampaging around the house and getting into everything. He tended to go from thing to thing, not concentrating on anything for very long, and when seen at four he also talked incessantly. At the clinic he was a cheerful, friendly boy but very disinhibited and lacking in persistence. Psychological testing showed that his intelligence was on the borderline of mild retardation. He was an only child and came from a happy, well-adjusted family. Mother especially was obviously very fond of Bruce. but both parents found his extreme overactivity very wearing and difficult to deal with.

Bruce showed the hyperkinetic syndrome and like many children with this disorder he was also somewhat delayed in his development and had evidence of organic brain dysfunction (as shown by the fits). The disorder arose from abnormalities in his intrinsic development rather than from any adverse experiences or stresses. It was important to bring the fits under control and he was immediately started on anticonvulsant medication. Stimulant drugs are often helpful with this kind of severe overactivity, so they were prescribed. Unfortunately they did little to help the overactivity, but they did make Bruce very miserable and tearful so they were stopped. This is a paradoxical side-effect sometimes seen in children. One of the major tranquillizers (see chapter 9) was used instead. This helped to calm Bruce and make him less active, but it was difficult to adjust the dose so that it did this without making him sleepy. Nevertheless for a year this made things more manageable at home and was worthwhile for this reason. In the meantime mother had been seen, to help her find better ways of coping with Bruce's overactivity by setting him clear limits or being firm on what was not allowed, by structuring a situation to reduce distractions and by encouraging concentration on games and tasks. At age five years he started at a special unit in an ordinary school and then later moved on to a school for educationally backward children. When last seen at age seven years he was making some progress at school and was less active but remained impulsive and showed poor persistence in his lessons. He liked and played with other children, but did not get on so well with those of his own age because he was rather bossy.

Some of Bruce's problems will probably persist into adolescence, but he showed very little in the way of secondary problems of behaviour, thanks to a very well-adjusted family in which the parents showed great affection but also knew how to deal firmly with his behaviour when that was required. In other cases the prognosis is much worse, either due to a more severe biological disturbance or a less adequate family. In Randolph's case both seemed to apply.

Randolph was first referred to the clinic at six years, although he had had previous psychiatric treatment when younger. He was grossly overactive, had very poor concentration and was aggressive to both adults and children. Immediately prior to referral he had been excluded from a special school because of his extremely disturbed behaviour. Randolph's birth had been normal, but mother had had a threatened miscarriage early in the pregnancy. Even as an infant he was difficult; he vomited when fed, slept fitfully and was very restless. Motor milestones, such as sitting and walking, were delayed and he did not speak until after he was three. During these early years he screamed frequently and banged his head. Mother was worn out by the boy's behaviour and used to shout and smack him in anger. When Randolph was nearly two years she took a job to get away from him, leaving him with a child-minder. The job lasted only six months. When Randolph was four he was placed in a special class for disturbed children where he remained for nine months. His play there was often purposeless, he was very overactive and enjoyed making a mess and was aggressive to the other children. As Randolph formed a close relationship with the teacher, his behaviour improved somewhat but when she left it deteriorated again. During the next year he was admitted to and suspended from three other schools. He remained severely overactive, was markedly clumsy, often dashed into the road regardless of traffic, was aggressive with other children and caused much damage by breaking things. The neighbours' children were no longer allowed to play with him. With his parents he was alternately loving and spiteful. He was dangerous with his younger brother whom he had once tipped out of a high chair, he was cruel to animals (squeezing a hamster to death on one occasion) and lied freely. He wet and soiled himself, had several fears and appeared unhappy.

At the clinic Randolph rushed in and out of rooms, turning lights on and off, picking up telephones and generally causing disruption wherever he went. His speech was limited and poorly articulated. On examination he was found to be clumsy and to have a poor appreciation of shapes. One brain-wave test was abnormal but a second test showed no unusual features. His IQ was at the borderline of mild mental retardation.

Father was a happy-go-lucky man with a regular job as a plumber. However, he felt Randolph's behaviour was specifically directed against him and he would lose his temper with the boy several times a week, hitting him in anger. Mother was an anxious woman who had become depressed and was distraught by her failure to deal with Randolph. The marriage was happy and there were two other normal children.

The severity of Randolph's problems meant that there was little alternative but to admit him to a children's psychiatric unit. His behaviour improved considerably in hospital but he remained overactive and aggressive. Stimulant drugs and then tranquillizers were given without effect on his behaviour. After nearly a year he was placed at a special day-school, but his behaviour soon deteriorated after returning home, as it had not proved possible to help his parents learn how to cope with Randolph's difficulties satisfactorily. For a year he had to have home tuition because a suitable school could not be found. Finally, after an unsuccessful placement at another special day-school, he started at a special boarding-school for children. He improved considerably whilst there but remained disinhibited and overactive. When last seen at age thirteen years his behaviour had much improved and he was no longer overactive, although his concentration was still poor and his scholastic attainments were far behind what they should be.

Although Randolph had improved greatly by the time he reached adolescence, he still had considerable social and educational problems. Drugs had made no difference and it had not been possible to help the parents learn how to deal with his aggression and overactivity. However, both while in hospital and at the special boarding-school Randolph's behaviour greatly improved and it was these placements in units where skilled staff knew how to combine structure, firmness and consistency with warmth and affection that the main progress was made. As Randolph improved, and with only school holidays to cope with, the parents gradually became more able to manage the situation and, by the time Randolph was a teenager, parent–child relationships were harmonious and settled. It is only a small minority of children with psychiatric problems who require in-patient care or residential schooling, but for these few children such services are invaluable.

8 Underachievement, Learning Inhibitions and Other Problems

Educational underachievement

Of all the problems seen in school-age children, learning disorders are among the most common. These disorders are first the responsibility of the school teacher and the school psychologist, but many children also get referred to psychiatric clinics. Sometimes this is because the child has additional emotional or behavioural problems (which are a common accompaniment of underachievement) and sometimes it is because underlying developmental disorders or medical disabilities are suspected. The subject of learning disorders, as dealt with in many textbooks, is both confusing and contentious. The literature is full of emotive controversies about the existence or non-existence of medical syndromes such as 'dyslexia' or 'word-blindness' and about the importance or lack of importance of 'emotional blocks' and 'learning inhibitions'. I will have something to say about these controversies later in the chapter, but most of the disputes lose their heat once the facts are made clear. So let me first consider some of the concepts and research findings concerning educational underachievement.

The concept of 'underachievement'

Originally the concept of underachievement involved for many people the assumption that a child was not performing up to his innate potential. An IQ was thought to reflect innate intelligence and the mental age was thought to indicate the maximum level of performance of which a child was capable. It was assumed that children rarely, if ever, achieved at a level above their mental age, and that the extent to which educational attainments fell short of mental age reflected the degree to which a child was performing below his capacity. These notions have not entirely disappeared, but they have been shown to be false.[167]

In the first place, children *do* achieve at a level well above their mental age (see below), so in practice as well as in theory the idea that mental age sets an upper limit on attainment is quite invalid. Also, although there can be no doubt that genetic factors are very important indeed in the development of intelligence, there is abundant evidence that the IQ is not a pure measure of innate ability. Severe environmental privation (both biological and psychological) can seriously impair intellectual development as represented in the IQ, as well as in other measures. The IQ score reflects a child's genetic endowment, but it also reflects the quality of his nutritional and experiential environment. Furthermore the IQ is not a test of 'potential', it is a test of *current* performance. Over the course of the school years, *on average*, a child's IQ goes up or down by some 15 points, so the IQ is far from fixed. The IQ simply provides a sample of the child's behaviour on a variety of tasks. In that respect it is basically no different from a test of reading. It just so happens that, because the behaviours cover a wide range of conceptual and reasoning skills which are not acquired as the result of direct teaching, IQ scores in practice constitute good predictors of children's educational attainments.

So, although the early notions of fixed innate potential have been discredited, the IQ remains a most useful measure of a child's current intellectual skills. Because the IQ is a good predictor of attainments, the child whose attainments are quite out of keeping with his IQ is unusual. Accordingly the concept of underachievement continues to have practical utility. The child whose reading is far below his intellectual level presents an educational problem which requires investigation and treatment.

Definition and measurement of educational underachievement

Obviously underachievement is not something that is simply

present or absent. It is a matter of degree. Very few children perform *exactly* at the level expected. Most have scholastic achievements somewhat below or above expectation and it is mainly when achievements are a lot below expectation that there has to be concern. The questions then are: What should be the expected level of attainment for any child? How do you decide what is a lot below that? The issues involved in these questions are complex and involve statistical considerations as well as psychological and educational concepts. However, the main points may be summarized here. [159, 167]

The simplest approach to defining underachievement is to compare a child's attainment with the average for children of the same age. That provides some guide to a child's scholastic progress, but it does not give a measure of what level of attainment should be 'expected', because it fails to take IQ or mental age into account. It is appropriate to expect a child of high IQ to have above average attainments, just as a child of low IQ may be expected to have below average attainments. That follows because there is a substantial positive correlation between intelligence and educational attainment.

For a long time it has been customary to take intelligence into account by comparing educational age with mental age. Thus, if a ten-year-old boy with a mental age of thirteen years had a reading age of twelve years, he might be said to be one year retarded in reading. While that sounds reasonable and while such an approach has been widely followed, it is in fact based on a misconception and gives rise to serious error. In reality, the boy should *not* be expected to have a reading age of thirteen years. Rather the expectation should be for a reading age of about twelve years – exactly what he had. The explanation for this apparent paradox lies in the 'regression effect'. If the correlation between reading and intelligence were unity (i.e. $+ 1.0$), then of course mental age and reading age should run exactly parallel. But, where the correlation falls short of unity (and that between IQ and reading is about $+ 0.6$), then the two will differ. A highly intelligent child will have above average attainment, but his attainment will generally not be as high as his intelligence. Conversely a retarded child will have below average attainment but his attainments will generally be above his intelligence. In short, in each case there is a 'regression to the mean' so that attainment is nearer average than is the intelligence. This has nothing to do with the qualities of intelligence or of reading but is simply a consequence of the fact that the correlation between intelligence and scholastic attainments is less than unity.

The conclusion that reading age and mental age should not run exactly parallel follows inexorably from the correlation between reading and IQ (or for that matter between any attainment and IQ, indeed between any two tests), and from the fact that overachievement occurs with approximately the same frequency as underachievement. But psychologists and teachers alike have been astonishingly reluctant to accept this fact. Nevertheless several surveys of the total school population have convincingly shown that it is a fact, in practice as well as in theory. The unavoidable conclusion is that studies based on either the achievement ratio or on discrepancies between achievement age and mental age are invalid and misleading. Fortunately there is an appropriate statistical procedure – a regression equation – which takes account of these effects and which can be used to estimate 'expected' levels of scholastic achievement. We need not be concerned here with the mathematics of this, but the important facts to bear in mind are that overachievement and underachievement occur with approximately the same frequency, and that the 'regression effect' means that a child's educational attainments may be expected to be a little nearer the average than his IQ score.

The next question is: How far below expectation must a child's attainments be before there should be concern about underachievement? Again statistical considerations are relevant and the 'regression equation' can be used to estimate the expected frequency of different degrees of underachievement. This allows underachievement to be defined in terms of a degree of educational failure which is relatively uncommon in the normal population.

In this connection it should be noted that epidemiological studies show that *extreme* degrees of underachievement in read-

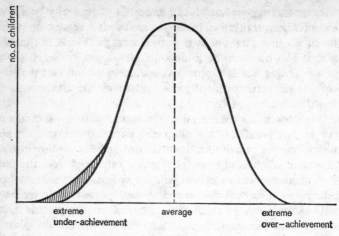

Fig. 4

ing are especially common and create a 'hump' at the bottom of the curve of distribution of achievement in reading (see Figure 4). Although, in general, overachievement and under-achievement occur with roughly the same frequency, *extreme* underachievement is considerably more common than *extreme* overachievement. It has often been said by educationalists that, because reading skills are 'normally' distributed (as they are for the most part), children with extreme underachievement are just the lower end of a continuum, with nothing remarkable about them. Some children must have scholastic achievements below average, just as some must be shorter than average. However, this argument is misleading because it is *not* just a continuum, as shown by the 'hump' at the bottom of the curve. There seems to be something special about this group at the extreme lower end of achievement – a group which constitutes somewhere about three to ten per cent of the population (if severe under-achievement is defined as reading skills which are the equivalent of more than thirty months below expectation at age ten years).

There needs to be concern about the child with extreme degrees of underachievement, not just because such degrees are uncommon but because the prognosis is poor. There must be most concern about the child who is unlikely to 'catch up' with his contemporaries. Follow-up studies have shown that there is a very poor outlook for most of the children in this extreme group. Children with severe reading retardation at age ten years are unlikely to 'catch up' by the time they leave school, and many will fall even further behind. This is so in the ordinary circumstances of schooling but whether it *has* to be so is something I shall consider later in the chapter.

Decisions on when and how to provide special help for the underachieving child must also depend on other educational considerations. The degree to which a child *suffers* from underachievement will depend not only on the degree of underachievement and the course of his scholastic progress but also on educational practice. The underachieving child is more likely to suffer from his disability in schools where educational failure results in segregation and opprobrium. Also the extent to which the underachieving child is at a psychological disadvantage will depend on the attainments of the other youngsters in his class, on the degree and nature of streaming and on the extent to which teaching is individualized rather than group based. In ordinary schools, reading failure is strongly associated with conduct disorders, but in certain special schools this has been found not to be the case. Probably this is partly a result of better, individual remedial help and partly it may be a consequence of a greater acceptance by the school that many of the children do have serious scholastic problems and that this may not be their fault.

Classification of different varieties of underachievement

In considering underachievement, three distinctions have to be made: between general backwardness and specific educational problems, between different types of special problem and between a failure to gain skills and a loss of these skills.[159]

The first distinction is between general backwardness (i.e. low achievement in relation to the average for that age, but without taking IQ into account) and specific retardation (i.e. achievement which is low after taking both age *and* IQ into account).

In the first case there tends to be low IQ and generally low attainments, whereas in the second there is a specific educational disability which is *not* explicable in terms of low intelligence. The distinction has been most studied with respect to reading, and has proved to be of crucial importance. As Rutter and Yule have shown,[167] specific reading retardation differs from general reading backwardness in terms of sex distribution, neurological correlates, developmental abnormalities, association with other educational problems and prognosis. Specific reading retardation is three to four times as common in boys as in girls, whereas general backwardness has a nearer equal sex ratio. General backwardness is often associated with overt neurological disorder and with a wider range of developmental disabilities in coordination, perception, constructural skills, speech and language. In contrast specific reading retardation is associated with a much narrower range of deficits in just speech and language, being very strongly associated with spelling difficulties, while attainment in other school subjects is less affected. Although the children with specific retardation are, on the whole, considerably more intelligent than those with general backwardness, they actually make *less* progress in reading. The specific difficulty in reading has a worse prognosis, in spite of the fact that the outlook with respect to progress in other school subjects is better. Underachievement in mathematics and in other aspects of schoolwork has been less investigated and it is not known whether the differentiation between general backwardness and specific retardation applies in the same way.

The second distinction involves classification according to the scholastic skill involved. Most attention has been paid to reading and spelling, two skills which are very closely associated. However, specific difficulties in mathematics do occur and, to a lesser extent, in other subjects also. Surprisingly little attention has been paid to the similarities and differences between underachievement in different scholastic subjects.

The third distinction is between failure to acquire educational skills and a loss of those skills. Specific reading retardation and general reading backwardness both apply to the former situation. The children have had difficulties in learning to read from the very outset. However, there is also the situation in which a child, having been well launched in his school work and having mastered the basic skills, later runs into educational difficulties and falls increasingly behind. Sometimes these later difficulties involve specific school subjects and sometimes they involve schoolwork generally, or even all learning. Either way, the disorder is of a quite different type from the variety in which there is a failure to acquire the initial skills.

Specific reading retardation

Specific reading retardation, then, is a term applied to disorders in which the child has a specific disability in reading, such that his attainments are well below those expected on the basis of his chronological age and IQ. This is a common problem[167] – a study on the Isle of Wight showed a prevalence among about four per cent of ten year olds and a similar study in an inner London borough found a rate over twice as high. Specific reading retardation is found in children from all types of social background. The children often have some difficulty with other school subjects (partly because the child needs to read to follow what is printed in his books or is written on the blackboard), but usually reading disability is much the most severe. The one exception is spelling which has a special association with reading. Children with specific reading retardation usually have severe spelling difficulties and often these remain even after the child has learned to read well. Claims have been made that the children show particular types of spelling difficulties, but there is no sound evidence that this is the case. On the other hand the matter has not been adequately investigated and the issue merits further study.

Developmental delays

Although there is no diagnostic pattern of intellectual performance, there is a well-established tendency for retarded readers to have impaired verbal skills, as assessed on the Wechsler intelligence scales. This finding is in keeping with the extensive evidence that speech and language difficulties are strongly associated with reading retardation. A characteristic story is that the child has been delayed in learning to speak, then shows great difficulties learning to read and later only severe spelling difficulties persist. The association with speech delay is basic and probably reflects causal influences. This is scarcely surprising since reading concerns written language and speaking involves spoken language: an impairment in one form of language is likely to be associated with impairment in other forms. Nevertheless it should be noted that the association also seems to apply to children who have defects in pronunciation yet have no detectable impairment in spoken-language skills as such.

Other developmental delays are also significantly associated with reading retardation. One of the most important concerns verbal coding and sequencing. It has been found that poor readers have difficulty matching either auditory or visual dot-and-dash patterns. This may be because they do not find it so easy to produce verbal codes for the patterns (e.g. one dot, two dashes and three dots) but have to remember the pattern as a picture. Indeed many have problems with any kind of task that involves putting things into an order or sequence. Thus children may find it hard to remember the order of the months. This sequencing problem is probably related, at least in part, to language deficits.

Another common difficulty involves the child's confusion between right and left. In spite of assertions to the contrary in textbooks, research has shown that specific reading retardation is *not* particularly associated with mixed-handedness, but it is associated with a difficulty in telling right from left, especially on other people. Reading difficulties are frequently associated with very poorly coordinated writing and may also be associated with a wide range of other developmental deficits including clumsiness and difficulties in differentiating shapes. However, although important in individual children, these are less common factors than speech, language and sequencing problems.

At least in some children, these various developmental delays seem to be due to biological factors involving brain function. It has been suggested that specific reading retardation may be due to a relative failure in the normal growth and maturation of certain specific functions of the brain cortex. The chief evidence in support of this view is that most of the development disabilities associated with reading retardation are normal in younger children and that these disabilities lessen in reading-retarded children as they grow older. However, the findings are far from conclusive at the moment, since brain maturation cannot be directly measured in living humans. It is a plausible hypothesis in that normally the brain does not develop at a uniform rate (see chapter 2). Ordinarily some parts are more advanced in maturation than others, and it would only be an extension of this observation to postulate that abnormal delays might also involve any certain specific brain functions. It is unknown, unfortunately, whether in fact this happens.

Family history

All studies have shown that reading difficulties frequently run in families. Although this is not conclusive evidence of heredity, there can be little doubt that in many cases genetic factors do play an important part in the causation of specific reading retardation. On the other hand it is not known whether reading *skills* are inherited or whether a specific *condition* of reading disability is transmitted through some gene.

As well as a biological inheritance, in some cases the family history may provide social transmission. For example, parents who themselves read badly may inculcate in the child a negative attitude towards reading, may be unable to instruct the child how to read, may provide inadequate verbal or other stimulation and may not establish a milieu in which books are available and libraries are visited.

Family size

That this kind of social transmission does indeed play some part is suggested by the association between specific reading retardation and large families and by the finding that a family history of reading difficulties is much more common in children from large families. Children with many brothers and sisters (three or four or more) tend to have both impaired verbal intelligence and poorer reading attainments. It has been suggested that verbal development is affected by the extent to which children, when learning to talk, come into contact with other preschool children, whose vocabulary and elementary grammar offer little verbal stimulation, rather than with adults, whose language is richer and more varied. On the other hand it may be the clarity and meaningfulness of stimuli rather than the complexity of stimulation which are most important. The often greater amount of conflicting cross-talk when a large family is gathered together may make it more difficult for the young child to make sense of what is being said.

Temperamental characteristics

Several studies have indicated that reading-retarded children lack concentration (even on tasks other than reading), are restless, distractable, impulsive and quick to jump to conclusions. As these temperamental attributes are evident during the preschool years it seems that in many cases they are not a response to reading failure but rather a contributory cause of the reading difficulties.

Geographical variation and school influences

It has already been noted (see page 275) that specific reading retardation was found to be over twice as common in inner London as on the Isle of Wight. The findings suggest that social factors are important in the genesis of reading retardation, but also that school factors are very important. It has been found, for example, that the proportion of socially deprived children, amount of teacher and child turnover and calibre and experience of the teachers are all influential. Curiously, large class size is, if anything, associated with better reading attainments. There are many good reasons for wanting to reduce class size, but this is unlikely in itself to improve reading standards. If the reduction in class size is to benefit reading, it is probably necessary for the teachers to provide more individual help. Specific teaching skills are also likely to be important. A pilot study suggested that the in-service training of junior-school teachers may increase the children's progress in reading.[166] On the whole the precise method of teaching reading is not very important, but an emphasis on phonetic methods at the start seems to lead to fewer serious reading problems.[34]

Association with antisocial behaviour

Several studies have shown a strong connection between reading retardation and disorders of conduct. Thus, in the Isle of Wight study, among the children with specific reading retardation one quarter showed antisocial behaviour – a rate several times that in the population at large. Other investigations have produced similar findings. Obviously the key question concerns the nature of the association. Is it that reading failure leads to antisocial problems, or do conduct disorders predispose to reading difficulties, or are both due to some third set of factors? No firm answer is yet available, but there is some relevant evidence. It appears that part of the explanation lies in the fact that adverse temperamental attributes, large family size and various other factors are important in the aetiology of both conditions. In part it is also due to the fact that, at least in metropolitan areas, family influences leading to reading retardation overlap with those leading to antisocial behaviour – an example of the truism that a depriving environment tends to be depriving in many respects, not just in one element. However, the evidence does indicate that in some children the reading retardation may predispose the child to develop conduct problems. Because reading is such an essential skill at school, reading failure may be a potent source of discouragement, loss of self-esteem and antagonism which may contribute to the development of delinquent activities. With status and satisfaction through schoolwork denied to him, the reading-retarded child may rebel and seek satisfaction in activities running counter to everything the school stands for.

Clinical assessment

As is evident from what has been said already, children with specific reading retardation do not form a homogeneous group. Many factors may be important in aetiology; frequently these involve developmental factors in the child himself, but environmental influences at home and at school are also important. It must also be said that in many cases it is not possible to determine the cause or even the nature of the basic disability. Three cases may serve to illustrate these points:

Roderick was referred to the clinic at age eleven years because he was virtually a non-reader. During his first seven years he had many moves of home, spending three periods of eighteen months or so abroad. There were several occasions when he lived with relatives for two or three months prior to moves. His birth was difficult and he was placed in an incubator for a week. He cried very frequently as an infant, there were many feeding difficulties, he was not put on solids until after his first birthday and was not fully weaned until age two years. His motor milestones were normal, but he was very delayed in speech, not producing distinct words until three years and not using sentences until four years. He had always been very clumsy and could not manage buttons until aged nine years. Roderick was an anxious, rather unhappy boy who was very afraid of his mother who frequently shouted at him and punished him for not doing his schoolwork properly. She was a very neurotic, uneducated woman who had periods of depression and who was very worried over Roderick's failure to read. Father, a manual worker, was fond of the boy and tended to spoil him. The parental marriage was not a very happy one. There were four other children in the family. Roderick generally got on well with other children and had plenty of friends.

Psychological testing showed that Roderick was of average intelligence, but that his reading attainments were only at the five-and-a-half-year level. His writing was slow, laboured, jerkily irregular and he used undue pressure. There were some problems in pronunciation and he had difficulty coordinating his breathing and talking. He was markedly clumsy and there were frequent jerky movements of his extremities. His right–left differentiation was poor. When he moved one set of muscles he tended also to contract many other unneeded muscle groups.

Roderick clearly had a mild neurological disorder, which probably stemmed from the difficulties at the time of birth and which had led to both a marked delay in speech and severe clumsiness. However, his problems were increased by a very unsettled early life, three moves of school in his first two years of education. His parents were not able to help him with his reading and mother's irritation and shouting at him when he couldn't manage to read undoubtedly aggravated his school difficulties.

Jerome first came to the clinic at age nine years because of reading difficulties. His early development was quite normal except that he did not use single words until after age two years and did not use phrases until three and a half years. His pronunciation during the preschool years was very poor and he received speech therapy up to age five years. He was a friendly, affectionate boy but very sensitive to criticism and this led to frequent altercations with friends at school. He was restless and markedly impulsive in his approach to work. His mother used to get cross with him because he could not read, and homework always ended in rows. Then, following advice, she left him to work on his own and there had been no rows of this kind in the last two years. Jerome often lied and there had been two recent episodes in which he slashed a chair with a razor and broke the lock on a door, both in temper. The father had a professional job, the parents got on well together and there were two other children, neither of whom presented problems.

At interview Jerome had a rather mature attitude and expressed his worries and misery over reading. He felt that he was not being helped much at school and was resentful about the fact that he could not read properly. There were no abnormalities on neurological examination, but he had a slight hesitancy of speech and was confused as to right and left. Psychological testing showed that he had good average intelligence, but was only reading at the six-year level. He did not know his alphabet properly, his writing was poor and his spelling very bad, with many letter reversals, words missed out and poor spacing.

With Jerome the problems lay in a developmental speech and language delay. As is often the case, by the time he came to the clinic there was no indication of current speech abnormalities but there could be no doubt that his marked speech delay in early childhood was the major factor leading to his present reading retardation. His restlessness and impulsiveness were contributory factors and mother's irritation when Jerome first started school may also have aggravated the situation. However, there was no evidence of neurological disorder and no important environmental components in aetiology. While Jerome showed no marked emotional or behavioural problems, his temper and resentfulness might constitute the early signs of a secondary conduct disorder if his reading difficulties were not treated adequately.

Raymond was not referred until age twelve years, although his reading difficulties had been recognized when he was much younger. At five and a half he was noted to be writing his name backwards and to be reading signposts from the bottom up. He was seen by a private psychologist whose testing showed a very high IQ. He was placed at a special private school for children with reading difficulties and the family moved house to enable him to attend. Unfortunately the facilities for remedial help at the school did not live up to expectations and after one year he had to leave because the local authority would not pay the fees and the parents could no longer afford to do so. He attended an ordinary local school for two years but received no remedial help and the family moved house again in order for Raymond to get the assistance he needed. He was put on the waiting list for a remedial class but then the parents' marriage broke up and mother moved with the two children to live with her parents. Raymond again attended an ordinary school, but it was only for the last two terms that he received any remedial help there. The school reported that his oral classwork was very good, but his written work was poor because of gross spelling errors. Raymond read science and other technical books with effort and some misunderstanding, but he never read fiction for pleasure. There were no emotional or behavioural difficulties. Mother was a warm, responsive, professional woman who was said to have been a late developer educationally. Father also had a professional job, but at school he had been behind his peers in schoolwork and had stayed down for one year. The marriage had been a basically happy one until father had an affair after the family moved house for the second time. Raymond had one brother who now presented no problems but who had had some reading difficulties in the infants' school.

Raymond was a slightly shy boy who talked easily and well. There were no abnormalities on either psychiatric or neurological assessment. Psychological testing showed him to have very high intelligence, but the scores showed a great discrepancy between his verbal skills which were extremely good and his visuo-spatial skills which were just average. He read at appropriate age level but his spelling was five years retarded.

It was evident that Raymond had some intrinsic reading difficulty, but its nature was obscure. Unlike the other two boys he had no speech or language difficulties. His perceptual abilities were normal by the time he was seen at twelve years, but the very unusual IQ pattern suggested that there had been more marked perceptual difficulties when he was younger. The story of educational problems in both parents, who were obviously of high intelligence, suggested the possibility of a hereditary disorder. In spite of the break-up of the parental marriage, Raymond's home life had been basically happy and he was a well-adjusted youngster. His mother had been able to give him a lot of help without putting him under undue pressure and in spite of the appalling lack of special educational treatment he had caught up in reading. Characteristically, however, he had been left with a very severe spelling difficulty and he still lacked confidence and pleasure in reading.

Treatment

Although much has been written about methods of teaching children with specific reading difficulties, evaluations of different techniques are lacking and very little is known about the merits and demerits of each approach. Most attention has focused on various types of perceptual training, but the investigations undertaken so far suggest that this is not very useful for most children.[167] As already indicated, the children show varying patterns of disability and varying effects of environmental influences. In planning treatment, it is obviously important to ameliorate adverse influences in the home or school. It is also necessary to adapt teaching methods to the child's particular disabilities. However, it remains uncertain how far instruction should concentrate on the child's strengths or on his weaknesses. Although evidence is lacking, it appears that it is desirable to utilize the child's assets in the first instance in order to put a premium on success and gain the child's confidence.

However, it will usually be necessary to provide special teaching to cope with his particular deficits and difficulties.

The published studies suggest that remedial or 'progress' classes are of very limited benefit for children with severe and specific reading retardation. Some kind of individualized approach in which the child is seen on his own or in a very small group will generally be required. There is a lack of evidence about the relative merits of different teaching methods, but it seems unlikely that there is one right method. The best techniques, however, seem to show certain common features. First, the teacher must gain the child's interest and give him confidence in his ability to succeed. As well as personal teaching qualities, a variety of 'gimmicks' may help in this connection. Second, the teacher must accurately appreciate just what the child knows and does not know. Third, the teaching programme should be broken down into a series of very small steps, both to make learning easier and to make it immediately apparent to the child that he is progressing. Fourth, the structuring of the programme should be such that it ensures early success. Reading-retarded children will have had many years of failure and discouragement and it is of the first importance that they learn that they can succeed. Fifth, both the teacher and pupil must have accurate feedback to ensure that they can recognize achievements and also identify areas of difficulty. Sixth, there must be systematic rewards for progress and accomplishments. These may consist of the child seeing his gains on a chart with stars or other markers for reaching various levels, of praise and encouragement specifically given by parents and teachers for each piece of successful work, or sometimes of material rewards. However this is organized, it is essential to change the usual emphasis on failure to emphasis on success.

Skilled remedial teaching will almost always be necessary. Unfortunately the existing facilities for this are woefully inadequate and many children who need help fail to receive it. However, particularly with some of the older children with reading retardation, the main problem may have come to be the lack of confidence, the sense of failure and the misery consequent upon years of being faced with their own lack of accomplishments. In these cases, counselling or psychotherapeutic techniques may come to be the most important elements in treatment. Usually this will need to be accompanied by specialized teaching, but sometimes the youngster may have learned more than he realized and, once his confidence and self-esteem have been restored, he may come to use the skills he was not aware of and so progress on his own.

It was noted earlier that the outlook for most children with specific reading retardation is not good. Although many improve to some extent, the majority continue to have reading problems in adolescence and nearly all show persisting spelling difficulties. How far this is inevitable is quite uncertain, in that so few children receive adequate help, and often the help which is provided is inappropriate. The fact that the developmental abnormalities underlying many cases of reading retardation greatly diminish as the child grows older suggest that, given both skilled teaching and encouragement, the children ought also to show marked gains in reading. Follow-up studies of children who have received skilled treatment are much needed. It seems likely that there is potential, but the nature of the problems may be such that, in spite of great improvements, it may be difficult for many youngsters to become really fluent and successful readers.

'Dyslexia'

The term 'dyslexia' (or 'word-blindness') is often applied to children with specific reading retardation.[43] The diagnosis is a medical one and it implies a condition based upon constitutional factors, often hereditary in type. The descriptions of 'dyslexia' are closely in line with the characteristics described for specific reading retardation: disorder of speech and language, severe and bizarre spelling errors, a family history of reading difficulties, right–left confusion, difficulties in the perception of space relationships, clumsiness and lack of coordination, directional confusion, disordered temporal orientation and difficulties in naming colours or recognizing the meaning of pictures. The introduction of the concept of 'dyslexia' was helpful initially in emphasizing (correctly) that many reading problems stemmed from specific biological handicaps in the child rather than any lack of general intelligence, poor schooling, privation in the home or 'emotional blocks'. Because of this, the term has some utility in showing that the child 'cannot help it' and that he needs skilled remedial help.

However, the concept has rightly been severely criticized.[167] The main criticisms are as follows: (1) The term suggests one unitary syndrome, whereas the evidence clearly indicates that there are at least several and probably many different patterns of disability. (2) The definition of 'dyslexia' indicates that the condition is only to be diagnosed in children of normal intelligence from non-depriving backgrounds who have had adequate schooling. However, research has shown that disorders fitting all the criteria of 'dyslexia' occur in children of *all* levels of intelligence, from bad as well as good homes and from poor as well as adequate schools. (3) The exclusive focus on biological factors tends to lead to a neglect of environmental influences. But the child with a biological handicap is *more,* not less, vulnerable to a depriving environment, and very often biological and experimental causes co-exist. Multifactorial determinance is common. (4) No unambiguous criteria for the diagnosis of 'dyslexia' have ever been put forward. (5) In practice the emphasis on whether the child is or is not 'dyslexic' is restricting. The question should not be posed in that form, but should be: Why can't this child read? and What are the current and past causal factors both in the child and in his environment?

The controversy over 'dyslexia' will go on, but it is important that fruitless battles over labels should not prevent *all* children with reading difficulties from getting the help they so badly need.

'Emotional Blocks'

It has often been claimed that reading retardation arises as a result of some form of neurotic conflict or 'emotional block'. However, this view is based on uncontrolled studies of mixed clinic populations and on highly speculative psychoanalytic interpretations, so that satisfactory supporting evidence is lacking. On the other hand there is substantial contrary evidence. It may be concluded that specific reading retardation has many important causal factors, although, except rarely, neurosis does not seem to be one of them. However, this does *not* mean that emotional factors are of no importance with respect to reading difficulties.[159]

In the first place, although emotional disorder rarely acts as a *primary* cause of reading retardation, as a secondary influence it is much more important. Children who fail to learn to read are likely to be continually faced with negative responses to their failure. School reports may say 'doesn't try', 'could do better' or 'not working up to his capacity', when from the child's point of view he is doing all that he can but without any sign of success. School becomes an unhappy experience strongly associated with failure and with the adverse social responses to his failure. By the time people are considering whether he needs special help he is likely to have 'given up', and the remedial teacher is faced with a discouraged, miserable child who lacks confidence and feels that he cannot succeed whatever he does. Although not the prime cause of reading retardation, emotional and motivational factors probably are important in the *continuation* of reading difficulties. As a consequence the remedial teacher's first task will usually be to increase the child's confidence and motivation to learn and to set about it in an appropriate way.

Second, although emotional factors may not constitute a primary cause of specific reading retardation, they may be much more important in the genesis of learning inhibitions which arise later in childhood.

Learning inhibitions

As well as disorders, such as specific reading retardation, which involve a failure to develop some scholastic skill, there are other conditions in which disorders of learning may arise later, after the child has made a successful start in schooling. These conditions, usually termed learning inhibitions, have been much less studied and there is no firm evidence about the mechanisms by which they arise. However, there are at least four which seem to be important.[159] They are: lack of motivation, avoidance of learning, impaired function and anxiety.

Learning requires attention and involvement in the task at hand and these variables will be influenced by the child's interest and motivation. These are increased by his identification with the person (either teacher or parent) associated with the learning process and by his seeking to please them by his learning success. Conversely, when a child has a bad relationship with his teacher, there may be a marked falling off in his scholastic attainments. More specifically the child may work less well because his attention is deflected onto other things. This may occur, for example, with worries about home, with sexual preoccupations, with daydreams or with obsessional ruminations.

Children may also show underachievement because of a positive avoidance of learning (either in general or with respect to a specific subject). Most obviously this is evident in those adolescents whose work falls off as part of a rebellion against adult values. Some intelligent children come to reject education as something not worth working for and, as a result, their educational attainment may suffer.

In other cases learning comes to be associated in the child's mind with pain or unpleasant feelings. This situation may arise when a parent or teacher keeps punishing a child for not learning properly. Eventually the child may come, by generalization, to associate learning with punishment and so avoid it. The same phenomenon may result if the child's peer culture regards schoolwork as cissy and to be despised. If the child is teased and tormented as a 'swot' by his friends when he does his schoolwork well, he may learn that scholastic success is to be avoided.

Alternatively it has been argued that schoolwork may be avoided because learning has become involved in a neurotic conflict. In these cases learning is inhibited because of its symbolic associations. Thus it has been suggested that reading is associated with sexual 'looking'. Or, in the case of arithmetic, psychoanalysts have suggested that this may result from castration anxieties. While this may occasionally occur, it remains quite unknown how commonly learning inhibitions arise on the basis of these or any other types of neurotic conflict. Probably, not often. On a more conscious basis, certain school subjects may come to have a masculine or feminine identity and be favoured or avoided for this reason.

It is usually said that a little anxiety helps learning, but too much anxiety interferes with it. Also it has been thought that high anxiety is most beneficial for simple tasks, but lower levels of anxiety are optimal for difficult tasks. Actually the evidence on these points is rather contradictory, but in some children scholastic performance seems to be impeded by severe anxiety.

Finally, learning inhibitions may arise because of a general impairment of a child's psychological function. This can occur with schizophrenia beginning in adolescence, but it is much more commonly seen with depressive disorders.

Elliot was referred by his school at age thirteen years because of poor concentration on his work. He had had an excellent scholastic record at his primary school and was in the upper half of the top stream in his first year at grammar school. Then over the course of about eighteen months his work fell off badly and at the time of referral he was bottom of the lowest stream with marks ten per cent below the next lowest boy. He had become increasingly unhappy and often cried. He was tearful if spoken to sharply, no longer seemed to enjoy life, had given up his hobby of chemistry, was badly teased at school and had become increasingly reluctant to attend. Homework took longer and longer and at the time of referral was taking four hours. At school his relationships with other boys were poor, he participated poorly in group activities and had become increasingly shy and withdrawn, seeming in a perpetual daydream. At home he mostly sat around and took hours to get off to sleep at night.

The parents were very non-intellectual people who did not share Elliot's interests. Father was a quiet, passive man and mother was an assertive, capable, rather masculine woman. The marriage was not very happy and father was prone to bouts of depression. When seen at the clinic, Elliot was distant and unresponsive, speaking slowly with long silences. He was a tall, gangly, awkward boy who looked a caricature of the 'intellectual'. He hesitantly described feeling extremely miserable. Psychological testing showed him to have superior intelligence.

Elliot had a severe depressive disorder which had led to a progressive withdrawal and increasing impairment of his ability to work at school. His intelligence was more than adequate for what he had to do, but he achieved less and less as a result of his incapacitating depression. At the time he was seen he was rapidly getting worse and it soon became necessary for him to be admitted to hospital. He responded to antidepressants and after some months was able to return to school and once again cope with the schoolwork. Unfortunately, soon after that his mother died and his father developed a severe depressive illness requiring hospital admission. As a result Elliot once more became very depressed and it was another eighteen months before he was managing schoolwork adequately.

Nocturnal enuresis

Another very common problem in the schoolchild is that of nocturnal enuresis, or bed-wetting.[96] Thus in this country at age seven years one child in five still wets his bed occasionally; at age ten years about one in fourteen does so, but by age fourteen to fifteen years only one child in thirty-three remains enuretic. This sharp fall in the rate of wetting as children grow older is typical of developmental disorders. All infants wet themselves, because they have not got the biological capacity to control their bladders, but, with maturation, control becomes possible and fewer and fewer children wet. The question then arises: why is it that some children gain control by age two years, whereas others do not do so until their late teens?

In spite of the frequency of enuresis, no entirely satisfactory answers are available. However, the evidence we have suggests that several factors may be operative. First, enuresis frequently runs in families, and twin studies suggest that a genetic factor may be important in some cases. Second, in some children enuresis is associated with delayed physical maturation (such as shown by late puberty or a brain-wave pattern typical of younger children). This indicates that there may have been a delay in the development of the biological brain mechanism needed for bladder control. The evidence suggests that it is decidedly rare for biological immaturity to directly *prevent* bladder control after the age of four years, but it may be indirectly influential either by making the acquisition of control more difficult or by the effect of the early delay on parental expectations. Third, stresses occurring between one and four years of age, when bladder control is normally achieved, may interfere with the acquisition of control. Douglas has shown that children with enuresis are more likely than other children to have had stresses such as severe burns, hospital operations or family break-up during the preschool years. Fourth, in some children bed-wetting is associated with frequency of urination during the day. In these children there may be some functional disorder in the bladder's filling and emptying mechanism, although what this might be remains quite uncertain. Fifth, in some children toilet-training may have been inadequate either because of a lack of concern or because of excessive punitiveness. Bladder control usually develops without any specific training so this is probably not an important factor in most cases. On the other hand it is striking that, for some reason, children reared in institutions tend to have a higher rate of bed-wetting than do children in the general population. Sixth, about a quarter to a third of enuretic children have emotional or behavioural difficulties – a rate well above that in the general population. This association is more marked in girls than in boys, and more marked in children who wet during the day as well as at night. In some cases the emotional disturbances may be secondary to the enuresis, but the evidence suggests that it is often primary, although the causes for the psychiatric disorder leading to wetting are rather uncertain. Seventh, the enuresis may be a result of some current environmental stress. It is very common, for example, for children to wet only at home but not when staying with relatives. Often this is simply a function of the child's greater motivation to be dry when away from home, but sometimes it is a direct result of stresses in the parent–child relationship. Finally, and rarely, bed-wetting may be associated with physical abnormalities in the urinary tract. The most important association in this connection is that with urinary infection in girls. Although cure of the infection does not normally stop the wetting, investigation and treatment of any infection is most important because, if untreated, it may lead to kidney damage.

Obviously, the treatment of enuresis depends on the nature of the child's situation and the relevant causal factors. However, although it is crucial to give help with any underlying emotional or physical disturbance and remove any stress factors (using the methods described in other chapters) it will often be necessary in addition to provide some direct treatment for the wetting itself. Several treatments are available. In the first instance it is almost always worthwhile trying simple measures, such as providing encouragement for dry nights by means of praise and a star chart. In many children this is quite enough to tip the balance, so that the child achieves control. However, in other cases it may be necessary to use either drugs or the 'bell and pad'.

A large variety of drugs have been tried in the treatment of enuresis, but the tricyclic antidepressants (for example 'tofranil') are the only ones shown to be effective. Many children treated with tricyclics improve considerably, but probably less than half become completely dry. The benefit, when it occurs, is usually evident within a couple of weeks, so that there is no point in persisting with this form of treatment for more than a month if improvement has not occurred by then. The main drawback to using tricyclics is that most children become wet once more as soon as the drug is stopped. This means that rather prolonged treatment will be required in most cases if drugs constitute the mainstay of treatment. On the other hand this limitation does not apply if the tricyclics are used, in conjunction with other methods, to bring about control for shorter periods when it is most needed – such as when the child is going away on holiday or to a school camp.

The tricyclics seem to work best in girls, in youngsters who wet the bed frequently and in those who have gained bladder control but then lost it (a very common occurrence). It is probably least useful in mentally retarded children. The means by which the drugs control enuresis, when they do, remains quite obscure. The tricyclics have many pharmacological actions (including effects on the sympathetic-parasympathetic nervous system, antidepressive effects, local-anaesthetic actions, sedative effects and actions on sleep), and which of these effects is responsible for the benefits is not known. The drugs are best known for their antidepressive actions, but it is likely that this is not the crucial mechanism, although further research is needed.

The other treatment of proven benefit is the 'bell and pad'. This is a simple piece of apparatus designed to wake the child as soon as urination occurs. The child sleeps on some form of special mat placed under his sheet. The pad is wired to a battery, so that, as soon as a spot of urine comes through the sheet or as soon as the sheet is wet, an electrical circuit is completed which leads to the ringing of a loud alarm or bell. This simultaneously wakes the child and stops him passing urine. The precise means by which this leads to bladder control is not known, but the immediate awakening of the child as soon as he passes urine is the crucial element. This treatment necessitates close supervision to ensure both that the alarm does not go off unnecessarily (as with the child's sweating) and that when it does go off the child wakes up properly. The effect of the 'bell and pad' is specific, in that waking the child at intervals during the night is not so effective (although it helps some children).

The 'bell and pad' provides the most effective remedy for enuresis so far devised. About three quarters of children stop wetting after two or three months of treatment. A third of children relapse after treatment has stopped, but most of these respond to a second course of treatment. For many children it is the treatment of choice, but it does require a good deal of parental cooperation and some families do not manage to follow through with what is required. Although the evidence is somewhat contradictory, the method seems less successful in those children with a great deal of emotional or behavioural disturbance in addition to their wetting. Obviously, too, there are certain requirements for treatment which are not present in all families. For example, the child must have a bed of his own. Also, if several children share a bedroom the amount of disturbance caused to the others by the alarm may make this form of treatment impractical.

The criteria for using the 'bell and pad' are that organic disease has been excluded, that there has been no satisfactory response to simpler measures, that the child is wetting at least two or three times per week, that the child understands the purpose of the routine and can readily carry it out (the alarm should be reset when it goes off) and the parents are prepared to cooperate actively and persist with treatment. If there are problems with shared beds, it may be possible to invoke social assistance to obtain an extra bed or to help the family in other ways.

Although these are the best established treatments, others, not yet adequately evaluated, have been used with benefit in some children. For example, if children also wet during the day or if they urinate over-frequently during the day, it may be helpful to train them to hold their urine longer. This may be done by getting the child to go the lavatory regularly and by then gradually increasing the intervals until the child is able to go three or four hours before emptying his bladder.

The general principles involved in planning treatment for the child with enuresis are the same as those for children with other conditions. In short, before embarking on treatment it is necessary to obtain a careful account of the child's problems and development and to understand the circumstances which affect the likelihood of the child wetting. It is important also to know what the child feels about the wetting and about its possible origins. On the basis of the assessment, and in terms of hypotheses about the nature of the child's disorder and about the underlying mechanism, treatment should be planned. In children in whom the bed-wetting is an isolated symptom, one of the direct treatments of enuresis may be tried straight away. It is nearly always best to start with simple measures such as star charts (perhaps combined with lifting and waking when the parents come to bed). In all cases the doctor needs to provide explanation for what is usually a worrying complaint and, by his concern and involvement, to reduce family tensions and create attitudes of constructive optimism. If there is day-time frequency, interval training may be used as well at this stage. If these simple measures are not effective, then the 'bell and pad' is usually indicated, or tricyclics may be helpful (these are better not combined). If the enuresis is part of a wider emotional or behavioural disorder, appropriate treatment of the wider disorder should be undertaken along the lines described in other chapters. However, the presence of such a disorder should not inhibit the psychiatrist from using physical methods of treatment – successful treatment of the enuresis often leads to improvement in the other symptoms.

Encopresis (soiling)

Soiling is a much rarer disorder than wetting, but even so about one child in sixty-five still soils himself at age seven to eight. Whereas wetting is rather commoner in boys than in girls, soiling is very much commoner, with a sex ratio of about five to one. To a greater extent than with enuresis, encopresis is frequently part of a marked psychiatric disorder with many other symptoms apart from the soiling. While there are a variety of patterns of disorder associated with encopresis, three main types are the most important[1] (see also chapter 1).

The first type, mainly seen in younger children, is when the child has failed to gain control over his bowels. The soiling is frequently associated with wetting and the motions are passed into the pants wherever the child is at the time he needs to have his bowels opened. Often such children come from socially disadvantaged homes, many are seriously behind in their schoolwork, frequently the child is socially aggressive, and in many cases the parents too have personality limitations. The treatment in such cases involves some form of bowel-training together with whatever is required to deal with the wider social problems.

The second type is different in that it involves a partial blockage of the bowel with secondary overflow of loose motions. It is the main variety associated with abnormal motions, and, if there is diarrhoea as well as soiling, it should always be considered. In addition, when the doctor feels the abdomen, the masses of bowel distended with faeces will be evident. This can arise in two quite distinct ways. In the first the young child develops some kind of lesion (such as an anal fissure) which makes it very painful for him to pass his motions. As a result he becomes afraid to go to the lavatory and holds back his motions with resulting constipation. If this becomes severe, two things happen. First the distention leads to a loss of the bowel reflex which brings the need to pass motions to the child's attention. Second, the accumulation of faeces leads to a partial blockage, so that only watery, offensive motions leak past the blockage. The other (probably less common) way retention develops is when there is a parent–child battle over toilet-training. The child rebels against over-pressuring and strict potty-training and refuses to open his bowels. This brings about a severe and punitive response from his parents and thereby bowel opening comes to be associated with unpleasant feelings, fear and resentment. This leads on to a continuing struggle between parent and child in which the child repeatedly holds back, eventually causing severe constipation and bowel distension, as in the first mechanism. Either way, the first priority in treatment is to clear the bowel blockage by enemas and bowel washouts (or by appropriate medicines in milder cases). Then the child must be taught to empty his bowels regularly. Mild laxatives may be useful at first in bringing this about. In addition, of course, if there is still some anal lesion, it must be treated appropriately, and if there is a continuing parent–child battle over toilet-training, the family must be helped to alter their pattern of interaction.

The third type of encopresis is when the child had gained bowel control but then starts soiling as part of a psychiatric disturbance. In this type the soiling is usually *not* associated with wetting, the motions are normal in form but are deposited in all manner of unsuitable places. Often the child is full of shame, anxiety and guilt, the family exhibit obsessive-compulsive traits and the toilet-training has been invested with a high level of both tension and importance. In this type of encopresis some form of psychotherapy is usually necessary to deal with widespread family problems. At least initially bowel-training has little place. However, at a later stage in treatment when family stresses have been reduced, it may be useful if it seems that the soiling is continuing simply as a habit.

Soiling is a complaint which arouses strong emotions in most people, especially if it is associated with smearing (as it often is). Accordingly the family responses are not always a good guide to how the soiling arose. In order to determine the type of encopresis, close attention needs to be paid to the pattern of soiling and of bowel-opening. Gloria's problems provide a good example of how severe secondary psychological components may arise even when the soiling has a physical basis.

Gloria was referred to the clinic at age eleven years, having soiled regularly for three years and intermittently from the age of five years. As an infant Gloria had frequently been constipated and this alternated with brief periods of loose stools. Nevertheless she became fully clean and dry by the age of two and a half. At the age of five years there was a brief period of soiling and she complained that it hurt her to pass motions. Over the next year there were two more episodes of soiling, but these cleared up without treatment and there was no more soiling until she was aged eight years, since when she had soiled several times during every day and night. This occurred at home and at school, during term-time and holidays, and there were no times when she was clean. She went to the lavatory repeatedly during the day and had baths every morning and evening, but still there were often motions under her nails and sometimes sheets were smeared. Sometimes Gloria hid soiled underwear and lied about having dirtied herself.

Gloria had not done well at school. There were no other indications of emotional or behavioural disturbance except that she manipulated her parents with threats and promises and that she got on very badly with her elder sister of whom she was jealous. The sister was an attractive, intelligent girl, strikingly neat and well turned out. Mother was a houseproud woman, very fond of Gloria and deeply distressed by her soiling. She blamed herself for the trouble and wept at interview when talking about Gloria's soiling. Father, a shopkeeper, was a very fussy, tidy, safety-conscious man who could not bear anything out of place. He constantly checked up that the family had done everything they should and he nagged at Gloria about washing, doing her teeth and brushing her hair. The whole family had to take off their shoes and put on slippers when they entered the house in case they brought in dirt. Father regularly examined Gloria's pants for signs of soiling and he supervised her bathing, sometimes washing her body himself. He openly admitted his anger with Gloria and his feelings that she soiled on purpose.

Gloria was a rather immature girl of average intelligence who appeared cheerful and relaxed. She talked freely except on the topic of soiling which she refused to discuss. However, she expressed her dislike of dirt and her revulsion at puppies which had not been house-trained. On physical examination she was found to have a markedly protuberant lower abdomen in which bowels distended with faeces were easily felt. Her motions contained mucus.

There were ample indications that the family were abnormally preoccupied with cleanliness, the father–daughter relationship revolved around bathing and checking for soiling, there was overt rivalry between Gloria and her very clean, attractive sister, and Gloria manipulated her parents to such an extent that she dominated the household. All these elements suggested the third, psychogenic, variety of encopresis. However, the motions were abnormally loose and mucoid and she clearly had a grossly distended and blocked bowel. This indicated retention with overflow, whatever the psychological complications. Accordingly treatment was directed to relieving the blockage. Laxatives were briefly tried but they did not help at all. Gloria was admitted to hospital where she had several bowel washouts. She was discharged on a combined laxative and softening agent. This brought about a return to normal motions and, apart from one occasion a few months later when she was physically ill with a high fever, there was no recurrence of soiling. This confirmed that the assessment had been correct with respect to the origin of the soiling. However, the preoccupation with cleanliness and the abnormal parent–child interaction continued, so that the physical treatment was combined with counselling the parents and psychotherapy with the girl over the next three months. The parents were encouraged to let Gloria take more responsibility and not to supervise her washing. It was suggested that father should no longer bath her and the parents were encouraged to lay greater emphasis on Gloria's positive behaviour and to check less. This led to an appreciable relaxation of tension. The father remained a rather fussy man, but this impinged somewhat less on Gloria. A follow-up six months later showed that the improvement had been maintained and there had been no further soiling.

9 Methods of Treatment and their Effects

Throughout previous chapters reference has been made to the treatment of children with psychiatric problems and to the range of techniques available. In this chapter there will be a more explicit focus on the principles underlying various treatments. Child psychiatry is sometimes associated with the use of psychotherapy and social casework; in fact there are many other treatment methods and even the terms psychotherapy and casework cover a wide range of therapeutic approaches.

It would be appropriate to begin by a systematic account of the research findings indicating the efficacy of and indications for each form of treatment. Regrettably this is not possible. It is only in very recent times that psychiatrists and other professionals dealing with children have come to realize the importance of evaluating the results of their therapeutic endeavours. As a result the research findings on treatment are sparse and inconclusive for the most part. Nevertheless there is evidence suggesting that various forms of treatment may be effective if used appropriately in the right circumstances.[142] So far as possible I will attempt to indicate the strength of the evidence on therapeutic efficacy and the directions in which the findings point.

It should be appreciated in this connection that, as in much of medicine, the goals of treatment are to relieve suffering and to hasten recovery. Only rarely can treatment be thought of as providing a cure for a condition which would otherwise prove chronic. Most psychiatric disorders of childhood will ultimately remit even without treatment, but in the absence of treatment they may last several years and cause considerable distress and disability. In these cases the purpose of treatment is usually to bring about an earlier remission, although in a few cases it may

be to cut short a disorder which would not have remitted spontaneously. With some of the less common and more severe psychiatric disorders, such as infantile autism, it is not realistic to
expect full recovery (except with the occasional child) even with
the best possible treatment. In these cases the object of treatment is to reduce handicaps and aid more normal development.
For all these reasons attempts to measure the overall outcome
of child psychiatric treatment are of little interest. Different
disorders require different treatments and involve different
goals. It is no more meaningful to consider the average success
rate of child psychiatric treatment than it would be to consider
the average success rate of general medical treatment in hospital. The results will differ according to whether the patients
have cancer, pneumonia or diabetes and according to whether
the right treatments are used in the right circumstances. So it is
with child psychiatry. Accordingly studies of global treatment
will not be considered. Rather, attention will be confined to the
very few investigations of specific treatments for specific problems.

Psychotherapy

Although a wide variety of other treatments have become available in the last twenty years or so, psychotherapy has long been
the method of treatment specifically associated with psychiatry.
This is as true of child psychiatry as it is of the treatment of
adults. People have argued over the correct definition of
psychotherapy, without resolving the issue. However, what is
generally agreed is that psychotherapy is a form of treatment in
which the main therapeutic agent lies in the communication and
in the relationship between the therapist and the patient. This
cannot be thought of as one method, because there are many
very different varieties of psychotherapy, which are distinguished both by the theories which lie behind the method and
by the ways in which the psychotherapeutic communication
and relationship are used to bring about improvement. In all
types of psychotherapy an understanding of the meaning of
behaviour plays an important role and the goal is to help the

patient himself develop better ways of dealing with his emotional problems.

In the beginning the main impetus for the development of psychotherapeutic methods came from psychoanalysis and from analytic psychology, which provided a theoretical framework in which psychiatric disorders were thought to have developed through unconscious processes. Thus psychoanalytically oriented psychotherapy places most emphasis on gaining insight with respect to these unconscious conflicts and mental mechanisms. Freud and Jung were the pioneers in these fields and, with respect to child psychotherapy, Anna Freud, Melanie Klein and Michael Fordham have done most to develop the subject in this country.

The use of psychoanalytic methods provided understanding of the workings of the human mind, and many of the insights thereby gained into mental mechanisms and psychological processes have been accepted to the point where they are now general knowledge and are an intrinsic part of almost any type of psychotherapy, regardless of theoretical orientation. It is widely appreciated that patterns of behaviour may have a symbolic significance or hidden meaning. In an earlier chapter we discussed the case of a boy who became severely depressed on the anniversary of his father's death. There were no particular objective stresses in April when he became depressed, but the coming of Easter served to remind him of his father's death the previous April. Sometimes children are aware of these connections but often they are not. The association is unconscious and its meaning is only understood later. Also almost everyone has come to accept the notion of mental mechanisms. A father's anger with his boss at work may be *displaced* on to his wife when he returns home from work. Appointments may be forgotten because really you did not want to go and the memory of the meeting was *repressed*.

Research into these various psychological processes has been rather fragmentary, so that the results are often inconclusive and open to different interpretations, as the recent books by Kline[95] and Eysenck[53] show. We do not know just how often the various mechanisms operate and evidence on the relative importance of each is lacking. This unsatisfactory state of affairs has led some academic psychologists to deny altogether the existence of unconscious processes and to reject the relevance of the meaning of behaviour. This seems too sweeping. Even leading behaviourist psychologists have come to accept the importance of the meaning of behaviour, and there are grounds for accepting the existence of both symbolism and unconscious mechanisms. An appreciation of these processes greatly aids an understanding of why people behave in the way they do.

Traditionally, psychoanalytic psychotherapy involved very frequent treatment sessions over a period of several years. The focus was exclusively on what went on during the treatment sessions, and in some clinics there was a deliberate refusal to pay any attention to what was happening in the child's life during the remaining twenty-three hours of the day, and a deliberate avoidance of any therapeutic contact with the parents or any other members of the family. This approach was exceedingly time-consuming and was based on the misleading assumption that the roots of disorder always lay entirely in intra-psychic processes, rather than in any aspect of current interpersonal relationships or in current environmental stresses or deficiencies.

As a result psychotherapeutic methods have developed and been modified in several important respects. The four main changes have been: (1) a move towards briefer methods of treatment, (2) a greater attention to conscious conflicts and the current environmental stresses, (3) a shift away from exclusive treatment of the individual child towards a focus on the family as a group of interacting members and (4) less preoccupation with the interpretation of intra-psychic mechanisms and a greater reliance on the therapist–child relationship itself as the main treatment agent.

In the first instance economic considerations led to an exploration of briefer methods of treatment. Clearly, frequent interviews over the course of several years was just not a practical proposition for most patients, and such methods inevitably meant that only a tiny proportion of children needing treatment could receive it. However, as experience with short-term psychotherapy increased, it became evident that there were actually positive advantages in these briefer methods. With brief therapy there had to be a clear focus of therapy and a setting of realistic treatment goals. Time limitations necessitated a more definitive therapeutic strategy, greater activity by the therapist and a more active role played by the family both between sessions and during the psychotherapeutic interview. The therapist needed to search for the family strengths and to encourage family members to use these strengths in coping with both the internal and interpersonal aspects of their lives. As well as observations, reflections and interpretations as in traditional psychoanalytic psychotherapy, therapists became prepared to use also reassurance, advice and directions whenever appropriate. Rosenthal and Levine[144] made a controlled comparison between brief psychotherapy and long-term psychotherapy and found that for most patients the shorter methods were equally effective, although, for some, more prolonged treatment may be required. This is in keeping with studies of psychotherapy in adults which suggest that prolonged and intensive treatments have little, if any, advantage over briefer methods.

There is very little evidence on how the benefits of psychotherapy compare with other methods of treatment, such as advice and reassurance, or behavioural techniques. Most of the attempted comparisons have such serious flaws that no weight can be attached to the findings. However, there are a few investigations which have used some kind of appropriate control. For example, there are a few studies of psychotherapy with institutionalized delinquents which indicate that this may be of some value, especially if it is combined with learning practical skills. Almost the only controlled study in an out-patient setting is that undertaken by Eisenberg and his colleagues.[51] They showed that brief psychotherapy led to significantly greater improvement in neurotic children than did simple assessment and advice. Unfortunately the methods used in psychotherapy were not described. Their results are encouraging, but until the results are confirmed or contradicted by other controlled studies, the findings must be accepted with reservations. Research into the efficacy of psychotherapy is difficult and complex, but further studies are greatly needed; indeed they are essential if our psychiatric services for children are to be planned on a rational basis.

In recent years there have been two important advances in psychotherapeutic research. First, it has been found that there are systematic differences between therapists in their therapeutic efficacy. Second, it appears that people with different personality characteristics may require different types of psychotherapy.

Most of the work on therapist variables has been conducted with adults or adolescents and it is uncertain how far the findings may be generalized to children. However, the findings are provocative and interesting and may well be relevant in younger age-groups. There is extensive evidence that the therapist's faith, interest, enthusiasm and optimism are important factors in leading to improvement when drugs are used in treatment, and similar findings have been reported with brief psychotherapy. Enthusiastic, involved therapists tend to have a greater success rate than do uninterested or pessimistic therapists. The importance of therapist variables has been most extensively explored by Truax and his colleagues[190] with respect to Rogerian counselling, which aims to be relatively non-directive in approach. Their findings indicate that effective therapists are those who are able to perceive and communicate accurately and with sensitivity both the feelings and experiences of the patient and their meaning and significance. In a way this is parallel to Kounin's finding[97] that the most effective teachers are those who are 'on the ball' and able to appreciate accurately what is happening in the classroom. However, of equal importance is the finding that effective therapists provide a trusting and open relationship in which they are warm and accepting. Obviously to some extent these characteristics are part (or not part) of someone's personality, but it also appears that to a considerable extent the skills may be learned. Clearly this has important implications for the training of psychiatrists. This is particularly so because the research also suggests that therapists who are not warm, empathic and open may actually make their patients worse!

The differing therapeutic needs of individuals have been most explored in the Californian treatment programmes for delinquents.[124, 192] Their findings suggest that anxious youths with feelings of guilt and inadequacy do better with more easygoing therapists who show interest in the boy's feelings about himself and about others. In contrast the tough delinquent conforming to sub-cultural norms or the manipulative anti-authority, non-conformist delinquent both respond better to direct, outspoken, more formal therapists who focus less on feelings and more on issues related to external controls and the setting of limits. Again the findings need replication by other workers and with different groups of youngsters, but the evidence certainly suggests that the type of therapy needs to be carefully tailored to individual needs.

Individual psychotherapy with children

Individual psychotherapy of children is most likely to be required when the child's problems stem from some form of emotional disturbance concerned either with internal conflicts and stresses or with the way he feels about some unalterable stress in the past or present. This applied, for example, to Margaret, the girl in chapter 3 (page 130) who had had a severe head injury, leaving her partially paralysed down one side and who became depressed in adolescence. Her difficulties derived from worries that she was unattractive to boys as a result of her injury, and from the conflicts between her wish to be an autonomous individual and her need to remain dependent on her parents. The family provided loving and harmonious relationships, so that there were no family stresses and her physical handicap, although fairly mild, could not be altered. The difficulties came from how Margaret *felt* about the situation. She responded first by depression and then by tentative expressions of sexual provocativeness. The therapist provided a trusting relationship and showed that he understood how Margaret felt and how these concerns were important to her. By discussing her conflicts over independence and her lack of confidence in her attractiveness, Margaret came to accept her minor physical limitations, and by being more relaxed and confident in her interpersonal relationships learned to overcome her disabilities to a considerable extent. She gained confidence through her trusting relationship with the therapist, and, by understanding the nature of her emotional conflicts, she was helped to find better ways of dealing with her difficulties.

The situation with Sandra, the promiscuous, antisocial girl discussed in chapter 7, page 255, was different in that not only was she in conflict over her developing identity as a young woman but also there were problems in her family due to lack of communication and understanding. In her case it was important to help the parents change too, though the central focus of treatment was the psychotherapy with the girl herself. It was important to her to have an adult therapist who accepted her as she was, and who showed warmth and understanding in spite of her deviant behaviour. Of course the acceptance of Sandra did not mean that the therapist had to approve of what she did. While not criticizing Sandra and while accepting that for the moment she had to act in the way she did, the therapist also indicated that he thought that her use of drugs and mixing with criminal young men carried dangers. By showing he realized that these were responses to her emotional difficulties, the basis was laid for helping her come to more adaptive solutions to her problems. Again both the warm relationship and the understanding which came from a discussion of her problems and her conflicts were important elements in therapy.

With Margaret and Sandra it was possible to discuss feelings, attitudes and behaviour in a relatively direct manner once trust had been established. However, in other cases more indirect means may be needed. For example, Dorothy was a shy, rather inhibited eleven-year-old girl who had recently reached puberty and who was referred because of an anxiety state accompanied by stomach pains. She found it difficult to express her feelings openly at first and, in particular, she was reluctant to talk about her feelings for her teacher at school to whom she had become very attached in a way which worried her. Communication became easier when Dorothy talked about her dreams. These provided both an expression of her feelings and a medium which allowed her to be frank in a way impossible for her when talking about real-life happenings. Dorothy was encouraged to tell the therapist about her dreams and then to discuss her feelings and thoughts about them. In view of both the content of her dreams and, more particularly, the feelings they aroused in Dorothy when talking about them it became clear that Dorothy had sexual feelings towards her teacher which aroused great guilt and anxiety. She was greatly relieved at being able to talk about these feelings which she had not been able to accept in herself, and both the stomach pains and anxiety feelings went as Dorothy came to realize that this sort of 'crush' was part of normal adolescence, and a sign neither of lesbianism nor of sin.

In younger children communication often has to be through play. This has sometimes led to the use of the term 'play therapy'. However, play itself does not constitute the therapy. Rather the play provides a mode of communication. This means that the toys available to the child in therapy should lend themselves to the expression of feelings and ideas. Paints, plasticine, puppets, family figures, toy soldiers and guns may all help the child communicate his thoughts. For example, Frank, a severely withdrawn seven year old, expressed his feelings through his drawings. He drew lively active pictures of animals fighting, and as he drew he gave them names of both family members and class mates at school. Feelings of hostility were expressed both in the representation of killings and also in the angry obliteration of figures by heavy scribbling. His own moods were accurately reflected in his choice of colours: black when he was depressed and red when things seemed more hopeful. Drawings provided a way of re-enacting unhappy interactions at home and school which could be given a different ending in fantasy. By discussion of his drawings it was possible to get Frank to recognize his social problems, which he denied if asked directly, and then to move on to the development of better ways of dealing with them.

Henry was an aggressive eight year old from an extremely deprived and unhappy family background. He put on a social front of 'couldn't care less' bravado but his great unhappiness was evident for all to see. He had been placed in care but still had intermittent contact with his family. Henry was very aware of the insecurities of his family relationships and would occasionally talk of his worries and distress that he had no one he could rely on when he needed them. However, most of the time he pretended that his family was just like everyone else's. In therapy he adopted a convention of using a toy theatre set to re-enact family scenes about a boy in exactly his situation. These both expressed his anger about his family and also served to explore new solutions. The therapist, who was inexperienced, at first drew the parallel with Henry's own family, but these comments were met by angry denial. The psychiatrist quickly learned that, so long as he did not actually say that he knew the boy in the theatre scene was Henry, he could discuss Henry's difficulties by talking about the boy in the play. Occasionally Henry slipped into saying 'I' when he meant the other boy and would grin sheepishly knowing that, although neither said so, both he and the therapist were well aware that it was really Henry who was being discussed. It was very important to Henry to know that he could always rely on the therapist and his trust was something he had not previously experienced. Of course the therapist could in no sense take the part of Henry's father who was rarely on the scene, but his relationship with the boy could be used to help Henry accept his appalling family situation and, in accepting it, to learn how to deal with it.

Different therapists use rather different approaches, but most would agree with the seven principles outlined by Reisman.[135] They are:

(1) A careful assessment of the nature of the child's psychological difficulties is an essential precondition to psychotherapy. The therapist must discover the actual psychological mechanisms which underlie each child's problems, rather than assuming some mechanism on the basis of theoretical considerations.

(2) The therapist listens to the child and allows him ample opportunity to express his feelings and beliefs. This implies both that the therapist does not impose his own views and that

the therapeutic situation is so structured as to facilitate communication.

(3) The therapist communicates his understanding of the child and his wish to be of help.

(4) The therapist and child should define the purpose or goals of their meeting. These are not necessarily the reasons why the child was referred, but it is important that the child appreciate that therapy has a point and a focus.

(5) The therapist must make clear what is ineffective or inappropriate in the child's behaviour.

(6) When dealing with behaviour that is dependent on social interaction, the therapist may modify it by focusing directly on the interaction. This means that when the trouble lies in family communication and relationships it may be more appropriate to use conjoint family therapy (see page 312) than individual therapy with the child. Similarly, if the difficulties lie in the school, treatment may best be conducted there, perhaps through consultation with teachers. Alternatively, if the child's difficulties concern his interaction with other children, group therapy may be indicated in which the child is seen as part of a group of children with similar or related problems.

(7) The therapist should plan ending the treatment when the advantages of ending outweigh the advantages of continuing. This sounds self-evident, but what it implies is that treatment may need to finish before the child is fully better. Complete recovery may not be realistic and it could be counterproductive to continue treatment past the point where it is having any effect.

Fundamental to the whole of psychotherapy is a clear identification of goals and objectives. This implies also a consideration both of whether psychotherapy is the most appropriate method of reaching the goals and also, if it is, what type of therapy is most appropriate. Psychotherapy should never be the automatic treatment of choice. It is the best approach in some circumstances but quite inappropriate in others. During therapy clear limits need to be set on the child's behaviour. Except in very unusual circumstances nothing is to be gained by allowing the child to be aggressive or destructive, and the child will feel more secure when it is clear what is allowed and what is not. In aiding communication and understanding it is usually better, when a child describes a situation or event, to respond to the child's feelings or relationships rather than to the specific set of circumstances. Thus, if a child says that he is tormented by other children, it would be better to respond by recognizing that this makes the child feel angry or hurt or by appreciating the implications in terms of his lack of friendships – not in the first instance by asking which children tormented him or in what classroom it occurred. It may be valuable later to know these details when helping the child learn how to cope with unpleasant teasing, but, if asked to begin with, it implies a lack of feeling and understanding of the child's plight.

The therapist may convey understanding and empathy by the appropriate use of interpretations of psychological processes or interpersonal interactions. Interpretations also serve to aid insight and understanding. However, it is important that these should be made in an inquiring way which helps the child to explore and understand his feelings, rather than as a dogmatic, *ex cathedra* statement. It is also necessary that the therapist use the language of the child at an appropriate level of both vocabulary and abstraction. Throughout treatment the therapist needs to focus on positive assets and constructive solutions rather than on deficiencies and failures. Although the child needs to recognize his failures and disabilities, it is essential that he be helped to find constructive solutions.

While the essence of psychotherapy lies in the child gaining understanding, it would be both blinkered and silly not to appreciate that often it may be helpful for the therapist to suggest ways of dealing with problems and to take steps to alter environmental stresses. This may mean that psychotherapy should be combined with educational methods, with environmental manipulation or with behavioural modification techniques. As already noted, the strengths of brief psychotherapy sometimes lie in this flexible bringing together of different therapeutic methods in order to gain the best leverage on the problem.

Conjoint family therapy

As psychiatrists have come to appreciate that in many cases the origin of children's problems lies in the family, conjoint family therapy has been more and more widely employed. This is a method of psychotherapy in which the whole family group is seen together and in which the focus is placed on family inter-action rather than on the problems of one individual child. An example was given in chapter 4, page 154. Up to now there have been very few systematic and controlled evaluations of family therapy and it is not yet possible to draw conclusions regarding its efficacy or its merits and demerits compared with other methods. Nevertheless what studies there have been suggest that the approach has value,[193] and clinical experience indicates that in appropriate cases it can be a most useful form of treat-ment. Unfortunately in some centres enthusiasm for family therapy has increased so much in recent years that a few psy-chiatrists have come to see it as an answer to all problems, which it is not. Children's psychiatric disorders may not be due at all to problems in the family and, even where they do arise through family difficulties, family therapy may not be the best way of dealing with the problems. Because it is a relatively new form of treatment, the criteria for its use are not yet adequately established. However, the chief indications seem to be:

(1) The main problems lie in family communication or inter-action: that is, there are difficulties in family members under-standing one another, or coming to agreements, or getting other people to listen or finding someone in whom to confide.

(2) This problem should be a major factor in the disorder which leads the family to seek help.

(3) There should be substantial emotional ties between family members. It is quite possible in family therapy to deal with angry feelings and with resentment, but this is not usually the right form of treatment where the predominant feelings are ones of hostility and rejection without compensatory warmth.

(4) There should be some wish or need for family members to remain together. If the parents are on the verge of divorce, or if the child is about to leave home, conjoint family therapy is not usually appropriate.

Family therapy should not be used where the child's problems are largely due to factors intrinsic to the child or extrinsic
to the family. This means that it is inadvisable to use a means of
diagnostic assessment which presupposes the need for family
therapy. It is always necessary to assess the importance of constitutional or physical factors in the child, of intra-psychic
conflict unrelated to family disturbance and of stress at school
or in the community. Although it is always informative to interview the family together, it is also usually necessary to see the
child and his parents individually.

A variety of techniques have been suggested for conjoint
family therapy, and many therapists use methods which combine several. However, there are probably three main approaches. Zuk[206] suggested two – a psychoanalytic approach
and a systems analysis approach – but a third, using behavioural methods, has been used increasingly in the last few
years. In the traditional psychoanalytic approach there is an
emphasis on unconscious processes, the current effects of past
events, the meaning of the relationship of different family
members with the therapist and the fostering of insight into
behaviour. The focus is on the meaning of what is said by each
speaker (rather than on its effect on other family members), and
direct suggestions are rarely offered. In the systems analysis
approach the main emphasis is on the *interaction* between
family members, as shown by the patterns of dominance, the
kinds of communications which are transmitted, the type of
feedback given to the speaker by other family members and
patterns of isolation or scapegoating. In short the family is
viewed as a miniature social system in which the therapist's task
is to understand the forces acting within the system as they lead
to maladaptive behaviour, and to alter the forces accordingly.
In this approach the therapist may comment on the exclusion or
victimization of certain family members and may want the
family to discuss why the child (or father or mother) is not
being given a chance to express his viewpoint or why conflicting
messages are being given and what is the effect of such messages.

In practice many of the leading exponents of conjoint family therapy (especially those with a background in group therapy, a form of treatment in which several patients are seen together for psychotherapy) combine both approaches. For example, Skynner[180] emphasizes the importance of re-establishing adequate family communication and developing an effective dominance hierarchy to provide a degree of control and consistent structure appropriate to the children's developmental stage. There is an assumption that the child's symptom represents some blocked communication. Role-playing and acting out family difficulties may highlight the problems in the way family members interact. There are probably four main differences between this type of conjoint family therapy and traditional psychoanalytic individual psychotherapy: (1) the focus in family therapy is more on the here-and-now interactions rather than on past events (although these are also considered); (2) there is an emphasis on communications between family members rather than on intra-psychic conflict in the single patient; (3) there is a deliberate expectation that the family will continue between appointments to discuss and develop the interactions during the therapeutic session (sessions are often at two- or three-week intervals to encourage this); (4) treatment is usually brief, with not more than a dozen or so meetings.

In order to focus better on current family interaction and communication some therapists deliberately avoid obtaining an account of what the parents are concerned about and avoid either interviewing or examining the individual child. While there may well be some advantages in starting straight away on family interaction, in my view this is undesirable because it starts with the quite unwarranted assumption that the child's problems must reside in family interaction and that family therapy is always the treatment of first choice. Unfortunately these assumptions and claims to universal applicability are frequent when new methods are brought in with a fanfare and become a fashion. Much the same thing has happened at various times with the use of drugs and behavioural treatments.

The third approach to conjoint family therapy is that based on a behavioural model using principles of learning. Liberman[105] is one of the foremost exponents of this method. He emphasizes three main areas of concern. First, creating and maintaining a positive therapeutic alliance. In this he follows the work of Truax and his colleagues[190] which has already been discussed and which maintains that a relationship based on warmth, empathy and concern is fundamental to all forms of treatment. Second, a behavioural analysis of the problem. This involves an identification of the changes that each person would like to see in other members of the family and the ways he would like to be different himself. This allows an identification of specific goals of treatment and often brings out the basic dissatisfactions in the family which have not previously been expressed in a clear and unambiguous fashion. The analysis also requires the identification of what environmental or interpersonal factors are leading to a perpetuation of maladaptive behaviour. Third, use of the principles of *reinforcement* (i.e. encouragement and reward as positive reinforcement, and unpleasant consequences or lack of attention as negative reinforcement) and of modelling (i.e. providing an example of the behaviour which is wanted to influence interpersonal interactions).

In bringing about change there is an explicit focus on specific goals and there is an emphasis on moving towards those goals by a series of small, carefully graded steps which are shaped by the appropriate use of encouragement and approval. The therapist aims to provide a shift towards more optimistic and hopeful expectations; to give the family an emphasis on doing things differently while giving the responsibility for change to each family member; to encourage the family to look at themselves and their relationships with one another; and to ensure that a record is kept of the changes that occur, so that everyone can see if things are moving in the right direction.

As in the other family approaches there is an emphasis on here-and-now interaction, and role playing or behavioural rehearsal may be used to bring about improved patterns of interaction. Also, as in other approaches, the therapist–family relationships are considered important to the solution of family problems in a conjoint affair. The main differences lie in the explicit identification of goals, the functional analysis to determine causes and effects in the family, the open recognition that there is a need to define family tasks and that each person needs to do things differently between sessions, and the explicit use of both small steps and encouragement to bring about changes in family interaction.

As with the other varieties of conjoint family therapy there is a lack of sound research evidence upon which to assess the efficacy of the method or its suitability for different types of problem. However, clinical experience suggests that it is a most useful technique in properly selected cases.

Group therapy with parents or with children

Group therapy seems to be particularly useful when the children's main problems concern interactions with other youngsters. It is often very difficult to deal with these problems in any type of individual therapy because the therapist inevitably has to rely on other people's accounts of what happens, rather than having the opportunity to observe the interactions himself. In these cases it may be particularly useful to see the child in a therapeutic group together with other children, usually of similar age. The therapist can note what it is the child does that leads to isolation, rejection, teasing, bullying or whatever the difficulty may be. Then, by focusing on the nature of the group interactions and communications, the child can be helped to modify his behaviour. The principles are similar to those outlined for family therapy and the methods used show similar variations. The main difference lies in the obvious fact that the child is interacting with strangers rather than with the group of individuals with whom he shares problems outside sessions. Because of this drawback it may sometimes be useful to work directly in the setting where the problems arise. The school-based treatment of the boy described in chapter 5, page 210, is an example of an approach of this kind. Very little research has been undertaken with respect to group therapy with children.

Other sorts of groups, not usually based on psychoanalytic principles, have been developed to deal with different sorts of problems. For example, many parents find it helpful meeting with other parents who share similar problems with their children. This may be particularly valuable for the parents of children with chronically handicapping disorders such as mental retardation, cerebral palsy or infantile autism. Such groups serve several purposes. First, parents may derive a good deal of comfort from talking with other parents in a similar predicament. People are very inclined to blame parents for shortcomings in their children and a group situation free of this blame can be very supportive. Second, both the therapist and other parents can help them to find ways of coping with their difficulties. Discussion of how other families have dealt with tantrums, sleeping difficulties, feeding problems and toilet-training difficulties may suggest how their own problems of a similar kind may be met. Third, feelings of guilt, anger, despair and frustration are the common lot of parents whose children show severe disorders. Frequently parents are very reluctant to admit these negative feelings, and not only is it reassuring to find that other parents have felt the same way but also discussion may aid an understanding of how these feelings arise and how they may be dealt with.

Another sort of group is that where several parents and their children meet together. This has been particularly used when mothers who have become depressed or who suffer from persistent neurotic or personality disorders find difficulty in knowing how to deal with their preschool children. In these circumstances it may not be a question of dealing with problematic behaviour in the child but rather of how to play and talk with children. By meeting together in a supportive group with a therapist, mothers may learn by example as well as by discussion how to enjoy their children and how to cope with the many common difficulties that young children present.

Unhelpful aspects of psychoanalysis

Psychoanalysis has made fundamental and lasting contributions to our understanding of problem behaviour and the workings of the mind, and has played an essential role in the development of methods of psychotherapy. Nevertheless, as Philip

Graham[87] has pointed out in a recent article, it would be misleading not to note that certain unhelpful attitudes have also drifted in on the tide of psychoanalysis. Perhaps the two most serious are the assumptions that *all* behaviour is explicable in psychoanalytic terms (which seems to lack modesty and is in any case out of keeping with the available evidence) and that the goal of treatment is to satisfy the therapists' own interests rather than to make the patient better (which appears blinkered, to say the least). Graham quotes Meltzer as claiming that the therapist should continue psychotherapy for the child so long as the treatment holds the therapist's interest and fulfils his professional desires.

The over-interpretation of children's behaviour in psychoanalytic terms is best illustrated by Graham's quotation from Michael Fordham: 'From this and various other indications it seemed clear that Alan's omnipotent defences, which had become very prominent, were defences against his ambivalent passive wishes. When this became clear to me, I made this interpretation: his anus sometimes felt that it wanted father's penis in it, just as he sometimes wanted mine also. But he feared that if it got inside it would turn bad and damage his like the faeces which were often like animal penises and that was why he expelled them (he suffered from encopresis).'

Of course Fordham's explanation could be correct, but it sounds implausible and far-fetched and is made in the (false) certainty that psychoanalytic theory is correct and that there is no need to consider other types of explanation or other theoretical viewpoints. Both Meltzer and Fordham are distinguished exponents of psychotherapy and have made important contributions to the subject, but this type of exclusive adherence to psychoanalysis as the incorporation of all that is good has no place either in science or in practical medicine. It has rightly brought certain aspects of child psychiatry into disrepute. Unfortunately some clinics still run on these rather limited lines. Undoubtedly they will provide valuable help for some families but for others they have little to offer and their failure to recognize that may prevent the families from getting the kind of treatment they need.

Casework

Casework is the tool-in-trade of the psychiatric social worker, and so far as child psychiatry is concerned it provides the range of techniques used by the social worker to help families and especially to help parents. Volumes have been written about the nature of casework and critics have not been slow to point out that much of the writing is vague, pompous and pretentious.[202] Great emphasis has been laid on 'the relationship' with the client and in some quarters there has been such heavy reliance on psychoanalysis that the social worker has become preoccupied with people's psychological inner world to the exclusion of the outer world of the social environment in which they live. It has to be admitted that these criticisms have substance, but it would be quite wrong to equate casework with its more extravagant claims, however eminent the writers may be. Casework provides an integral and essential part of child psychiatric services and the role of the psychiatric social worker is frequently crucial in treatment.

The central characteristic of casework is its emphasis on the *social* context of people's behaviour. Children's development is seen primarily in terms of their relation to interpersonal interaction, particularly in the family but also outside it. This interaction takes place in a social and community framework, so that the social worker is as much concerned with the ways in which social forces, resources and attitudes influence people's behaviour, as with the intra-psychic conflicts of an individual person. The scientific background of the social worker is in the social sciences, and the scientific basis of social work is to be found in sociology, social anthropology, social administration and social psychology. The social worker in a child psychiatric clinic will have had (or should have had) extra training and experience both with the issues special to psychiatry and with the needs and problems in child development. In recent years there has been a shift to a broad generic training for all social workers regardless of the field in which they are going to work. However, it is being increasingly appreciated that, in addition, there is a need for more specialized training tailored to the particular concerns in each of the sub-specialities of social work.

As in any of the helping professions, but particularly in those dealing with people's psychological problems, there is a need for a warm, empathic, honest but accepting and non-critical relationship, as already discussed with respect to psychotherapy. This provides a basis for the wide range of techniques that the social worker may use in helping families with their various problems.

When considering how to help any particular family, the social worker will want to determine how their social circumstances impinge on their life and how they have reacted to their life situation. In this he will be concerned with such items as housing, finances, neighbours, community leisure facilities and schooling. The social worker is an expert on both the social provisions that are available and also the wide range of state facilities and voluntary organizations that may be used to provide the necessary help. He will know how to arrange for the care of children at times of crisis, how to provide holiday placements for mentally handicapped children, what nursery-group or special-school facilities might be appropriate and how to get in touch with the relevant parent organizations (such as those involved with mentally handicapped, autistic, speech-impaired or cerebral palsied children). He will provide material help when this is needed, but the overall aim will always be to enable people to help themselves. The social worker will want to determine not only what social resources are lacking but whether people are making the best use of the resources they already possess. This is partly a question of how people respond psychologically to any particular situation but also partly of how they organize themselves in their community to deal with the issues that face them all. Although the social worker's prime responsibility must be to the particular family he serves, he will always be concerned with the adequacy of community resources and hence has a responsibility to the community as a whole. With this responsibility he will be aware of the importance of organizations such as Shelter or Child Poverty Action, which exist both to improve social conditions and to reduce the suffering of poor families. The social worker will want to work with these organizations and in some situations may need to be active within them.

In these actions it is the 'social' in social casework which receives emphasis. However, the special skills involved in casework are rather different, but complementary. The therapeutic techniques are varied, but those specially characteristic of casework are ones concerned with understanding and influencing the way in which people interact and behave in social situations. The interview is the main therapeutic tool, but the ways in which it is used are based on several different bodies of knowledge: on the understanding of how people interact and how small groups function, deriving from social psychology; on the insights into psychodynamics, provided by psychoanalysis; on the methods of influencing behaviour, which stem from clinical psychology; and on the therapeutic use of the relationship, deriving from the field of counselling. Although the social worker may often interview parents on their own, the principles and skills employed are very close to those used on conjoint family therapy, and indeed he may often use that method of treatment. He will have a range of techniques to help people alter their environment and their ways of interacting, and may take a specifically educational role in suggesting or demonstrating ways of dealing with particular problems in child-rearing – how to encourage self-help, how to ignore attention-seeking behaviour, how to cope with the child's demands, how to play and talk with a young child.

Casework differs from behaviour therapy in being more concerned with how people relate and interact than with the modification of individual items of behaviour. Nevertheless, the social worker should have a full understanding of behaviour modification techniques and will sometimes make extensive use of these methods in the course of casework. The importance of these approaches in social work has been well argued by Jenu.[85]

Casework differs from psychotherapy in that it is not primarily concerned with intra-psychic conflict. Rather it places greater emphasis on interpersonal conflict. Nevertheless the skills involved in psychotherapy are essential to casework, the social worker must understand intrapsychic mechanisms and in some circumstances he will practise straightforward psychotherapy, as already described.

In common with all these methods of therapy, casework shares the need for an accurate diagnostic formulation, a precise delineation of goals, a clear appraisal of what methods will be used to reach the goals and a systematic monitoring of treatment to determine whether the initial formulation was correct and how far the aims are being achieved.

That these are indeed the right requirements is suggested by a well-controlled evaluative study by Reid and Shyne.[134] They studied families presenting difficulties in marital or parent–child relationships and found that the results were significantly better with planned, short-term casework (up to eight interviews within a three-month period) than with a continued or open-ended approach involving up to a hundred interviews within an eighteen-month time-span. The advantages of the brief casework seemed to lie in its focus on and definition of goals as much as on its brevity.

Reid and Shyne's study stands in refreshing contrast to most others. Although it is likely that short-term intervention will prove inappropriate and ineffective in many chronic and complex situations, the emphasis on a planned approach probably has wide applicability.[66] Mullen and his colleagues[115] have made a useful appraisal of the available evaluations of social intervention (only a few of which were concerned with children) and have shown that, although there have been some successes, for the most part studies have failed to demonstrate the efficacy of the methods used. This shortcoming seems to stem largely from a failure to define goals and values and a general diffuseness and vagueness about the therapeutic techniques employed. The studies provide a warning concerning the need to get away from general waffle and 'do-goodery'.

The ways in which casework often combines different techniques is best illustrated by considering a particular family.

Maureen was a two year old referred because of sleeping problems and difficulties separating from her mother. The sleep problem began when she was six months and had continued ever since. She shared a room with her mother and kept her mother awake half the night insisting that she play with her. Maureen was very clinging and, if anybody visited the home, she screamed and held on to

mother. She appeared frightened of all adults and would only sometimes separate from mother to play with her cousins. There were
tantrums each evening and she was particularly irritable when
father (who lived elsewhere) did not visit, as well as when he left
after visits.

Mother was an unmarried Irish woman living on her own, who had
been brought up with her sister in a harsh and very strict orphanage
since infancy, after the death of her own mother. Her father had remarried when she was a schoolgirl and she and her sister had then
returned home. She did not get on at all well with her stepmother
and left home as a teenager to come to London. In her early
twenties she had an affair with a married man, which lasted for six
years until Maureen was born and the man returned to his wife. He
still visits mother several times a week. He wanted a son very much,
was disappointed that Maureen was a girl, and still has very mixed
feelings about her. Mother became depressed while Maureen was an
infant, and was put on antidepressants. These made little difference
and she remained miserable, eating and sleeping poorly. Mother
had not told her father about Maureen and was frightened he would
find out. Maureen and her mother lived in a small, one-bedroomed,
basement flat. Mother found Maureen very difficult and had little
idea of how to play with her.

The difficulties seemed to centre around the mother–child
interaction. The immediate problem concerned mother's depression which was adversely influencing the way she dealt with
Maureen. However, other problems stemmed from mother's
own deprived and unhappy childhood, so that she had little
basis upon which to build her mothering of Maureen. Mother
felt quite guilty about Maureen's birth and this led to some
ambivalence in her feelings towards Maureen. Her relationship
with Maureen's father was frustrating and unsatisfactory. She
had religious objections to birth control and tended to use Maureen's presence as a contraceptive. The bedtime routine was
hopelessly unsatisfactory and the sleeping arrangements
became even worse when the cot broke and Maureen had to
share her bed. Mother had no job, so that finances were
difficult, and also she had no social outlets.

Casework with mother constituted the main treatment and, as
is often the case, there had to be a mixture of approaches:

psychodynamic, behavioural and welfare. The psychodynamic element consisted in helping mother to come to terms with her unhappy childhood, her illegitimate child and her current liaison with Maureen's father. It was necessary for her to recognize her guilt over these in order to overcome her feelings of being a failure as a mother and as a woman. But also it was necessary that she decide what solution she wanted and then take the necessary steps to bring it about. After a few months she let her father know about Maureen and was much relieved when he responded positively and helpfully. She visited the housing department and had her name put down on the housing list and obtained a part-time job. This was beneficial in giving her more social contacts and in giving her some hours away from Maureen. Practical help was provided by the clinic in supporting her housing application and arranging for Social Security to provide a cot when Maureen's broke beyond repair. Mother was helped to work out ways of coping with Maureen's sleeping problem and it was suggested that the cot be put in the hall to make this easier. For one week only both mother and Maureen were given sedatives at night to help re-establish a more normal sleep routine. A plan of dealing with the tantrums was established. Mother and Maureen were seen jointly to help mother learn how to play with the child. Then there was a planned separation in which the social worker saw mother while the doctor (who had participated in the joint sessions) went off with Maureen. After a brief initial protest this worked well. Eight months after the initial referral mother was' no longer depressed and Maureen was much better with respect to both sleeping and tantrums, but the future of mother's relationship with Maureen's father had yet to be resolved.

Traditionally casework has involved social workers seeing mothers. However, that is much too narrow a view for present-day practice. In the first place, work with parents will usually involve fathers as well, and sometimes it is most appropriate for the social worker to see the child rather than the parent. In the second place, social workers frequently have contact with schools as well as a wide range of community agencies. But most important of all, casework skills are needed by the psychiatrist and psychologist as well as by the social worker. Similarly, as already noted, social workers now use behavioural treatments as well as casework.

Behaviour therapy

Behaviour therapy is the term applied to a wide range of focused treatment approaches, designed to modify specific behaviours and broadly derived from learning theories. It includes many very different therapeutic techniques which utilize quite disparate learning principles; but an important element of all the techniques is a systematic manipulation of the environment to encourage or discourage particular forms of behaviour. Accordingly an essential prerequisite is a careful analysis of the factors that influence the behaviour of the particular child being treated. Although behavioural techniques have been employed sporadically for many years, it is only in the last two decades that they have been used at all widely and the application to children's problems is even more recent than that. New methods are being developed all the time and the evaluation of older methods is still being undertaken. As a result it is still too early to provide an adequate assessment of the value of all the types of behaviour therapy. Nevertheless there is in fact more evidence on the effects of these methods of treatment than on the longer-established casework and psychotherapies.[63, 146, 147, 148] Much of the evidence comes from the detailed study of just a few cases. These studies convincingly demonstrate that behaviour therapy can produce quite dramatic changes in behaviour even when the problems have been resistant to other treatment methods. By showing that the changes in behaviour occur and only occur in a strict time-relationship to the application of treatment, it can be demonstrated that the changes are not just *associated with* treatment but are *due to* treatment. Some examples of studies of this kind will be mentioned. However, a proper evaluation also requires an assessment of how the treatment compares with other treatment methods, how much better it is than doing nothing and how far the benefits of treatment persist. There have been few studies of this kind in children, although there have been more in adults.

For example, several studies have shown that behavioural methods are considerably superior to psychotherapy in the treatment of specific phobias in adults.[108] As the results in children seem so similar, it would appear that behaviour therapy should usually be the treatment of choice in these circumstances, even though psychotherapy has been the traditional approach used in the past. Or again, it has been clearly shown that the 'bell and pad' method of treating bed-wetting is superior to other methods and should therefore usually be preferred.[96] Thus, although the subject of behaviour therapy is still in its infancy, there is already sufficient evidence to indicate it has considerable value and, although no panacea, in some circumstances it is demonstrably superior to other methods.

Desensitization

Desensitization has been used in the treatment of phobias for many years and it is probably the best established of the behavioural methods. Two principles are involved: (a) the pairing of the anxiety-evoking stimulus with the experience of relaxation and pleasure, which is to some extent incompatible with fear, (b) the systematic progression through an anxiety hierarchy from the least fear-provoking situation to the most frightening stimulus. This method was exemplified in chapter 6, page 220 by the treatment of the boy with a dog phobia. He was first introduced to small furry animals, like guinea pigs, which produced scarcely any anxiety and then, step by step, having got accustomed to this stimulus, he progressed up to the point where he was meeting and touching large frisky dogs without fear. The point of the treatment lay in moving through a series of small, carefully graded steps so that the child never became more than slightly anxious. Every time he moved up a step to a slightly more frightening situation, anxiety was reduced by means of relaxation, encouragement and food. In this case the child progressed up the anxiety hierarchy by means of real-life situations, but the procedure may also be employed by doing the same thing in imagination. The technique of desensitization has been used with great effect in the treatment of such conditions as animal phobias, fear of water, school phobia and fear of eating. Studies in adults have shown it to be more effective than psychotherapy for these conditions.[108] The only study in childhood produced the same finding, but defects in the study design mean that the finding needs to be checked by better-planned investigations.

Modelling and vicarious effects

Bandura and his colleagues have produced evidence to show that watching someone else progressively approach and cope with feared objects may also serve to eliminate phobias.[4, 5] They showed that children who were afraid of dogs became much less fearful if they watched other children or adults (who were unafraid) go up to dogs and in a carefully graded manner progress from saying hello to the animal in a pen up to playing with it and feeding it. This effect worked both if they watched the model in real life and also if they watched him on film. Comparable groups of children who watched the model without dogs, or dogs without models, or who just saw cartoon films did *not* show this reduction in fear, demonstrating that it was really seeing someone else approach dogs which had caused the fear reduction.

Modelling was an important element in the treatment of Joseph, an eleven year old about to transfer to secondary school, who was referred because of a fear of water. He was a shy, rather withdrawn boy who had two good friends but was reluctant to join in group activities or to play organized sport. This reluctance stemmed in part from a dislike of undressing in front of other boys. At age five years he had had a period of school refusal with stomach-aches each school morning but subsequently adjusted well to school. He is said to have become frightened at seven years, after falling into a shallow pond. His father, a passive man now in his mid-sixties, was also severely afraid of water (since being pushed in as a child) and his mother and two sisters were all reluctant to swim. Joseph's birth had not been planned, and since then mother and father had rather drifted apart although there was no overt tension. Mother turned to Joseph as a response to this relative estrangement and their relationship was a very close one. There were three much older sisters, all of whom were in their mid-twenties. Swimming was said to be compulsory at the secondary school to which Joseph was due to go and the fear of water was making the boy very apprehensive about the new school generally. He was afraid he would be mocked by other children, and mother was concerned that this reflected on his manhood. In view of this possible adverse effect on his already rather limited social relationships, treatment was thought necessary. The important background factors were his overly dependent relationship with his mother (which was mutual) and the lack of an adequate father-figure at home. The reason for the specific fear of water lay in the similar fears showed by the rest of the family. Joseph was seen twice a week for the next two or three weeks and he developed a good relationship with his therapist. His anxieties were discussed with him and it was agreed to treat his fear of water directly by taking him to the hospital swimming bath. The plan was to use a combination of modelling (provided by the therapist going into the water first) and desensitization (by introducing him gradually). On the first session he changed with some embarrassment and then eventually got into the shallow end, splashed his face and made swimming movements while being held by the therapist. Visits to the swimming bath were repeated every two or three days over the next fortnight with Joseph being encouraged to do more each time. At the same time his mother was seen by the social worker who discussed with her how to build up Joseph's confidence and how to respond to his fears. He then went on holiday with the family and an adult friend of the family who could swim. For the first time in his life he entered the sea and went 'swimming' every day with enjoyment. On his return he started at secondary school. For the first few weeks he had nausea on school mornings, but he went, joined in with other children and participated in both swimming and sport. By the end of term he was making good progress and was more confident and outgoing in his social behaviour.

'Flooding'

An apparently quite different approach to the treatment of phobias is provided by the technique of 'flooding'. This consists, after establishing a relationship and discussing the details of treatment, of going straight into the *most* frightening situation. Usually this is done in fantasy by getting the patient to imagine himself in a panic in the situation he fears most, and then by getting him to enter the same situation in real life. In a way this is the equivalent of the technique of 'throwing the child in at the deep end', in which, by directly facing the feared object, the child finds that it was not as frightening in fact as he had imagined it might be. Although systematic comparisons have not been made in children, controlled studies with adults have shown that 'flooding' is an effective treatment of phobias and, furthermore, that the results are as good as those obtained by desensitization.[108] This was a surprising finding at first because 'flooding' violates all the principles thought to be important in desensitization. 'Flooding' was originally thought to depend on the induction of very high levels of anxiety in intensely frightening situations, whereas desensitization relies on the avoidance of anything more than minimal anxiety. However, further research has shown that the rationale of 'flooding' was wrong and that the results are not quite as paradoxical as they seemed at first sight. There have now been several investigations which have shown that 'flooding' was *more* effective if it was combined with a tranquillizer to keep anxiety levels *low*. In short, it is not the induction of anxiety that matters but rather the exposure to the feared object.

There is continuing theoretical dispute over the precise mechanisms by which these rather disparate treatments operate in the elimination of phobias. That they are effective has been clearly demonstrated, but we are not sure exactly how they work. The one essential element seems to be exposure to the phobic stimuli, preferably in a therapeutic situation which allows the patient to receive support in coming through unscathed. Perhaps what is important is that, one way or other, the patient learns how to master the situation. This may be accomplished by 'getting used to it' gradually, as in desensitization; by gaining confidence through seeing someone else successfully deal with the feared object, as in modelling; by going straight in at the deep end and finding that nothing terrible happens, as in 'flooding'; or by being taught specific skills which increase the child's mastery over the feared situation. This last technique was used with the child in chapter 6 with a fear of maths who conquered the fear partly as a result of coaching which showed her that she could easily do all that was required of her in maths lessons. In the same way social-skills training may be very helpful for youngsters who are afraid of meeting people.

The technique of 'flooding' is exemplified by the treatment of James, a fourteen year old who presented with claustrophobia. At age six years, when in hospital, he became very upset about having his cot sides up and got into quite a panic. This soon settled down on return home and there were no further difficulties until age nine years when he became trapped in a lift for a few minutes. Since that time he was very afraid of lifts and also started to avoid underground trains. When he had to go on the subway, he was tense, anxious, tremulous and sweated profusely. When he was thirteen he was accidentally locked in a room at school and became very panicky. A year later there was a further episode in which a classroom door jammed and thirty children were trapped for about ten minutes. James became severely distressed and when let out he was in such a bad state that he had to be taken home. It was this episode that led to referral, as since then James had been teased a good deal about what happened and he had become very frightened of being in any room with the doors closed.

James was a happy, sympathetic, sensitive, cautious boy with many interests and plenty of friends. He became rather anxious at times of stress (such as during school examinations) and would sometimes sleepwalk then. He was also rather afraid of heights and walking over bridges, but there were no other emotional or behavioural problems of note. Father was a shopkeeper, a slightly shy but generally demonstrative man who was very fond of his family and spent a lot of time with them. Mother also got on well with the family, but it was noteworthy that she had been very anxious as an adolescent and on one occasion as a young adult she had been off work three months for an anxiety state which was treated by her family doctor. She was afraid of enclosed buildings. James had two older brothers neither of whom had had any psychiatric problems.

This was a relatively isolated phobia and, following discussion with James and his parents, it was decided to use 'flooding' in treatment. However, in keeping with the principles already outlined, the 'flooding' was graded to avoid undue anxiety and the technique was combined with other methods designed to give James confidence in and mastery of the situations which he feared. In order to give James and his therapists feedback on what was happening, a polygraph was used initially in which skin electrodes attached to a meter reflected the physiological components of anxiety. In addition a 'fear thermometer' was devised, so that James rated his anxiety on a special scale every five minutes. The first two sessions were spent discussing with James what was to be done and getting him accustomed to the whole proceedings. In the third session James was placed in a room on his own but with an intercommunication system to the psychologist and psychiatrist in an adjoining room. Sessions lasting about an hour were held two or three times per week, in which the stresses were increased by locking the room, turning the lights out and moving to a still smaller room. James was very anxious in the early sessions, but as the sessions progressed he became more relaxed. The psychologist stayed with James on several occasions to give him confidence and show him what to do. In later sessions James had to find the key in the desk in order to let himself out of a locked room. The same procedures were followed with lifts which were stopped between floors, using the emergency stop button. James repeatedly underwent the frightening experiences until he was no longer afraid. Throughout, great care was taken to ensure that James knew what was to be done and was happy to proceed, and he was given practical training in exactly what to do in various entrapped situations. With James's agreement various unexpected aspects were introduced, so that he could learn to cope with these too. In this connection Nature added her help by causing the door to jam unexpectedly on one occasion. James coped well. The same general procedure was followed with the underground, but, because what happened was more outside our control, two other elements were added. First, James was taught how to relax and, second, a minor tranquillizer was used to reduce anxiety on the first few occasions. Practical experience in feared situations was combined with rehearsal in imagination. Altogether, treatment lasted for nineteen sessions spread over two months. At the end of this time James was no longer anxious in enclosed spaces and was confident of his ability to cope if accidentally entrapped. A few further sessions were spent dealing with James's fear of bridges and his examination 'nerves' in the same way. Follow-up a year later showed that James had remained symptom-free and was doing well in all respects.

Graded change

Desensitization can be considered a specific example of the more general technique of 'graded change' in which major alterations in behaviour may be accomplished by progressing through a carefully graded series of steps, each of which is so small that the difference is scarcely noticeable. Marchant and her colleagues[107] have reported how this may be employed with the abnormal attachment to objects shown by many autistic children. One seven-year-old autistic boy was handicapped in his activities through his insistence on always carrying a large leather belt. It was suggested that mother should shorten the belt by an inch or so each night and that she should insist that he put down the belt at certain pleasurable times, such as at meal times. Two weeks later the child was content with a four-inch piece of leather which he was prepared to put down when necessary. He was then gradually induced to vary the objects he carried. The abnormal attachment remained (it usually does in a severe condition like autism), but he was no longer attached to specific objects, the objects were small and so did not interfere with his life, and he was prepared to relinquish the objects temporarily in order to undertake other activities. The whole procedure was achieved without the child becoming upset, because changes were introduced gradually in small steps.

The same procedure has been followed in the treatment of obsessional rituals and stereotyped routines. By the progressive introduction of flexibilities into the routine and by making a graded series of very small changes it has been possible to change a rigid and handicapping ritual into a much more varied way of doing things which no longer interferes with the child's daily activities.

Feedback approaches

Sometimes the main factor preventing a child from overcoming a problem is that he is not properly aware of what is happening. A variety of ingenious pieces of apparatus have been devised to correct this. When the feedback on what is happening involves providing the child with information on his body physiology the term 'bio-feedback' is usually employed.[172] This technique was used with Gilbert.

Gilbert was an adolescent boy with a neurological disorder giving rise to a constant twisting and distortion of his neck, associated with pain and tension in his neck muscles. This was causing some embarrassment at school and also interfered with his ability to work. Although the basic disease process could not be altered, it was thought that Gilbert's situation could be improved if he could learn how to relax the neck muscles which were in spasm. This he could not do because he did not know which muscles were affected and it was difficult to relax muscles which went into this abnormal spasm. Accordingly a treatment programme based on bio-feedback was planned by the psychologist. This simply means that a device is found which will give the person feedback on what his body is doing. The device in Gilbert's case was an electrode which when placed on the skin recorded the electrical activity in the muscle. The electrode was connected up to a dial which Gilbert could see, so that by watching this he could learn which muscles were relaxed and which were tense. This was used to teach Gilbert how to relax his neck muscles, and by combining it with the use of a mirror it was possible to teach him how to hold his head relaxed in the normal upright position looking straight ahead. The treatment could not remove the medical problem and Gilbert's neck still tended to go into spasm, but it did enable him to relax more readily and it brought the spasms a little more under his control.

The 'pressure pen' is a much simpler piece of apparatus also designed to give feedback. Sometimes children's writing is very bad because of undue tension resulting in a cramped, inconsistently sloped series of letters which are badly formed and pressed together by the use of heavy pressure from a taut hand. The pen is designed so that the point retracts into the casing whenever it is pressed too hard.

This was used with Gordon, an intelligent adolescent who became anxious under stress and whose schoolwork, especially in examinations, was ruined by appalling handwriting. His fingers began hurting two or three minutes after starting to write and his hand became very tight whenever he had to write under stress. He had tried to relax but the difficulties always reappeared. Treatment consisted of teaching him how to relax, giving him instruction in examination techniques (planning his answers, etc.) and the use of the pressure pen. The pen was necessary because, regardless of his anxiety, Gordon had got into a maladaptive habit of writing. The principle of the pen was explained to him and he was given the pen to use regularly for all writing. In addition he was shown better writing techniques and given practice with these. Four months later he had a clear, cursive style of writing and his excessively strong grip and pressure had been wholly eliminated. There were no further pains in his arm. It was no longer necessary for him to use the pressure pen and a follow-up after some months showed that the improvement had been maintained and that Gordon was happy and relaxed.

Another ingenious piece of apparatus is the musical potty. Some children with mental retardation or with severe developmental disorders seem unaware of when they are wetting themselves. Before they can learn to use the toilet properly, it is necessary for them to appreciate clearly when they are passing urine. A special potty has been designed to help with this learning. It is so wired that when a stream of urine goes into the pot it sets off a bell which makes an interesting noise. Children learn that whenever they urinate into the pot they can make this noise, and by means of this amusing feedback they can be helped to gain awareness of their bladder function.

The much more familiar 'bell and pad' treatment for bedwetting (see chapter 8) is most conveniently considered here, although it still remains uncertain exactly what learning mechanism leads to the child gaining bladder control. In the usual case of night-time bed-wetting the child wets in his sleep and doesn't wake up until later to find that he is lying in a wet bed. The principle of the 'bell and pad' is the quite simple one of ensuring that the child wakes *immediately* he starts to pass urine. Comparative investigations have shown that this treatment is considerably superior to psychotherapy.[96] Although some of the improvement comes from non-specific influences (as shown by the short-term benefits of randomly waking the child during the night), the main benefit is contingent upon the use of the apparatus to bring about immediate waking. Using an unconnected apparatus (the 'gadget-effect') or just waking the child intermittently does not work as well.

Another type of feedback is provided by the use of videotape in social training, as described in chapter 5. Many social difficulties stem from people not being aware of what they do wrong and, if they can see what they do by watching a videotape of themselves, this provides the necessary basis for eliminating bad social habits and gaining the necessary social skills.

Encouragements and discouragements

It is a general principle of human behaviour that particular behaviours are more likely to recur if they bring about something pleasant (that is they are rewarded) and are less likely to recur if they either fail to bring about anything pleasant or if they give rise to something unpleasant (that is they are discouraged or reprimanded). This principle is well known to parents and teachers who regularly use praise and encouragement to get children to do the 'right' things and who use expressions of regret and disappointment, or use punishment to stop them doing the 'wrong' things. This principle operates in all forms of treatment and the therapist will always be wise to ensure that whatever mode of therapy is being employed the child is getting appropriate rewards from doing what is expected of him. However, in some cases the principle is elevated to constitute the main element in treatment. When this is done, it is usually advisable to combine the systematic use of 'reinforcements' (i.e. encouragements and discouragements) with a carefully graded programme in which the desired behaviour is reached by a series of very small steps. In this way the child's behaviour is *shaped* by a series of successive approximations to what is eventually required. The art, as well as the science, in this approach lies in breaking down the behaviour into small steps, in ensuring that the programme is arranged to bring about a maximum of successes and a minimum of failures, in providing the child with immediate feedback on his successes and failures, in organizing the environment so that the child is most likely to do what is wanted and in a careful study of the individual child to find out what is and is not rewarding for him. Children are motivated in many different ways and the therapist has to discover what is most likely to encourage each particular child.

Much the most useful approach in most instances is to concentrate on providing encouragement for doing the right thing. When a child shows psychological difficulties, often he is in a situation where, whatever he does, someone shouts at him or complains. Ingenuity has to be exercised in picking out the 'good things' in what he does and concentrating on giving maximal encouragement for these. Encouragements most often take the form of adult interest, praise and approval, but material rewards (or points which may be exchanged for material rewards) may also be useful in some cases.

This usually has to be combined with a systematic attempt to ensure that 'bad' behaviour does *not* bring rewards. It may be sufficient to just ignore the child when he is doing the wrong thing, or the point may be emphasized by a deliberate turning away from the child and a lack of interest and pleasure in what he does. However, sometimes it is necessary to go a stage further by what is called a 'time-out' procedure. This simply means that the child has to have a short time without anything pleasurable. This may be brought about by taking the child away from his toys or his play for a few minutes or by actually sending him to a room on his own. Obviously, for this to work, the child must be doing something pleasurable and it is very important to place a high premium on ensuring that for most of the time life is pleasurable for the child. The use of this type of 'cooling off' period should be explained to the child in advance, the 'time-out' should be very brief (two to three minutes) to avoid a punitive content and it should be followed by praise and encouragement as soon as the child stops misbehaving. It should be done under careful professional supervision and should be systematically monitored to ensure that it is having the desired effect.

In order to help children understand what behaviours are unacceptable, disapproval, corrections and reprimands may be necessary. However, although occasionally important, punishment as such is much less useful. If given some time after the event, it tends not to be very effective because there is a danger that it will be associated with the wrong thing in the child's mind. So, if used, it should be immediate. However, punishment, if at all marked, carries disadvantages. First, what may seem a punishment may actually be rewarding. For example, the child who is shouted at in class may get reward from the notoriety, from the teacher's attention or from the amusement it gives to other children. Second, punishment may be disruptive in its effects by causing panic or resentment. The child who is frequently shouted at may get into a state of constant anxiety and, although he tries to avoid punishment by doing the right thing, the anxiety so disrupts his behaviour that in practice he often does the wrong thing. Alternatively the child who is humiliated by corporal punishment will certainly try to avoid getting caught again, but also his anti-authority attitude may be intensified by his resentment and anger at what was done to him. Third, many punishments set a bad example. Thus the use of smacking (or, even more so, caning in school) may provide a model which suggests aggression and violence as the solution to problems. Fourth, severe punishment, especially if physical, may be harmful to the person who administers it. Striking another person may induce feelings of guilt, anger or even pleasure which can be destructive in their effects. This does not mean that systematic discouragements and reprimands have no place in bringing up children. To the contrary, some use of discouragement and disapproval is very necessary. However, it does mean that punishments as such should be used very sparingly and that they should very rarely form the basis of treatment.

The literature on treatments based on reinforcement principles, or operant conditioning as it is sometimes called, is very off-putting to many people because of both the excessive use of jargon and the impression given of a mechanical, impersonal approach. The jargon is unnecessary for the most part, but it is a common feature in any new science, and the impression of mechanical objectivity is seriously misleading. If the approach is to be successful, it requires a warm, responsive therapist who will be rewarding the child and an individually tailored approach to meet individual needs. Because of its emphasis on success and pleasure, it is an enjoyable form of treatment for the child, and it is very personal in its avoidance of abstract theory and its focus on the individual.

The methods may be employed either to build up positive patterns of behaviour or to eliminate undesirable ones. Examples of each have already been given in previous chapters. Thus reinforcements were strategically employed in the classroom to discourage tantrums in the boy described in chapter 5 (see pages 210–11) and to encourage speaking in the girl with elective mutism described in chapter 6 (see pages 225–7). In the former case the teacher went out of her way to praise the boy for whatever he did well, but she just ignored the disruptive behaviour. This led to a dramatic decrease in tantrums and a gradual building up of improved social behaviour and better attention in class. In the latter case both praise and a points system were used to get the girl to speak at school. In order to avoid undue anxiety, this was done by very small stages, giving a lot of encouragement for each step forward. Again the improvement was very striking.

It should be emphasized that the use of reinforcements should be combined with a carefully graded programme using a series of steps working forward in a systematic manner, and with accurate and immediate feedback to the child and therapist on what has been achieved. The point may be illustrated by considering the old-fashioned approach of blackboard teaching at the front of the class and with yearly (or termly) exams. Because the teacher is instructing the class as a whole, he is probably going too fast for half the class, too slowly for the other half and with only a few children in the middle is he proceeding at just the right pace. He has no means of knowing which children are learning and which are not, other than by the haphazard means of picking out children to ask them questions. The yearly exams are useful in grading children, but the feedback comes at a time when the child is moving on to other things and so it is too late to influence learning in any substantial way. The child gets his marks, but he is rarely told exactly what he got right and what he got wrong, so he has little opportunity to benefit from his mistakes.

Programmed learning, in contrast, aims to be individualized, with the teaching tailored to the child's level of accomplishments. Also there is immediate feedback, so that the child only moves on to something new when he has shown he has learned what precedes it. Each step forward is small and so planned that the chances that the child will succeed are very great. The procedure tends to be associated in the mind of the public with teaching machines, but these are only one special example of the technique which can be applied to ordinary teaching and to the modification of behaviour.

Staats and Butterfield[181] applied reinforcement principles in the treatment of a fourteen-year-old boy with a long history of anti-social behaviour and school failure. Reading was a particular problem. After an analysis of what the boy did and did not know, a carefully tailored programme was devised to teach him reading. Success was rewarded by tokens which could be exchanged for money. After forty hours of treatment he had gained two years in reading, was succeeding in his schoolwork for the first time and no longer showed any misbehaviour. As he improved, the tokens ceased to be necessary because reading itself became pleasurable and self-rewarding.

This approach was followed with Jacqueline who was having great difficulty in arithmetic and had become both discouraged and anxious. The various arithmetical tasks were broken down into a series of many small steps. These were taught her stage by stage. Throughout the coaching she had very many small 'tests' both of her multiplication tables (which were causing her trouble) and of the different arithmetical tasks. Her results on these tests were graphed by Jacqueline herself, so that she could see the steady progression. The rising graph itself was very rewarding, but special prizes were also given when particular levels were reached. This served three purposes. First, both the teacher and child had immediate and frequent feedback on what Jacqueline did and did not know. This enabled teaching to be focused on the areas where help was most needed and ensured that Jacqueline could always be working at the right level. Second, the graphing and prizes provided constant encouragement and rewards. Because she was always competing with herself rather than with others, she had all the benefits of the stimulus provided by competition without any of the disadvantages associated with failure. She could only go forwards and hence there was a premium on success. Third, because Jacqueline took part in the graphing of her results and because the graphs were made interesting with pictures and the like, Jacqueline's whole attitude to arithmetic changed. She became interested in the subject as a whole as well as in her progress, and this change in motivation was a crucial factor in her success.

Material rewards played only a very small part in Jacqueline's treatment: success was its own reward. This is more strikingly exemplified by Jack, a fifteen-year-old boy who had become afraid that his bowels were not properly emptied. In his case the important things were breaking down the task into small manageable units and providing immediate feedback.

For the last two years Jack had had difficulty with his bowel movements. It started with abdominal pain and he was off school for two weeks. After that he continued to have discomfort each morning. He spent half an hour straining at stool and would often return to the lavatory several times for further half-hour periods, feeling that his bowels were not properly emptied. His motions were rather loose and he passed occasional blood and small amounts of mucus. Inordinate amounts of toilet paper were used and there were frequent family arguments over Jack's excessive time in the toilet. On school mornings he got up very early to allow himself several hours in the toilet but on Sundays, when he got up at a normal time, he was not free of visits to the lavatory until 11 a.m. If going out in the evening, he would again sit on the lavatory at least once and often several times for ten to fifteen minutes before leaving the house. For the last year he had not been on any form of public transport for fear of what would happen if he needed to use the toilet. As a result of these difficulties his social life had become much restricted. He was chronically late for school and had dropped out of sports and other activities. Although Jack was rather shy and inclined to worry, there were no other emotional or behavioural problems. The family was a happy one and there were no difficulties other than the rows over Jack's excessive use of the toilet. Jack himself was very worried about his bowel problem but had come to feel that nothing could be done to help. Before referral, medicines had been given to reduce his anxiety and to make his motions more firm. They had succeeded in this but Jack continued to spend hours in the toilet.

Adequate physical investigation had been carried out pre-viously by a paediatrician and it was clear that there was no physical cause for the bowel problem. The looseness of the motions and the mucus were the result of worry and anxiety. Initially the excessive time on the toilet was a response to abdominal discomfort, but it had become a habit which served to reduce anxiety regarding his bowels. However, it was also a cause of anxiety in that any departure from the prolonged periods in the toilet led to panic.

Jack was asked to to keep a daily diary of the times spent on the toilet and to cut down this time minute by minute. A graph was maintained to show his progress in this respect. In addition he and the therapist worked out a graded series of tasks which involved not going to the toilet for specific intervals, travelling on buses, waiting at bus stops and going out without going to the lavatory first. By advancing in a series of small steps Jack learned that he could ac-complish these tasks without needing to use the lavatory. His tran-quillizers were also gradually reduced and then stopped. The tablets to avoid diarrhoea were reduced, but it was found necessary to keep Jack on a small maintenance dose. After the first few weeks Jack was never late for school and he recommenced his sporting and social activities. His time in the toilet was reduced to less than ten minutes per day, his stomach pains disappeared, he relaxed when passing motions and his use of lavatory paper returned to normal. Altogether he was seen only eight times and when last seen six months after his first attendance he was remaining well. Once Jack understood what was required he worked out most of the steps himself and his steady progress constituted its own reward.

Behavioural approaches in the home and school

When behavioural therapies were first introduced, they usually involved treating the child himself in the clinic or hospital. While this is still entirely appropriate for many children, an increasing emphasis has been placed on working with teachers at school and parents at home. There are several reasons why this shift of emphasis has occurred, but two are especially im-portant. First, it is largely at home or at school (rather than at the clinic) that children show most of their difficulties, and it seemed logical to focus treatment on the situations where the problems are manifest. As noted in chapter 1, many disorders are relatively specific to a situation. Second, while the therapist can only see the child for an hour or so per week at most, parents and teachers are with the child very many hours each week. It seemed that, if they could be assisted in developing better ways of helping the child, this might be more effective. Preliminary findings suggest that this shift of emphasis has been worthwhile for many children.

Work with teachers was described in chapter 5, page 210 and a further case example was given in chapter 6, page 225. Much has still to be learned about this method of helping children, but the evaluative studies so far undertaken are very encouraging.[12]

Work with parents has been undertaken with respect to various types of problem including severe conditions with a strong constitutional component (such as infantile autism[80]), and also conduct disorders in which environmental factors play a larger part. Patterson and his colleagues[128, 133] in Oregon, mainly using encouragements and discouragements as described above, have been pioneers in developing therapeutic approaches for the latter group. The treatment of aggressive children has already been shown to be worthwhile. A particular point has been made of finding out just how parents and children do interact at home, in order to determine what things make positive social behaviour more likely. One of the most important things in many families has been getting them to use more praise and encouragement and to pay more attention to the good things their child does.

Medication

Over the last twenty years an astonishing number of drugs have been produced, which are supposed to be of benefit to children and adults with psychiatric disorders. Few of these drugs have been adequately assessed and much remains to be learned of their action. Nevertheless there is sufficient evidence to suggest that they have an important role in the treatment of selective cases.[38] Eisenberg[50] has succinctly summarized the main principles to be followed when using drugs to treat child psychiatric disorders:

(1) All the available drugs treat symptoms not diseases, so that the use of medication must always be preceded by a full and careful diagnostic appraisal. Symptom relief is an essential part of treatment, but attention should also be paid to causal factors. This means that medication is rarely a sufficient treatment on its own. (2) Most effective drugs also have toxic side-effects, so that no drug should be employed without a firm indication for its use. (3) An old and familiar drug is to be preferred to a new one unless there is good evidence for the superiority of the latter. (4) Drugs also have placebo effects (that is, effects due to expectations rather than to pharmacological actions), so that skill in the use of drugs requires sensitivity to their psychological implications. (5) Drugs can be effective in controlling symptoms not managed by other means, so that there should not be a reluctance to use them if the indications are appropriate. Drugs are not panaceas and not poisons; they are very useful therapeutic agents within a limited field.

(a) Hypnotics (sleeping medicine).

One of the common problems in early childhood is sleep disturbance. This is also one of the main symptoms in depression. In young children the main treatment of sleeping problems involves attention to why the child is not sleeping and modification of the factors interfering with sleep. Sleeping medicines are rarely an answer in themselves, partly because they do not affect the causes of disturbed sleep and partly because children habituate to the action of the drugs, so that after a few weeks (or even days) the effects wear off. Nevertheless hypnotics can be very useful adjuncts to treatment if used sparingly and selectively. Generally the best approach is to give them for a few nights at a time, in order to help the child get back into a normal sleep routine once the causal factors of sleep disturbance have been dealt with. In addition the drugs can be kept for use for the occasional nights when it is essential for the parents to have undisturbed sleep or when they need to catch up on their rest.

Barbiturates are much used for this purpose in adults, but

they are not satisfactory in children because they tend to lead to excitability and restlessness. In young children one of the chloral derivatives (such as 'welldorm' or 'tricloryl') or one of the sedative antihistamines (such as 'benadryl' or 'phenergan') are safest and most effective. In older children and adolescents nitrazepam ('mogadon') is one of the most satisfactory drugs.

(b) Sedatives.

Sedatives are not often required for children, but occasionally they are valuable in reducing anxiety and tension, especially in adolescence. Clinical experience suggests that diazepam ('valium') is most generally useful for this purpose, but there is a lack of sound research evidence on the merits and demerits of any of the sedatives with children. What little evidence there is suggests that diazepam is not of much help with pre-adolescent youngsters. Barbiturates are not recommended because of their excitant effect in some children.

(c) Stimulants.

In childhood stimulant drugs such as dextroamphetamine and ritalin have been shown to have the effects of improving attention and concentration in hyperkinetic children. It is this group of drugs which have given rise to both the best and the most research, and there is no doubt that stimulant drugs can have a significantly beneficial effect in children who are very restless and who concentrate poorly. Particularly in the USA these drugs have been used very widely for this purpose, and they have a definite place in treatment. However, although they improve behaviour in the short-term, it is uncertain whether the drugs do anything to improve the long-term prognosis. Because of this, and because there are some important side-effects, the drugs need to be used with care and selectivity. Sometimes they impair appetite and weight gain, occasionally they cause transient misery and depression (perhaps particularly in children with brain damage) and there is a very slight risk of addiction (although this seems quite small when the drugs are used in younger hyperkinetic children).

(d) Major tranquillizers.

There are several studies which have shown that the major

tranquillizers may be quite effective in controlling *severe* over-activity, in diminishing seriously disturbed behaviour and in reducing psychiatric manifestations in schizophrenia. In short the main indications for use are in the most severe, and hence less common, psychiatric disorders. In these conditions they may even form the main treatment and are certainly of proven efficacy. Chlorpromazine ('largactil') and thioridazine ('melleril') are the safest and most generally useful drugs, but the more powerful trifluoperazine ('stelazine') and haloperidol ('serenace') are occasionally to be preferred.

Although the major tranquillizers are useful for symptom control, evidence suggests that they may have bad effects on learning, so their use should be restricted to the few serious disorders where they are of definite benefit. They are very rarely indicated in the more everyday disorders of emotions and behaviour discussed in this book.

(e) Antidepressants.

Drugs are of proven value in the treatment of depressive disorders in adults, but less is known about their value in child psychiatric disorders. The studies which have been undertaken are on rather heterogeneous groups of children, which makes evaluation difficult. Nevertheless it has been shown that anti-depressants aid the treatment of school refusal and that they are superior to barbiturates in the treatment of a mixed bag of children with depressive symptoms. Thus there is some evidence that antidepressants are useful in the treatment of childhood depression, but further studies are required to delineate their merits and demerits. They are most obviously useful in the depressive disorders in older children and adolescents, but they are also occasionally useful in younger ones. Clinical experience suggests that the tricyclic derivatives, such as amitriptyline, nortriptyline or imipramine, are most generally safe and effective, but controlled trials are still needed to assess their efficacy and to compare their merits.

(f) Other uses.

As noted in chapter 8 one of the best-established drug actions is that of imipramine ('tofranil') in controlling bed-wetting. In the short term it has proven a most effective treatment, but most of the children relapse when the drug is stopped. This makes it less useful as the *main* treatment for bed-wetting, although it may be used for this purpose, but it has an important role in bringing about short-term control at key times such as when the child goes to school camp or the family go on holiday. The mode of action of imipramine (which is a complex drug with many pharmacological effects) in controlling bed-wetting is quite unknown and research into it might throw useful light on the mechanisms involved in enuresis.

For reasons which are ill understood, haloperidol ('serenace') has been found to be effective in reducing tics. In children with very severe tics this is a worthwhile drug to try, but it is not advisable in milder disorders because of its frequent side-effects.

Special schools, in-patient units and other facilities

In this book emphasis has been laid on the understanding and treatment of common disorders and on the forms of therapy undertaken by the psychiatric clinic, although not necessarily *at* the clinic. Several examples have been given where the main focus of treatment has been at school or in the child's own home. In addition to these out-patient approaches, day-hospital care or in-patient treatment may be needed for some children. There are several reasons for admitting children. These include: disorders too severe to be managed outside hospital; the need for relief for the parents when family stress has become too great; the necessity for special treatment methods only available in hospital; the need for a specialized and controlled group living experience to deal with difficulties in social relationships; the presence of an associated medical condition requiring in-patient treatment; the need for prolonged observation or special tests to assist in diagnosis. The use of day-hospital and in-patient facilities is an important part of psychiatric practice but one largely outside the scope of this book. However, a brief period of in-patient care may occasionally be a useful ingredient in a broader programme of out-patient treatment and an example of its use in this way is given on page 350. Even when the main treatment, hospital care is very rarely adequate in itself and the coordination between in-patient and out-patient care is an essential element in the treatment programme.

Special schools (both day and residential) also have an important part to play in helping the child with psychiatric problems. They provide a specialized group living experience planned to aid the development of children with emotional or behavioural problems, skilled remedial help for children with learning problems, the provision of individual psychiatric treatment (at a few of the special schools) and a useful break from home for the child from a severely disturbed family.

In addition there is a wide range of other facilities which may help the child with psychiatric problems. These include many local-authority and voluntary social services, foster-care, children's homes, special classes, hostels, holiday camps, adventure playgrounds, counselling and a variety of advisory services. The psychiatric clinic will be in touch with all of these and will make use of them in appropriate cases.

It would not be practical for all children with psychiatric disorders to be treated at psychiatric clinics, even if this were desirable, which it is not. Many children can be helped perfectly adequately by family doctors, teachers, social workers and the wide range of other professionals who deal with children. The psychiatrist, and other clinic workers, have a role here, helping other people to help the child. Their way of working in this connection is quite different from that of the clinic. The purpose is not usually to provide a diagnosis for the individual child nor even to teach others how to give psychiatric treatment. Rather the aim is to help other people do their own job better by means of discussions aimed at enabling them to understand what might be going wrong and what might be done to improve the situation. Again this aspect of psychiatric services is outside the scope of this book.

Combining treatments

In this chapter, so far, individual treatments have been separately considered. In practice it is very common for several quite different approaches to be combined together. The following case illustrates the need for this and also the use of interdisciplinary collaboration which is central in the treatment of child psychiatric disorders.

Stewart was a twelve year old referred because of school refusal. He had transferred to secondary school a year earlier and had always been worried and lacking in confidence at the new school. During his first year there he had not actually refused to go, although he was near to doing so on occasions. His mother fussed a good deal over this and went to see the housemaster about him. The boy was then given a letter to carry around with him which told teachers that he had been under a strain and that they were to treat him with kindness and understanding. After that, whenever he worried, he showed the teacher his letter. In spite of that, the worries got worse. Every Sunday evening Stewart would spend an hour checking his school bag and each school-day morning (but especially on Mondays) he got up at 6.30 a.m. He would go to the lavatory and open his bowels four or five times during the next two hours, he would not eat breakfast and he moaned and sometimes cried. Mother contacted the school several more times, there were more letters and mother got increasingly anxious and upset herself. Then, at the start of the second year at secondary school, things came to a head and Stewart became even more distressed on school mornings, crying for a couple of hours before going off red-eyed. Then a month after term started he began to refuse to go to school.

During the summer holidays father had been made redundant. He had what he thought was cancer and felt he could never work again. Always a bit of a worrier, he now became increasingly depressed and did not return to see his family doctor. During the first interview at the clinic he wept several times. Mother was an anxious, worrying person who had become increasingly depressed in the last month, being very concerned over her husband as well as over Stewart. She also wept when interviewed.

Stewart had been a very much wanted child and the parents had had to wait many years before conception. When he was born Mother was forty and father rather older. Mother doted on Stewart and was overprotective and solicitous with him. Her own memories of an unhappy three months in hospital as a child with rheumatic fever made her very distressed and sensitive about separations and the fact that Stewart did not talk until he was two years made her fuss over him. Stewart was very dependent on his parents and had a close relationship with them, especially with his mother. He had always been rather anxious away from them and when admitted to hospital at age eight years he cried so much that he had to be discharged early.

There were no marked difficulties at school, but Stewart was teased a bit about being thin and he worried a good deal over French lessons, becoming upset at the beginning of the second year over a change in French teacher.

When Stewart began to refuse to go to school, Mother took him there, as she had been advised. She was both anxious and self-conscious over this and would creep along after the boys were in assembly, hiding behind pillars and in doorways if she saw anyone coming. She became very distressed at parting from Stewart (who was tremulous and tearful at these times) and she would press him to enter the school, uttering reassurances as tears rolled down her cheeks.

There were important background features in relation to Stewart's school refusal. He was overprotected by his mother and, as with Levy's cases (see pages 148–53), this had its origins in her own childhood experiences (the unhappy separation), the difficulties in conception, so that the child was especially valued and the early problems in the boy's development. Even before the school refusal there were indications of Stewart's separation anxiety. However, he had managed to cope until the start of the new school year. The teasing and the change of French teacher may have played some part, but the major factor seemed to be father's illness and loss of job. Father was quite markedly depressed and was doing nothing about his supposed cancer. Stewart was undoubtedly worried over this, but mother was more noticeably affected and she also became depressed. Her emotional troubles made her more uncertain, worried and indecisive in her dealings with Stewart, who in turn spent his time at school worried about how his parents were at home.

Treatment was planned on the basis of this formulation. Arrangements were made for father to see a cancer specialist, and both mother and Stewart were seen at the clinic. Mother was helped by the social worker to see how her anxieties were impinging on Stewart, and practical help was given in coping with the boy's distress and his reluctance to go to school. It seemed important to get Stewart back to school quickly, so that his fears over school would not be worsened by a long absence. Equally, however, the whole family were in a distressed state and it was thought necessary to do this gradually. The school were contacted and it was agreed that in the first instance he need only attend for his favourite lessons. Mother was in no state to cope with taking Stewart to school, so it was organized that someone from the school would accompany him. This worked on a few occasions, but it soon became clear that the situation was deteriorating. Both parents were increasingly anxious and depressed, Stewart spent his time crying and shivering and eventually just clung on to a pillar and refused to go into school. When he did go into school, he was so upset he was sent home. Although the refusal had not originally arisen on the basis of depression, it was evident that Stewart now had a generalized depression which was manifest at home and at school. Even when there was no question of school attendance, he remained miserable and withdrawn. Both mother and Stewart were then put on anti-depressants. Father was told by the specialist that he probably did not have cancer, and he became less depressed. Stewart was now at home, not attending school, and mother said she did not see how he would ever get back. It was agreed that a short-term admission to hospital might help. The parents and Stewart were very anxious over this but agreed. In hospital Stewart was tearful at first but soon established good relationships with the other children. He became a popular leader, which gave an enormous boost to his confidence and self-esteem. Also, however, he did not like being away from his parents and he determined to return to school. After two weeks he went to school from hospital and then after two days of this he decided he could manage and insisted on going home. This was agreed with a lot of apprehension as to whether he would cope. However, he did. Father now knew that he did not have a growth, he ceased to be depressed and obtained a new job. This and Stewart's short hospital stay proved to be turning points. Mother brightened and relaxed perceptibly and the family as a whole improved in morale. There was one further day when Stewart missed school. Mother handled this well and there were no further difficulties. The whole period of treatment took just four months, and follow-up a year later showed that Stewart was attending school and generally getting on well. He still did not like his French teacher, but this caused no problems. In the mornings he tended to ask his mother if she would worry about him and, on being told no, he would go off to school happily. There were mild anxieties at the beginning of a new school year, but Stewart coped well. Father remained healthy and was happy in his new job.

This case shows how there may be a combination of causal factors and how several treatment methods may have to be employed. Antidepressant drugs reduced the depression in both Stewart and his mother, but it was only when father became well and returned to work that either of them really turned the corner. It was important to help mother with her anxieties over separation and to give her practical advice on what to do when Stewart became upset. Equally this was not enough in itself until Stewart received a boost to his confidence from his success with other children in hospital. The admission to hospital also served to indicate everyone's resolve to help Stewart get back to school and this provided the necessary incentive for him to take matters into his own hands and go off on his own, proving to himself that he could. From then on things went much more smoothly.

In conclusion

Child psychiatry is still a speciality in its infancy, or at least early childhood. It does not have answers for all the psychiatric disorders shown by children and much has still to be learned about child development, both normal and abnormal. Nevertheless knowledge has greatly increased in recent years and a wide range of treatments are now available to help children with emotional and behavioural problems. In the past these have all too often been wrapped in mysticism and secrecy. I have tried to show here that this is not necessary. An understanding of children and their development may be applied to the problems shown by an individual youngster. Knowledge based on systematic research may be brought to bear on these individual problems and a start, albeit a modest start, may be made on a rational planning of treatment.

Further Reading

MUSSEN, P. H., CONGER, J. J., and KAGAN, J., (1974) *Child Development and Personality*, fourth edition, Harper International. (A large but very readable book on child development, which gives an extensive coverage of relevant research.)

QUAY, H. C., and WERRY, J. S., (eds.) (1972) *Psychopathological Disorders of Childhood*, Wiley. (A sound and comprehensive review of the research undertaken in selected areas of child psychiatry.)

RUTTER, M., (1972) *Maternal Deprivation Reassessed*, Penguin. (A discussion of the evidence on the ill-effects of those adverse childhood experiences usually included under the general heading of 'maternal deprivation'.)

RUTTER, M., and HERSOV, L., (eds.) (1977) *Child Psychiatry: Modern Approaches*, Blackwell Scientific. (Accounts of current child psychiatric practice with an emphasis on recent developments.)

RUTTER, M., and MADGE, N., (1976) *Cycles of Disadvantage*, Heinemann Educational. (A review of various forms of disadvantage and of the ways in which it may continue from one generation to the next.)

RUTTER, M., TIZARD, J., and WHITMORE, K., (eds.) (1970) Education, Health and Behaviour, Longman. (This report of the Isle of Wight survey gives findings on the frequency and distribution of various childhood troubles. There is a special emphasis on the overlap between educational, physical and psychiatric problems and the implications for provision of services.)

SHIPMAN, M. D., (1968) *Sociology of the School*, Longman. (A useful paperback describing the school as a social organization and the ways in which teachers and children interact.)

WEST, D. J., (1967) *The Young Offender*, Penguin. (A very clear and interesting account of juvenile delinquency.)

WOLFF, S., (1973) *Children Under Stress*, Penguin.
(A very readable account of the acute and chronic stresses faced by children and the ways in which they may lead to emotional and behavioural disorders.)

References

1. ANTHONY, E. J., (1957), 'An experimental approach to the psychopathology of childhood: encopresis', *British Journal of Medical Psychology*, vol. 30, pp. 146–75.

2. ARGYLE, M., (1967), *The Psychology of Interpersonal Behaviour*, Penguin.

3. BANDURA, A., (1969), 'Social-learning theory of identificatory processes', in D. A. Goslin (ed.), *Handbook of Socialisation Theory and Research*, Rand McNally.

4. BANDURA, A., and MENLOVE, F. L., (1968), 'Factors determining vicarious extinction of avoidance behavior through symbolic modelling', *Journal of Personality and Social Psychology*, vol. 8, pp. 99–108

5. BANDURA, A., GRUSEC, J. E., and MENLOVE, F. L., (1967), 'Vicarious extinction of avoidance behavior', *Journal of Personality and Social Psychology*, vol. 5, pp. 16–23.

6. BECKER, W. C., (1964), 'Consequences of different kinds of parental discipline', in M. L. Hoffman and L. W. Hoffman (eds.), *Review of Child Development Research*, vol. 1, Russell Sage Foundation, New York.

7. BECKER, W. C., MADSEN, C. H., ARNOLD, C. R., and THOMAS, B. A., (1967), 'The contingent use of teacher attention and praise in reducing classroom behavior problems', *Journal of Special Education*, vol. 1, pp. 287–307.

8. BENAIM, S., HORDER, J., and ANDERSON, J., (1973), 'Hysterical epidemic in a classroom', *Psychological Medicine*, vol. 3, pp. 366–73.

9. BERECZ, J. M., (1968), 'Phobias of childhood: etiology and treatment', *Psychological Bulletin*, vol. 70, pp. 694–720.

10. BERENDA, R. W., (1950), *The Influence of the Group on the Judgements of Children*, King's Crown Press.

11. BERGER, M., (1972), 'Modifying behaviour at school', *Special Education*, vol. 61, issue 2, pp. 18–21.

356 References

12. BERGER, M., (1973), 'Early experience and other environmental factors: an overview. 1. Studies with humans', in H. J. Eysenck (ed.), *Handbook of Abnormal Psychology*, 2nd edn, Pitman Medical.

13. BERNSTEIN, B., (1965), 'A socio-linguistic approach to social learning', in J. Gould (ed.), *Social Science Survey*, Penguin.

14. BIRCH, H. G., (1972), 'Issues of design and method in studying the effects of malnutrition on mental development', in *Nutrition, the Nervous System and Behavior*, Proceedings of the Seminar on Malnutrition in Early Life and on Subsequent Mental Development, Jamaica, 1972, Pan American Health Organization/World Health Organization.

15. BIRCH, H. G., and GUSSOW, J. D., (1970), *Disadvantaged Children: Health, Nutrition and School Failure*, Grune & Stratton.

16. BLAKEMORE, C., and MITCHELL, D. E., (1973), 'Environmental modification of the visual cortex and the neural basis of learning and memory', *Nature*, vol. 243, pp. 467–8.

17. BOWLBY, J., AINSWORTH, M., BOSTON, M., and ROSENBLUTH D., (1956), 'The effects of mother–child separation: a follow-up study', *British Journal of Medical Psychology*, vol. 29, pp. 211–47.

18. BOWLBY, J., (1971), *Attachment and Loss, Vol. 1: Attachment*, Penguin.

19. BRACKBILL, Y., (ed.) (1967), *Infancy and Early Childhood*, Free Press.

20. BRIDGER, W. H., and BIRNS, B., (1968), 'Experience and temperament in human neonates', in R. Newton and S. Levine (eds.), *Early Experience and Behavior*, Chas. C. Thomas.

21. BRONFENBRENNER, U., (1972), 'Is 80% of intelligence genetically determined?' in U. Bronfenbrenner (ed.), *Influences on Human Development*, Dryden Press.

22. BRONFENBRENNER, U., (1973), *Is Early Intervention Effective?, A report on the longitudinal evolution of preschool programs*, US Department of Health, Education and Welfare.

23. BROWN, J. D., (ed.) (1967), *The Hippies*, Time-Life.

24. BROWN, R., CAZDEN, C., and BELLUGI-KLIMA, U., (1969), 'The child's grammar from I to III', in J. P. Hill (ed.), *Minnesota Symposia on Child Psychology*, vol. 2, University of Minnesota Press.

25. BRUNER, J. S., OLIVER, R. R., and GREENFIELD, P. M., (1966), *Studies in Cognitive Growth*, Wiley.

26. BRYANT, P. E., (1974), *Perception and Understanding in Young Children*, Methuen.

27. CALDWELL, B. M., (1964), 'The effect of infant care', in M. L. Hoffman and L. W. Hoffman (eds.), *Review of Child Development Research*, vol. 1, Russell Sage Foundation.

28. CAMPBELL, D., (1974), Personal communication.

29. CAMPBELL, E. H., (1939), 'Social-sex development of children', *Genetic Psychology Monographs*, vol. 21, pp. 463–552.

30. CAMPBELL, J. D., (1964), 'Peer relations in childhood', in M. L. Hoffman and L. W. Hoffman (eds.), *Review of Child Development Research*, vol. 1, Russell Sage Foundation.

31. CANTWELL, D., (1977), 'Hyperkinetic syndrome', in M. Rutter and L. Hersov (eds.), *Child Psychiatry: Modern Approaches*, Blackwell Scientific.

32. CAPLAN, H. L., (1970), 'Hysterical "conversion" symptoms in childhood', M.Phil. Diss., University of London.

33. CENTERS, R., RAVEN, B. H., and RODRIGUES, A., (1971), 'Conjugal power structure: a re-examination', *American Sociological Review*, vol. 36, pp. 264–78.

34. CHALL, J., (1967), *Learning to Read: The Great Debate*, McGraw-Hill.

35. CHESS, S., THOMAS, A., and BIRCH, H. G., (1965), *Your Child is a Person: A Psychological Approach to Parenthood Without Guilt*, Viking Press.

36. CLEGG, A., and MEGSON, B., (1968), *Children in Distress*, Penguin.

37. CONGER, J. J., and MILLER, W. C., (1966), *Personality, Social Class and Delinquency*, Wiley.

38. CONNERS, C. K., (1972), 'Pharmacotherapy of psychopathology in children', in H. C. Quay and J. S. Werry (eds.), *Psychopathological Disorders of Childhood*, Wiley.

39. COOPER, R. M., and ZUBEK, J. P., (1958), 'Effects of enriched and restricted early environments on the learning ability of bright and dull rats', *Canadian Journal of Psychology*, vol. 12, pp. 159–64.

40. CORBETT, J. A., MATHEWS, A. M., CONNELL, P. H., and SHAPIRO, D. A., (1969), 'Tics and Gilles de la Tourette's syndrome: a follow-up study and critical review', *British Journal of Psychiatry*, vol. 115, pp. 1229–42.

41. CRELLIN, E., PRINGLE, M. L. K., and WEST, P., (1971), *Born Illegitimate: Social and Educational implications*, NFER.

42. CRESSEY, D. R., (1964), *Delinquency, Crime and Differential Association*, Martinus Nijhoff, The Hague.

43. CRITCHLEY, M., (1970), *The Dyslexic Child*, 2nd edn, Chas. C. Thomas.

358 References

44. CUMMINGS, S. T., BAYLEY, M. C., and RIE, H. E., (1966),
'Effects of the child's deficiency on the mother: A study of mothers
of mentally retarded, chronically ill and neurotic children',
American Journal of Orthopsychiatry, vol. 36, pp. 595–608.

45. DALTON, K., (1969), *Menstrual Cycle*, Penguin.

46. DOBBING, J., (1968), 'Vulnerable periods in developing brain', in
A. N. Davison and J. Dobbing (eds.), *Applied Neurochemistry*,
Blackwell.

47. DOUGLAS, J. W. B., (1964), *The Home and The School*,
McGibbon & Kee.

48. DOUGLAS, J. W. B., ROSS, J. M., and SIMPSON, H. R., (1968),
All Our Future, Peter Davies.

49. EISENBERG, L., (1958), 'School phobia: A study in the
communication of anxiety', *American Journal of Psychiatry*, vol.
114, pp. 712–18.

50. EISENBERG, L., (1968), 'Psychopharmacology in childhood: A
critique', in E. Miller (ed.), *Foundations of Child Psychiatry*,
Pergamon.

51. EISENBERG, L., CONNERS, K., and SHARPE, L., (1965), 'A
controlled study of the differential application of outpatient
psychiatric treatment for children', *Japanese Journal of Child
Psychiatry*, vol. 6, pp. 125–32.

52. ERIKSON, E. H., (1963), *Childhood and Society*, 2nd edn, Norton.

53. EYSENCK, H. J., and WILSON, G. D., (1973), *The Experimental
Study of Freudian Theories*, Methuen.

54. FERREIRA, A. J., and WINTER, W. D., (1968), 'Information
exchange and silence in normal and abnormal families', *Family
Process*, vol. 7, pp. 251–76.

55. FLACKS, R., (1967), 'The liberated generation: An exploration of
the roots of student protest', *Journal of Social Issues*, vol. 23, pp.
52–75.

56. FLANDERS, N. A., and HAVUMAKI, S., (1963), 'Group compliance
to dominative teacher influence', in W. W. Charters and N. L.
Gage (eds.), *Readings in the Social Psychology of Education*, Allyn
& Bacon.

57. FREUD, A., (1966), *Normality and Pathology in Childhood*,
Hogarth Press.

58. FREUD, S., (1905), 'Three essays on the theory of sexuality', in
J. Strachey (ed.), *The Standard Edition of the Complete Works of
Sigmund Freud*, vol. 3, Hogarth Press.

59. FRIEDLANDER, B. Z., (1971), 'Listening, language and the auditory environment: Automated evaluation and interventions', in J. Hellmuth (ed.) *The Exceptional Infant, vol. 2, Studies in Abnormalities,* Bruner/Mazel.

60. FROMMER, E. A., and O'SHEA, G., (1973), 'Antenatal identification of women liable to have problems in managing their infants', *British Journal of Psychiatry,* vol. 123, pp. 149–56.

61. GALLE, O. R., GOVE, W. R., and MCPHERSON, J. M., (1972), 'Population density and pathology: what are the relations for man?', *Science,* vol. 176, pp. 23–30.

62. GATH, D., COOPER, B., and GATTONI, F. E. G., (1972), 'Child guidance and delinquency in a London borough', *Psychological Medicine,* vol. 2, pp. 185–91.

63. GELFAND, D. M., and HARTMANN, O. P., (1968), 'Behavior therapy with children: A review and evaluation of research methodology', *Psychological Bulletin,* vol. 69, pp. 204–15.

64. GESELL, A., (1946), 'The ontogenesis of infant behavior', in L. Carmichael (ed.), *Manual of Child Psychology,* Wiley.

65. GIBSON, E. J., (1965), 'Learning to read', *Science,* vol. 148, pp. 1066–72.

66. GOLDBERG, E. M., (1973), 'Services for the family', in J. K. Wing and H. Häfner (eds.), *Roots of Evaluation: The Epidemiological Basis for Planning Psychiatric Services,* Oxford University Press.

67. GRAHAM, P., (1974), 'Child psychiatry and psychotherapy', *Journal of Child Psychology and Psychiatry and Allied Disciplines,* vol. 15, pp. 59–66.

68. GRAHAM, P., RUTTER, M., and GEORGE, S., (1973), 'Temperamental characteristics as predictors of behavior disorders in children', *American Journal of Orthopsychiatry,* vol. 43, pp. 328–39.

69. GRONLUND, N. E., (1959), *Sociometry in the Classroom,* Harper.

70. GURIN, G., VEROFF, J., and FELD, S., (1960), *Americans View Their Mental Health,* Basic Books.

71. HALL, R. V., LUND, D., and JACKSON, D., (1968), 'Effects of teacher attention on study behavior', *Journal of Applied Behavior Analysis,* vol. 1, pp. 1–12.

72. HARGREAVES, D. H., (1967), *Social Relations in a Secondary School,* Routledge & Kegan Paul.

73. HEISEL, J. S., REAM, S., RAITZ, R., RAPPAPORT, M., and CODDINGTON, R. D., (1973), 'The significance of life events as contributing factors in the diseases of children. III. A study of pediatric patients', *Journal of Pediatrics,* 83, pp. 119–23.

74. HERSOV, L., (1977), 'School refusal', in M. Rutter and L. Hersov (eds.), *Child Psychiatry: Modern Approaches*, Blackwell Scientific.

75. HERZOG, E., and SUDIA, C. E., (1973), 'Children in fatherless families', in B. M. Caldwell and H. N. Ricciuti (eds.), *Review of Child Development Research*, vol. 3, University of Chicago Press.

76. HETHERINGTON, E. M., and MARTIN, B., (1972), 'Family interaction and psychopathology in children', in H. C. Quay and J. S. Werry (eds.), *Psychopathological Disorders of Childhood*, Wiley.

77. HEWITT, L. E. and JENKINS, R. L., (1946), *Fundamental Patterns of Maladjustment: The Dynamics of Their Origin*, State of Illinois, Springfield.

78. HINDE, R. A., and DAVIES, L., (1972), 'Removing infant rhesus from mother for 13 days compared with removing mother from infant', *Journal of Child Psychology and Psychiatry and Allied Disciplines*, vol. 13, pp. 227–37.

79. HINDE, R. A., and SPENCER-BOOTH, Y., (1970), 'Individual differences in the responses of rhesus monkeys to a period of separation from their parents', *Journal of Child Psychology and Psychiatry and Allied Disciplines*, vol. 11, pp. 159–76.

80. HOWLIN, P., MARCHANT, R., RUTTER, M., BERGER, M., HERSOV, L., and YULE, W., (1973), 'A home-based approach to the treatment of autistic children', *Journal of Autism and Childhood Schizophrenia*, vol. 3, pp. 308–36.

81. HUNT, A., FOX, J., and MORGAN, M., (1973), *Families and Their Needs*, HMSO, London.

82. HUTT, C., (1972), *Males and Females*, Penguin.

83. ILLSLEY, R., and THOMPSON, B., (1961), 'Women from broken homes', *Sociological Review*, vol. 9, pp. 27–53.

84. IRWIN, O. C., (1960), 'Infant Speech: effect of systematic reading of stories', *Journal of Speech and Hearing Research*, vol. 3, pp. 187–90.

85. JEHU, D., HARDIKER, P., YELLOLY, M., and SHAW, M., (1972), *Behaviour Modification in Social Work*, Wiley-Interscience.

86. JENKINS, R. L., (1960), 'Psychiatric syndromes in children and their relation to family background', *American Journal of Orthopsychiatry*, vol. 36, pp. 450–57.

87. JERSILD, A. T., (1954), 'Emotional development', in L. Carmichael (ed.), *Manual of Child Psychology*, 2nd edn, Chapman & Hall.

88. JOHNSON, S. M., WAHL, G., MARTIN, S., and JOHANSSON, S., (1973), 'How deviant is the normal child? A behavioral analysis of the preschool child and his family', in R. D. Rubin, J. P. Brady and J. D. Henderson (eds.), *Advances in Behavior Therapy*, Vol. 4, Academic Press.

89. JUDD, L. L., (1965), 'Obsessive-compulsive neurosis in children', *Archives of General Psychiatry*, vol. 12, pp. 136–43.

90. KANNER, L., (1957), *Child Psychiatry*, 3rd edn, Chas. C. Thomas.

91. KANTOR, M. B., (1965), 'Some consequences of residential and social mobility for the adjustment of children', in M. B. Kantor (ed.), *Mobility and Mental Health*, Chas. C. Thomas.

92. KELVIN, P., (1970), *The Bases of Social Behaviour*, Holt, Rinehart & Winston.

93. KENISTON, K., (1967), 'The sources of student dissent', *Journal of Social Issues*, vol. 23, pp. 108–37.

94. KLAUS, M. H., JERAULD, R., KREGER, N. C., MCALPINE, W., STEFFA, M., and KENNELL, J. H., (1972), 'Maternal attachment: importance of the first postpartum days', *New England Journal of Medicine*, vol. 286, pp. 460–63.

95. KLINE, P., (1972), *Fact and Fantasy in Freudian Theory*, Methuen.

96. KOLVIN, I., MACKEITH, R. C., and MEADOW, S. R., (eds.) (1973), *Bladder Control and Enuresis*, Clinics in Develop. Med. Nos. 48–9, Heinemann/SIMP.

97. KOUNIN, J. S., (1970), *Discipline and Group Management in Classrooms*, Holt, Rinehart & Winston.

98. LAMBERT, J. R., (1970), *Crime, Police and Race Relations*, Oxford University Press/Institute of Race Relations.

99. LANGNER, T. S., and MICHAEL, S. T., (1964), *Life Stress and Mental Health*, Collier-Macmillan.

100. LEIDERMAN, P. H., LEIFER, A. D., SEASHORE, M. J., BARNETT, C. R., and GROBSTEIN, R., (1973), 'Mother-infant interaction: effects of early deprivation, prior experience and sex of infant', *Proceedings of the Association for Research in Nervous and Mental Disease*, vol. 51, pp. 154–75.

101. LEIFER, A. D., LEIDERMAN, P. H., BARNETT, C. R., and WILLIAMS, J. A., (1972), 'Effects of mother–infant separation on maternal attachment behavior', *Child Development*, vol. 43, pp. 1203–18.

102. LEVITT, M., (ed.) (1959), *Readings in Psychoanalytic Psychology*, Appleton.

103. LEVY, D. M., (1943), *Maternal Overprotection*, Columbia University Press.

104. LEVY, D. M., (1958), *Behavioral Analysis: Analysis of Clinical Observations of Behavior as Applied to Mother–Newborn Relationships*, Chas. C. Thomas.

105. LIBERMAN, R., (1970), 'Behavioral approaches to family and couple therapy', *American Journal of Orthopsychiatry*, vol. 40, pp. 106–18.

106. McCANDLESS, B. R., (1960), 'Rate of development, baby build and personality', *Psychiatric Research Reports*, vol. 13, pp. 42–57.

107. MARCHANT, R., HOWLIN, P., YULE, W., and RUTTER, M., (1974), 'Graded change in the treatment of the behaviour of autistic children', *Journal of Child Psychology and Psychiatry and Allied Disciplines*, vol. 15, pp. 221–7.

108. MARKS, I. M., (1974), 'Research in neurosis: a selective review, II. Treatment', *Psychological Medicine*, vol. 4, pp. 89–109.

109. MARSHALL, W. A., (1968), *Development of the Brain*, Oliver & Boyd.

110. MASTERSON, J. F., (1967), *The Psychiatric Dilemma of Adolescence*, Churchill.

111. MAYS, J. B., (1954), *Growing Up in the City*, Liverpool University Press.

112. MEDAWAR, P., (1969), *Induction and Intuition in Scientific Thought*. Methuen.

113. MILLAR, S., (1968), *The Psychology of Play*, Penguin.

114. MITCHELL, S., and SHEPHERD, M., (1966), 'A comparative study of children's behaviour at home and at school', *British Journal of Educational Psychology*, vol. 36, pp. 248–54.

115. MULLEN, E. J., DUMPSON, J. R., and associates, (1972), *Evaluation of Social Intervention*, Jossey-Bass.

116. MURRELL, S. A., and STACHOWIAK, J. G., (1967), 'Consistency, rigidity and power in the interaction patterns of clinic and non-clinic families', *Journal of Abnormal Psychology*, vol. 72, pp. 265–72.

117. NEWCOMB, T. M., (1963), 'Persistence and regression of changed attitudes: long range studies', *Journal of Social Issues*, vol. 19, pp. 3–14.

118. NEWMAN, S., (1973), *Defensible Space*, Architectural Press.

119. NEWSON, J., and NEWSON, E., (1968), *Four Years Old in an Urban Community*, Penguin.

120. NIELSEN, J., and CHRISTENSON, A.-L., (1974), 'Thirty-five males with double Y chromosome', *Psychological Medicine*, vol. 4, pp. 28–37.

121. O'LEARY, K. D., BECKER, W. C., EVANS, M. B., and SAUDARGAS, R. A., (1969), 'A token reinforcement program in a public school: a replication and systematic analysis', *Journal of Applied Behavior Analysis*, vol. 2, pp. 3–13.

122. OLIVER, J. E., and TAYLOR, A., (1971), 'Five generations of ill-treated children in one family pedigree', *British Journal of Psychiatry*, vol. 119, pp. 473–80.

123. OSOFSKY, J. D., and O'CONNELL, E. J., (1972), 'Parent–child interaction: daughters' effects upon mothers' and fathers' behaviors', *Developmental Psychology*, vol. 7, pp. 157–68.

124. PALMER, T. B., (1971), 'California's community treatment program for delinquent adolescents', *Journal of Research in Crime and Delinquency*, vol. 8, pp. 74–92.

125. PATTERSON, G., (1973), 'Reprogramming the families of aggressive boys', in C. Thoreson (ed.), *Behavior Modification in Education 72nd Year Book*, Part I, University of Chicago Press.

126. PATTERSON, G. R., and COBB, J. A., (1971), 'A dyadic analysis of "aggressive" behaviors', in J. P. Hill (ed.), *Minnesota Symposia on Child Psychology*, vol. 5, University of Minnesota Press.

127. PATTERSON, G. R., JONES, R., WHITTIER, J., and WRIGHT, M. A., (1965), 'A behaviour modification technique for the hyperactive child', *Behaviour Research and Therapy*, vol. 2, pp. 217–26.

128. PATTERSON, G. R., and REID, J. B., (1973), 'Intervention for families of aggressive boys: a replication study', *Behaviour Research and Therapy*, vol. 11, pp. 383–94.

129. POLLAK, M., (1972), *Today's Three Year Olds in London*, Heinemann/SIMP.

130. POWER, M., ASH, P., SHOENBERG, E., and SIREY, C., (1974), 'Delinquency and the family', *British Journal of Social Work*, vol. 4, pp. 13–38.

131. POWER, M. J., BENN, R. T., and MORRIS, J. N., (1972), 'Neighbourhood, School and Juveniles before the Courts', *British Journal of Criminology*, vol. 12, pp. 111–32.

132. PROSHANSKY, H. M., ITTELSON, W. H., and RIVLIN, L. G., (eds.) (1970), *Environmental Psychology: Man and His Physical Setting*, Holt, Rinehart & Winston.

133. REID, J. B., and HENDRIKS, A. F. C. J., (1973), 'A preliminary analysis of the effectiveness of direct home intervention for treatment of predelinquent boys who steal', in F. W. Clark and L. A. Hamerlynck (eds.), *Critical Issues in Research and Practice*, Proc. 4th Banff Int. Conf. on Behav. Modif., Research Press.

134. REID, W. J., and SHYNE, A. W., (1970), *Brief and Extended Casework*, Columbia University Press.

135. REISMAN, J. M., (1973), *Principles of Psychotherapy with Children*, Wiley.

136. RICHARDS, M., and BERNAL, J., (1974), 'Why some babies don't sleep', *New Society*, vol. 27, pp. 509–11.

137. RIESEN, A., (1965), 'Effects of early deprivation of photic stimulation', in S. F. Osler and R. E. Cooke (eds.), *The Biosocial Basis of Mental Retardation*, Johns Hopkins Press.

138. ROBERTSON, J., (1970), *Young Children in Hospital*, 2nd edn, Tavistock Publications.

139. ROBERTSON, J., and ROBERTSON, J., (1971), 'Young children in brief separations: a fresh look', *Psychoanalytic Study of the Child*, vol. 26, pp. 264–315.

140. ROBINS, L. N., (1966), *Deviant Children Grown Up*, Williams & Wilkins.

141. ROBINS, L. N., (1972), 'Follow-up studies of behavior disorders in children', in H. C. Quay and J. S. Werry (eds.), *Psychopathological Disorders of Childhood*, Wiley.

142. ROBINS, L. N., (1973), 'Evaluation of psychiatric services for children in the United States', in J. K. Wing and H. Häfner (eds.), *Roots of Evaluation: The Epidemiological Basis for Planning Psychiatric Services*, Oxford University Press.

143. ROFF, M., SELLS, S. B., and GOLDEN, M. M., (1972), *Social Adjustment and Personality Development in Children*, University of Minnesota Press.

144. ROSENTHAL, A. J., and LEVINE, S. V., (1971), 'Brief psychotherapy with children: process of therapy', *American Journal of Psychiatry*, vol. 128, pp. 141–6.

145. ROSENZWEIG, M. A., (1971), 'Effects of environment on development of brain and of behaviour', in E. Tobach, L. R. Aronson and E. Shaw (eds.), *The Biopsychology of Development*, Academic Press.

146. Ross, A. O., (1972), 'Behavior therapy', in H. C. Quay and J. S. Werry (eds.), *Psychopathological Disorders of Childhood*, Wiley.

147. RUBIN, R., and HENDERSON, J. D., (1972), *Advances in Behavior Therapy*, vol. 3, Academic Press.

148. RUBIN, R., BRADY, J. P., and HENDERSON, J. D., (1973), *Advances in Behavior Therapy*, vol. 4, Academic Press.

149. RUTTER, M., (1965), 'Classification and categorization in child psychiatry', *Journal of Child Psychology and Psychiatry and Allied Disciplines*, vol. 6, pp. 71–83.

150. RUTTER, M., (1966), *Children of Sick Parents: An Environmental and Psychiatric Study*, Institute of Psychiatry Maudsley Monograph No. 16, Oxford University Press.

151. RUTTER, M., (1970), 'Sex differences in children's responses to family stress', in E. J. Anthony and C. Koupernik (eds.), *The Child and His Family*, Wiley.

152. RUTTER, M., (1971), 'Parent–child separation: Psychological effects on the children', *Journal of Child Psychology and Psychiatry and Allied Disciplines*, vol. 12, pp. 233–60.

153. RUTTER, M., (1971), 'Psychiatry', in J. Wortis (ed.), *Mental Retardation: An Annual Review*, vol. 3, Grune & Stratton.

154. RUTTER, M., (1971), 'Normal psychosexual development', *Journal of Child Psychology and Psychiatry and Allied Disciplines*, vol. 11, pp. 259–83.

155. RUTTER, M., (1972), 'Childhood schizophrenia reconsidered', *Journal of Autism and Childhood Schizophrenia*, vol. 2, pp. 315–37.

156. RUTTER, M., (1972), *Maternal Deprivation Reassessed*, Penguin.

157. RUTTER, M., (1972), 'Relationships between child and adult psychiatric disorder', *Acta Psychiatrica Scandinavica*, vol. 48, pp. 3–21.

158. RUTTER, M., (1973), 'Why are London children so disturbed?', *Proceedings of the Royal Society of Medicine*, vol. 66, pp. 1221–5.

159. RUTTER, M., (1974), 'Emotional disorder and educational underachievement', *Archives of Diseases in Childhood*, vol. 49, pp. 249–56.

160. RUTTER, M., BIRCH, H. G., THOMAS, A., and CHESS, S., (1964), 'Temperamental characteristics in infancy and the later development of behavioural disorders', *British Journal of Psychiatry*, vol. 110, pp. 651–61.

161. RUTTER, M., GRAHAM, P., and YULE, W., (1970), *A Neuropsychiatric Study in Childhood*, Clinics in Develop. Med. Nos. 35–6, Heinemann/SIMP.

162. RUTTER, M., GRAHAM, P., CHADWICK, O., and YULE, W., (1976), 'Adolescent turmoil: fact or fiction?' *Journal of Child Psychology and Psychiatry and Allied Disciplines*, vol. 17, pp. 35–56.

163. RUTTER, M., LEBOVICI, L., EISENBERG, L., SNEZNEVSKIJ, A. V., SADOUN, R., BROOKE, E., and LIN, T.-Y., (1969), 'A tri-axial classification of mental disorders in childhood', *Journal of Child Psychology and Psychiatry and Allied Disciplines*, vol. 10, pp. 41–61.

164. RUTTER, M., and MARTIN, J. A. M., (eds.) (1972), *The Child with Delayed Speech*, Clinics in Develop. Med., No. 43, Heinemann/SIMP.

165. RUTTER, M., SHAFFER, D., and SHEPHERD, M., (1973), 'Preliminary communication: An evaluation of the proposal for a multi-axial classification of child psychiatric disorders', *Psychological Medicine*, vol. 3, pp. 244–50.

166. RUTTER, M., TIZARD, J., and WHITMORE, K., (eds.) (1970), *Education, Health and Behaviour*, Longmans.

167. RUTTER, M., and YULE, W., (1973), 'Specific reading retardation', in L. Mann and D. Sabatino (eds.), *The First Review of Special Education*, Grune & Stratton.

168. RUTTER, M., YULE, W., and BERGER, M., (1974), 'The children of West Indian migrants', *New Society*, vol. 27, pp. 630–33.

169. SCHAFFER, H. R., (1966), 'Activity level as a constitutional determinant of infantile reaction to deprivation', *Child Development*, vol. 37, pp. 595–602

170. SCHAFFER, H. R., (1971), *The Growth of Sociability*, Penguin.

171. SCHOFIELD, M., (1968), *The Sexual Behaviour of Young People*, Penguin.

172. SCHWITZGEBEL, R. L., and SCHWITZGEBEL, R. K., (eds.) (1973), *Psychotechnology: Electronic Control of Mind and Behavior*, Holt, Rinehart & Winston.

173. SCOTT, P. D., (1965), 'Delinquency', in J. G. Howells (ed.), *Modern Perspectives in Child Psychiatry*, Oliver & Boyd.

174. SCOTT, P. D., (1973), 'Fatal battered baby cases', *Medicine, Science and the Law*, vol. 13, pp. 197–206.

175. SEIDEL, U. P., CHADWICK, O., and RUTTER, M., (1975), 'Psychological disorders in crippled children: A comparative study of children with and without brain damage', *Developmental Medicine and Child Neurology*, vol. 17, pp. 563–73.

176. SHAFFER, D., McNAMARA, N., and PINCUS, J. H., (1974), 'Controlled observations on patterns of activity, attention and impulsivity in brain-damaged and psychiatrically disturbed boys', *Psychological Medicine*, vol. 4, pp. 4–18.

177. SHEPHERD, M., OPPENHEIM, B., and MITCHELL, S., (1971), *Childhood Behaviour and Mental Health*, University of London Press.

178. SHERIF, M., HARVEY, O. J., WHITE, B. J., HOOD, W. R., and SHERIF, C. W., (1961), *Intergroup Conflict and Cooperation: The Robbers' Cave Experiment*, University of Oklahoma Press.

179. SHIELDS, J., (1973), 'Heredity and psychological abnormality', in H. J. Eysenck, (ed.), *Handbook of Abnormal Psychology*, Pitman Medical.

180. SKYNNER. A. C. R., (1969), 'A group-analytic approach to conjoint family therapy', *Journal of Child Psychology and Psychiatry and Allied Disciplines*, vol. 10, pp. 81–106.

181. STAATS, A. W., and BUTTERFIELD, W. H., (1965), 'Treatment of nonreading in a culturally deprived juvenile delinquent: an application of reinforcement principles', *Child Development*, vol. 36, pp. 925–42.

182. STACEY, M., DEARDEN, R., PILL, R., and ROBINSON, D., (1970), *Hospitals, Children and Their Families: The Report of a Pilot Study*, Routledge & Kegan Paul.

183. STEVENS, A., (1975), *Attachment and Polymetric Rearing*, Thesis for DM, University of Oxford.

184. STOTT, D. H., (1960), 'Delinquency, maladjustment and unfavourable ecology', *British Journal of Psychology*, vol. 51, pp. 157–70.

185. SUGARMAN, B., (1967), 'Involvement in youth culture, academic achievement and conformity in school', *British Journal of Sociology*, vol. 18, pp. 151–64.

186. TANNER, J. M., (1962), *Growth at Adolescence*, 2nd edn, Blackwell.

187. TARJAN, M. D., TIZARD, J., RUTTER, M., BEGAB, M., BROOKE, E. M., DE LA CRUZ, F., LIN, T.-Y., MONTENEGRO, H., STROTZKA, H., and SARTORIUS, N., (1972), 'Classification and mental retardation: issues arising in the Fifth WHO Seminar on Psychiatric Diagnosis, Classification, and Statistics', *American Journal of Psychiatry*, vol. 128, pp. 34–45 (Suppl.).

188. THOMAS, A., CHESS, S., and BIRCH, H. G., (1968), *Temperament and Behavior Disorders in Children*, New York University Press.

189. TIZARD, B., COOPERMAN, O., JOSEPH, A., and TIZARD, J., (1972), 'Environmental effects on language development: a study of young children in long stay residential nurseries', *Child Development*, vol. 43, pp. 337–58.

190. TRUAX, C. B., and CARKHUFF, R. R., (1967), *Toward Effective Counseling and Psychotherapy: Training and Practice*, Aldine.

191. WALLIS, C. P., and MALIPHANT, R., (1967), 'Delinquent areas in the county of London: ecological factors', *British Journal of Criminology*, vol. 7, pp. 250–84.

192. WARREN, M. Q., (1969), 'The case for differential treatment of delinquents', *Annals of the American Academy of Political and Social Science*, vol. 381, pp. 47–59.

194. WELLS, R. A., DILKES, T. C., and TRIVELLI, N., (1972), 'The results of family therapy: a critical review of the literature', *Family Process*, vol. 11, pp. 189–207.

194. WEST, D. J., (1967), *The Young Offender*, Penguin.

195. WEST, D. J., and FARRINGTON, D. P., (1973), *Who Becomes Delinquent?*, Heinemann.

196. WHITE, R. K., and LIPPITT, R., (1960), *Autocracy and Democracy: An Experimental Enquiry*, Harper.

197. WINNICOTT, D. W., (1953), 'Transitional objects and transitional phenomena', *International Journal of Psycho-Analysis*, vol. 34, pp. 89–97.

198. WOLFF, S., (1971), 'Dimensions and clusters of symptoms in disturbed children', *British Journal of Psychiatry*, vol. 118, pp. 421–7.

199. WOLFF, S., (1973), *Children Under Stress*, 2nd edn., Penguin.

200. WOODWARD, J., and JACKSON, D., (1961), 'Emotional reactions in burned children and their mothers', *British Journal of Plastic Surgery*, vol. 13, pp. 316–24.

201. WOODWARD, W. M., (1971), *The Development of Behaviour*, Penguin.

202. WOOTTON, B., (1959), *Social Science and Social Pathology*, Allen & Unwin.

203. YARROW, L. J., (1963), 'Research in dimension of early maternal care', *Merrill-Palmer Quarterly of Behavior and Development*, vol. 9, pp. 101–14.

204. YARROW, M. R., CAMPBELL, J. D., and BURTON, R. V., (1968), *Chil' Rearing: An Enquiry into Research and Methods*, Jossey-Bass.

205. YUDKIN, S., and HOLME, A., (1963), *Working Mothers and Their Children*, Michael Joseph.

206. ZUK, G. H., (1971), 'Family therapy during 1964–1970', *Psychotherapy: Theory, Research and Practice*, vol. 8, pp. 90–97.

Subject Index

Author Index

FOR THE BEST IN PAPERBACKS, LOOK FOR THE

In every corner of the world, on every subject under the sun, Penguin represents quality and variety – the very best in publishing today.

For complete information about books available from Penguin – including Pelicans, Puffins, Peregrines and Penguin Classics – and how to order them, write to us at the appropriate address below. Please note that for copyright reasons the selection of books varies from country to country.

In the United Kingdom: For a complete list of books available from Penguin in the U.K., please write to *Dept E.P., Penguin Books Ltd, Harmondsworth, Middlesex, UB7 0DA*

In the United States: For a complete list of books available from Penguin in the U.S., please write to *Dept BA, Penguin, 299 Murray Hill Parkway, East Rutherford, New Jersey 07073*

In Canada: For a complete list of books available from Penguin in Canada, please write to *Penguin Books Canada Ltd, 2801 John Street, Markham, Ontario L3R 1B4*

In Australia: For a complete list of books available from Penguin in Australia, please write to the *Marketing Department, Penguin Books Australia Ltd, P.O. Box 257, Ringwood, Victoria 3134*

In New Zealand: For a complete list of books available from Penguin in New Zealand, please write to the *Marketing Department, Penguin Books (NZ) Ltd, Private Bag, Takapuna, Auckland 9*

In India: For a complete list of books available from Penguin, please write to *Penguin Overseas Ltd, 706 Eros Apartments, 56 Nehru Place, New Delhi, 110019*

In Holland: For a complete list of books available from Penguin in Holland, please write to *Penguin Books Nederland B.V., Postbus 195, NL–1380AD Weesp, Netherlands*

In Germany: For a complete list of books available from Penguin, please write to *Penguin Books Ltd, Friedrichstrasse 10 – 12, D–6000 Frankfurt Main 1, Federal Republic of Germany*

In Spain: For a complete list of books available from Penguin in Spain, please write to *Longman Penguin España, Calle San Nicolas 15, E–28013 Madrid, Spain*

Maternal Deprivation Reassessed
Michael Rutter

Twenty years have passed since 'maternal deprivation' was first greeted with a storm of controversy. Some early views have been modified, but the basic proposition – that lack, loss or distortion of child care has a very important effect on psychological development – has received substantial support.

Why and how are children adversely affected? Dr Rutter reviews the qualities of mothering needed for normal development, and both the short-term and long-term effects of 'maternal deprivation' are considered. Dr Rutter concludes that the term covers a wide range of *different* experiences with quite *different* effects on development.

What is now needed, Dr Rutter argues, is a more precise description of the different aspects of 'bad' care and 'bad' effects. In starting on these tasks and in reappraising briefly and clearly the whole concept of 'maternal deprivation', Dr Rutter has written a book which will be necessary reading for all those concerned with the upbringing, care, teaching or treatment of children.

Juvenile Delinquency
Michael Rutter and Henri Giller

Based on a report commissioned by the Home Office and the Department of Health and Social Security, this is an important and timely analysis of the factors underlying juvenile delinquent behaviour.

Written by an eminent psychiatrist and a criminologist, *Juvenile Delinquency* examines in detail the concepts of delinquency, the developmental trends and the historical trends. The authors go on to consider the influences on delinquency of sex, class and race, and then analyse the predisposing individual characteristics and the wide range of psychosocial factors associated with delinquency. They conclude with a look at the means of prevention and intervention, and an assessment of the implication for research, policy and practice.

Juvenile Delinquency is essential reading for criminologists, psychiatrists, sociologists, psychologists, social workers – in short, for anyone concerned with the problems of youth and delinquent behaviour.

The Psychology of Childhood and Adolescence
C. I. Sandström

In this concise study of the processes of growing up, Professor Sandström has produced a book which, although it is perfectly suited to the initial needs of university students and teachers in training, will appeal almost as much to parents and ordinary readers. His text covers the whole story of human physical and mental growth from conception to puberty.

Outlining the scope and history of developmental psychology, Professor Sandström goes on to detail the stages of growth in the womb, during the months after birth, and (year by year) up to the age of ten. There follow chapters on physical development, learning and perception, motivation, language and thought, intelligence, the emotions, social adjustment, and personality. The special conditions of puberty and of schooling are handled in the final chapters.

Throughout this masterly study the author necessarily refers to 'norms of development': these neatly represent the average stages of growing up, but (as Professor Mace comments in his introduction) they must only be applied to individual children with caution.

The Child, the Family, and the Outside World
D. W. Winnicott

Long clinical experience gave Dr Winnicott a unique standing in child psychiatry and few experts did more to present the world of children and parents to the general public.

Beginning at the natural bond between mother and child – the bond we call love, which is the key to personality – Dr Winnicott deals in turn in this volume with the phases of mother/infant, parent/child, and child/school. From the problems – which are not really problems – of feeding, weaning, and innate morality in babies, he ranges to the very real difficulties of only children, of stealing and lying, and of first experiments in independence. Shyness, sex education in schools, and the roots of aggression are among the many other topics the author covers in a book which, for its manner of imparting knowledge simply and sympathetically, must be indispensable for intelligent parents.

'His style is lucid, his manner friendly, and his years of experience provide much wise insight into child behaviour and parental attitudes' – *British Journal of Psychology*

Child Care and the Growth of Love
John Bowlby

In 1951, under the auspices of the World Health
Organization, Dr John Bowlby wrote a report on *Maternal
Care and Mental Health* which collated expert world
opinion on the subject and the issues arising from it – the
prevention of juvenile and adult delinquency, the problem
of the 'unwanted child', the training of women for
motherhood, and the best ways of supplying the needs of
children deprived of their natural mothers. This Pelican is
a summary of Dr Bowlby's report, freed from many of its
technicalities and prepared for the general reader.

This revised edition contains chapters based on an article
by Dr Mary Salter Ainsworth, written in 1962 also for the
World Health Organization when it once again made an
important study of child care.

'It is a convenient and scholarly summary of evidence of
the effects upon children of lack of personal attention, and
it presents to administrators, social workers, teachers and
doctors a reminder of the significance of the family' –
The Times

Children Under Stress
Sula Wolff

The way in which children experience major crises in their lives has a profound effect on their emotional and psychological development.

Beginning with a discussion of personality development and the origins of behavioural disorders, Dr Wolff goes on to examine in detail a number of stressful situations. She looks at the principles of child psychotherapy and at the way society as a whole can contribute to the prevention and relief of psychiatric problems in children. Throughout, Dr Wolff aims not only to inform, but also to assist everyone concerned with children towards a greater awareness of the individual child's inner world.

'This is an admirable book, which deserves to be widely read, not only by those who are professionally concerned with disturbed and unhappy children, but by that very large number of parents who are worried from time to time about their children's behaviour and who are uncertain about when to seek expert advice . . . It is the best summary known to me of what can be achieved by child psychiatry, and an excellent account of the causes and common manifestations of emotional disturbance in children' – Dr Anthony Storr